BYTE/McGraw-Hill, 70 Main Street, Peterborough, NH 03458

Library of Congress Cataloging in Publication Data

Swanson, Paul
    Microcomputer disk techniques.

    Includes index.
    1. Microcomputer—Programming.   2. Data
disk drives.   I. Title.
QA76.6.S916   001.64'42   82-1313
ISBN 0-07-062582-4   AACR2

10 9 8 7 6 5 4 3 2

Edited by Bruce Roberts.
Cover Design and Production Supervision by Ellen Klempner.
Cover Photo by Paul Avis.
Drawings by Eddie Germano.
Production Editing by Tom McMillan.
Production by Mike Lonsky.
Typesetting by Debi Fredericks, Donna Sweeney, and Valerie Horn.
Printed and Bound by Halliday Lithograph Corp.
                    Arcata Company
                    North Quincy, Massachusetts

ACKNOWLEDGMENTS

I would like to thank my wife, Eleanor, for her help in proofing and in selecting illustrations for this book. I would also like to thank my mother-in-law, Petroneli Sanda, not only for her help in the proofing, but also for the glossary, as she selected each word in it.

TABLE OF CONTENTS

INTRODUCTION

Over the past few years, the cost of purchasing a computer system has plummeted, and, as a direct result, many people have purchased computer systems for personal use at home and many others have bought systems for small business. But because the cost of the software, or programming, has not dropped that much, if at all, many of these new computer owners have decided to program the machines themselves. These people have had varying success, but most have discovered the difference between an amateur programmer and a professional one. The net result is thousands of very under-programmed computers, computers whose programs are not nearly sophisticated enough to make full use of their powers.

The inexperienced or amateur programmer needs to have years of instruction and experience to know enough to increase the sophistication of the programs. If the computer is there, the experience is possible. But adequate instruction is not that easy to get. The various manuals and other instructional materials that come or can be purchased with the computer do a very good job of teaching the basic concepts behind the language the computer uses, usually Beginner's All-Purpose Symbolic Instruction Code (BASIC). By trial and error the amateur programmer can usually become quite proficient at programming the basic model of the computer. The real confusion begins when the amateur adds a disk drive. Adding a single drive to a computer transforms it into a system with greatly increased power and flexibility, particularly in comparison to that of a tape cassette player. This increase is due to the availability of fast data storage and retrieval that the disk provides. The problem is that, although the basics of the language are described well in the manuals, the various techniques required to make effective use of the disk are not there.

By discussing disk drives with amateur programmers and observing what literature and programming aids are available to them, I have learned that the average owner of a personal computer knows how to handle the disk in a relatively primitive way. The fault is in the items that are available. This book will show some fairly sophisticated methods of using disks in microcomputer systems.

The first part of this book is basically a long introduction to disks. In it are descriptions of the disk itself and how the computer physically uses it and how the operating system in the computer is written to make using the disk simpler. The rest of the book is divided into four sections, each section building on the information presented in the preceding one.

The first section starts where most disk manuals stop. It explains the random-access file, one of two types of files available on almost every disk-based computer. The random-access file is the type of file responsible for the increased flexibility the disk affords. The other type of file, the sequential file, is also used in the book for some required functions, but sequential files are like tape files (which, technically, are one form of a sequential file) and have the same basic restrictions. The contents of the first section represent the approximate limit most personal computer owners achieve using the learning material that comes with the computer system.

Section II deals with three different types of key files. Each of the three is used in professionally written programs for different purposes. Each one has its strong and weak points, so all should be examined to see which of the three types to use. The key file is a more sophisticated use of the random-access file than is explained in Section I. It has an index, which is a look-up table. The data is stored and retrieved by name instead of by number.

Section III adds to the programs developed in Section II. It explains what parameter-driven subroutines can do and increases the flexibility of a key-file system developed in Section II.

Section IV deals with the program itself. It shows how to effectively structure the program and the data to increase a system's usability. This section also deals with such subjects as using program overlays to segment the functions of a program system.

This book is not meant for the professional programmer, who either is familiar with most of the information presented here or uses larger computer systems that have more automatic, built-in methods for handling the disk. Instead, it is meant for the amateur programmer who is serious about learning how to effectively use a disk drive on a microcomputer system.

Microcomputer Disk Techniques

EDDIE GERMANO

PART ONE

CHAPTER 1

THE DISK AND DISK DRIVE

Deciding whether to add a disk drive to an existing computer system or to buy a new computer system with disks is confusing. Almost all of the microcomputers can have disk drives, but many of them give you choices that, unless you know a lot about computers, mean little. And although disks are made of very simple parts, there are many of those very simple parts. That is complicated.

A disk is often compared to a phonograph record, but this analogy is flawed. First, a record has two grooves on it—one on each side. A disk does not have grooves. It does, however, have something comparable—tracks that are the magnetic equivalent of grooves. The analogy fails here in that the disk has several concentric tracks instead of the single spiral pattern that is on a record. Also, while records cannot be erased, disks can, and information can be recorded over whatever was there, much the way a tape recorder can record over the former contents of a tape. Although there is really no analogy to the disk drive that explains it, you can explain the disk simply enough without an analogy.

Most disks are metal or plastic platters coated with a material that can be magnetized. Recording tapes are coated with a similar material. But unlike the tape recorder and player, the mechanism used to read and write the information on a disk can select a portion of the surface by a mechanical index. The logic circuits that control the disk drive, which is the mechanical part, can select how far the reading arm goes out across the surface of the disk by number. Each number on this index corresponds to an area of the disk that takes the shape of a circle. There are many of these circles on the disk, each one having its own index number. These circles are known as tracks.

A track may contain thousands of characters of information. In order to handle this information more easily, the logic that controls the disk can break down the information in each track into smaller units called sectors. Every track on a disk will have the same number of sectors as every other track on the same disk. Some disks are *hard sectored*, which means the tracks on the disks are mechanically divided into sectors, usually by a series of equally spaced holes on the disk. Others are *soft sectored*, which means that there is only one hole on the disk. This hole, and one selected hole on a hard-sectored disk, are called timing holes. A timing hole lets the logic handling the disk know where the tracks begin. Usually, the disk interface logic circuit handling the disk requires the computer to give it the number of the track and sector along with a code telling it whether it should read or write and the information to write. But remember, most of the physical properties of the disk are invisible to the computer program and to the computer programmer.

Several types of disks are on the market. They range in size from the small disk to the large hard disk. All of them use the same method of reading and writing.

The types of disks fall into two general categories. There are the *hard disks*, which are, as the name implies, rigid platters. On hard disks the mechanism used to read and write (called the read/write head) does not make contact with the platter. Instead, it literally flies over the surface on a bed of moving air continuously pumped across the disk platter. This read/write head flies at such an incredibly low altitude that a smoke particle will not fit between it and the surface of the disk platter. Some hard disk drives contain platters that are not removable but are permanently fixed inside the drive, while others have the disk platters enclosed in removable hard plastic cartridges. The most popular hard disk drives are a combination, having one platter fixed in the drive and another fixed in a removable cartridge. This type is quite logically called a *fixed/removable* disk drive.

The other general category of disks, much more common with microcomputers, is the flexible diskette or floppy disk. This disk is flexible, although your testing this quality will soon destroy the disk. The main difference between this type and the hard disks is that, on the flexible disk, the read/write head is in contact with the disk platter when it is in use. Although this allows the circuitry driving the mechanics to be a lot simpler, it also allows the disk platters to wear out. While hard disks will almost never wear out, floppy disks will.

There are two basic sizes of floppy disks available. The older of the two forms is 8 inches in diameter. The other, usually called the minifloppy, is 5¼ inches in diameter. Both are enclosed in an envelope that should never be removed. This envelope protects the surface of the disk against dirt and contact with materials that may mar the surface. It also has a material on the inside that constantly wipes the surface of the platter so that it will not accumulate dust particles. If dust were to accumulate, the read/write head, pressing on the dust particles, could scratch the magnetic material off the surface, making the platter unreadable. Even with this protection, the surfaces do wear out. Their life spans are usually fairly long, although this does seem to depend upon the logic circuits that read and write the information. If these circuits are not very sensitive, a disk that would work on a more sensitive system may not be readable. Unfortunately, many of the microcomputers on the market, because of efforts to keep costs down, do not have the best access circuitry and are not sensitive enough. Chapter 3 contains some information on the proper care of floppy disks that will help you make yours last a little longer.

There are also many differences in the individual drives that can further complicate the operation. The main difference is alignment. This is more of a problem on hard disks than on floppy disks because on hard disks data are stored in a more compressed form than on floppy disks. But floppy disks can also have alignment problems. Alignment refers to the index that allows the computer to find a given track. The index is the distance that the arm moves out onto the disk. If this index is off, the disk is said to be out of alignment. This is relative. Depending on how far out of alignment the disk drives are in relation to each other, a disk that is out of alignment might be able to read information that it stored itself, but may not be able to read information stored by another disk drive. There are standard alignment distances that are used so that most disks can read data stored by other disks and the alignment, if off, can be adjusted.

The idea of floppy disks wearing out brings me to backup, another important topic. Backup is an extra copy of software, normally kept on file in case the original program is damaged or lost. One rule on backups is that they should not be used just when the main disk becomes unusable. In that case a copy of the backup disk should be used. That way, the backup disk stays on file and is not destroyed. Backups of more important information should be made often. But because the information on a disk can be lost over time, even when the disk is not being used, a backup disk should be periodically refreshed by again copying it from the main disk. Refreshing also helps avoid reliability problems with disks, particularly microcomputer disks. Even systems that have good reliability records can have a disk that becomes, on occasion, unreadable. But always keeping two or three copies of all-important disks guards against this problem, too.

Another basic difference between the floppy and the hard disk is that some hard disks can store more data than any floppy disks. Here are some details. Both hard and floppy disks are divided into tracks and sectors. Although the sizes of the tracks are different on different types of disks, the sizes of the sectors are generally the same. All measurements are usually in bytes and all information used in most computers is stored in bytes. One byte is composed of 8 binary digits called bits (a bit is either a 1 or a 0, which are the binary digits) and stores a value between 0 and 255. On the disks, one sector is usually 256 bytes. The track is no longer important in that the computer will take care of the division into sectors. Hard disks can store 1,000,000 bytes of information (1 megabyte) and up while floppy disks usually store 1 megabyte or less.

The floppy disks, being the most commonly used disk on the microcomputers, require more discussion. There are several different types of floppy disks. The basic type is the single-density, single-sided floppy disk. The density refers to how compactly the data is stored. There are single-density and double-density drives. The double-density drives, as their name implies, store twice the amount of data as the single-density equivalent. Double-sided floppy disks simply use both sides instead of just one side. This requires two read/write heads in each drive. This also doubles the amount of information that can be stored on the floppy disk. The 8-inch floppy disk can have a capacity of about 250,000 bytes if it is single-sided and single-density. The capacity increases if the disk is either double-sided or double-density to about 500,000 bytes. If it is both double-density and double-sided, the capacity is about 1 megabyte. Minifloppy disks have similar options. The basic, single-sided, single-density minifloppy disk stores about 90,000 bytes. Dual-density and double-sided minifloppy disks are newer to the market and are not as widely available, but a minifloppy disk that is double-density or double-sided will store about 180,000 bytes, and one that is both double-density and double-sided will store 360,000 bytes.

The type, size, and number of disk drives required depend upon the intended application. Two minifloppy disks on a system with 32K (K stands for kilobytes—1 kilobyte is 1024 bytes) of memory create a very powerful personal computer system and will handle many small businesses. A single-drive system has its uses, but it also has many built-in handicaps. Backups, for example, are not as easy to make. To make a backup on a one-drive system usually requires removing and inserting the old and new disks several times. This also adds some extra wear to the disks and to the disk drives. Most users I know who started with a single drive system have purchased a second drive. A one-drive system is not a bad system on which to learn about disks, but if you purchase a one-drive system or add only one disk to a system that had no disks, expect to purchase another drive later. Planning it that way may be a good way to spread out some of the expense, in that the purchase price of the second drive is delayed until you learn how to handle the disk.

Knowing what a sector is helps in designing the programs, but the other physical information about the disk is only background. Most of the microcomputers use a dynamic allocation type of system, which is explained in the next chapter.

CHAPTER 2

DISK OPERATING SYSTEMS

Understanding the physical properties of the disks is only a beginning. Another important thing to know about is the operating system, the program built into the computer that supervises the disk's activities. It is this part of the computer that understands all of the commands listed in the manual.

To understand the disk operating system, you may need an overview of all of the systems operating and all the layers of languages present in the computer. At the lowest level is an understanding of the internal workings of the microprocessor chip itself. In that one chip is a full central processing unit (CPU), the brain of the computer, and some memory of its own, not available to the computer system in general. The CPU in the microprocessor is programmed to understand the microprocessor's machine language. When a machine language command is executed by this chip, it is read into the chip's internal memory and there triggers a series of commands inside the chip. These are simple commands. One command may be to get the contents of a register (a register is a temporary storage place where 8 bits can be stored), or to place a byte (8 bits) into a register. This language is called microcode and to computers it is the lowest-level language. A machine language can be used in the memory that is outside of the chip, and this memory is referred to as the computer's memory. BASIC and the disk operating system are both written in this language. Usually, an assembler is used to program the BASIC interpreter and the disk operating system. An assembler is simply a way of using a series of letters (called *mnemonics*) to represent the machine language commands. This makes it easier to program the machine language by making the computer do some of the computations involved in the programming.

Because the computer is usually precoded to accept some predetermined machine language, the computer's user cannot use the microcode. The machine language, however, generally is available to the user. BASIC is an interpretive language, which means that the computer looks at each command while the program is running, decides what to do, and then does it. There are also compiled languages, which first convert the program into machine language commands and then run the machine language. Compiled languages are normally faster than interpretive languages, but debugging is easier on the interpretive languages. What is actually happening when the program executes an instruction in an interpretive language like BASIC is that the machine language commands look up the instruction, then use a code found in this look-up table to branch to a series of machine language commands. In turn, the microprocessor interprets the machine language by using the microcode in the same way. This seems like a very long, involved process and, in fact, there are machines available that have the BASIC interpreter written directly in the microcode. These machines will run a BASIC program faster than those that have the BASIC interpreter written in machine language.

There is a good reason why these languages are built up like this. A very low-level language is very difficult to program. Five or six microcode statements may be required just to read 1 byte from memory. Machine languages can do this in one statement. BASIC can very easily move hundreds of bytes from one place in memory to another in one statement. This makes it much easier to program in BASIC than in any of the lower-level languages. There are also higher-level languages that are written in BASIC that can do even more in one statement. Each statement in a higher-level language causes many statements in the lower-level language in which it is written to be executed.

The disk operating system is a specialized set of instructions that, at times, acts as an interpretive language and at other times acts as a supplement to BASIC. There are commands in that language that can copy entire disks for backup, or can read the disk directory that lists the names of what has been written on the disk. Each disk operating system will have a specific way to set up the disk so that access is easier.

In almost any disk system, the disks are divided into files. A *file* is any collection of data that is called by a name. This name is chosen by the operator when the file is formed. The directory keeps track of where the file is on the disk. The collection of data may be data from a program and the file is called a data file, or it may be a BASIC program, in which case it is called a program file. There are also machine language program files and disk operating system command files. All of these are stored in the same manner on the disk.

Storing the files on the disk can be done in many ways. The simplest is for the disk operating system to have a directory at the beginning of the disk and, when a file is saved on the disk, store the name and the starting and ending sectors in the directory, along with some other information that the computer may require about the file. In this system, the size of the file must be determined first. Most of the microcomputers use a more sophisticated system called dynamic file allocation. In this system, there is an index in which only the starting sector is noted. The file is saved in small parts called records. The first record is placed where the index points, then a pointer is added to the first record to show where the second record will be. When the file becomes larger, it simply tacks on a few more records. If the file is altered in such a way that it becomes smaller, some records are freed up so that the operating system can use them for other files. If a file is completely eliminated, all of the records are freed for other files to use as they are needed.

Disks also require formatting before they are used. Some disks (for example, the one with the disk operating system on it) are already formatted. New blank disks must be formatted. The formatting is usually done by a command in the disk operating system. What formatting does is write some system information on each sector to identify it for the operating system. In addition, particularly in a dynamic allocation system, an index is created. All of this is done so that the operating system can keep track of where everything is and can go on the disk.

All of this information will be used to form some very efficient and easy-to-use methods of storing and retrieving data on the disk. The logic behind the interpreter is very similar to that behind using subroutines in a program. A subroutine is a series of statements that can be called by a statement in the program. It will perform a specific task determined by the programmer. That task could be to find a record on the disk and convert it to the form required in the program. There are several chapters in this book that explain ways to effectively use subroutines in programs to make programs easier to read (and therefore debug) and to also make programs much more effective.

There are generally several names and versions of any method used on computers. I chose the names in this book to be descriptive, so they can be more easily applied to the methods. If you read another text dealing with disk files, it may use other names and might describe a different variation of the method.

CHAPTER 3

TAKING CARE OF THE DISKS

There are some very simple, sensible rules about caring for the diskettes. The flexible disk is not as indestructible as it may look. Here it can be compared to a phonograph record, which also stores information.

Diskettes and records both do not like heat. Both can be warped and, given enough heat, can melt. Heat can also cause diskettes to lose information, even when there isn't enough heat to cause any visible damage. As with phonograph records, keep diskettes away from obvious heat sources such as radiators and the sun, as well as some not-so-obvious sources such as the tops of computers or other electronic devices. If the temperature of the diskette gets above 95° F, data may be lost to the heat. If you allow a diskette to get over 110°, you'd better have a duplicate of the data on it.

Diskettes, both the floppy and the minifloppy, are described as being flexible. This does not mean that you are supposed to bend them. The information stored on the diskette is stored on the very thin film of magnetic material on the plastic disk's surface. If the diskette is bent enough, this film will crack and the computer will not be able to read it. This does not mean that a disk that has been bent is automatically no good. I have had the unusual experience of mailing a disk to someone who received it folded in half by the U.S. Postal Service to fit into a mailbox. He unfolded the diskette and put it into the drive, and it worked. All of the information was still on it. This was an extremely lucky diskette, the only one of the several I know of that were received folded in half that actually worked. A diskette has flexibility so that the disk drive can use a contact head to read it. A rigid platter, on the other hand, would scratch more easily, not to mention break.

Always keep the diskette in its paper storage envelope when it is not in use. This is an extra protection against such things as dust. It also helps to prevent anything from touching the read/write window where a small portion of the surface is exposed. Never touch or allow anything else to touch this exposed disk surface. Anything that is left on this surface can become a weapon against the thin magnetic film, causing scratches that may render part of the diskette unusable. Anything left on the surface could also lead to a very expensive mistake by scratching the disk drive's read/write head. Also, never attempt to remove the envelope immediately around the diskette. This envelope is permanently sealed and is used to both protect and clean the surface. The cleaning is done by the inside surface of this envelope, which is covered with something resembling felt.

The disk is a magnetic medium, much like a cassette tape only more sensitive. Never get a disk near any magnetic field unless you want to erase it. Erasing can be done by running a magnet over both sides of the diskette (do not scratch the diskette through the read/write window). Avoid getting the disk near things like electric motors, television screens (which includes the screen on the computer), and transformers, as they all produce magnetic fields.

There is either a label or a place to put one on the diskette envelope. Since the disk is always inside this envelope, do not write on it with anything that requires any pressure, or the writing will be embossed onto the surface of the diskette. Use a felt-tip pen or write on the label before applying it to the diskette envelope.

Store diskettes like you would your best phonograph records. Do not pile them too high or put anything on top of them. Wire racks that are sold to keep 45 RPM records are good for storing the diskettes. They store best vertically. Also, the boxes that diskettes are sold in when they are bought in small quantities (usually a box contains 10 diskettes) are quite good for storing the diskettes.

PART TWO

SECTION I

INTRODUCTION

There are basically two types of files available on microcomputers: the sequential file and the random access file. The sequential file is very much like a tape file, which is actually one type of sequential file. For most disk applications, this file type is too clumsy, as the entire file must be rewritten to alter any data in it. There are some uses that this type of file will be employed to perform in this book, and further explanation will be saved for that application. The random-access file is the one responsible for the flexibility of the disk drive and this is the one that is explored in the section to follow.

Random access files consist of a series of numbered records, or spaces to store data. Each record must be the same size as all the other records in the same file, but the records may be read from or written to the disk independently from any other record in the file. Compare this to the sequential file, where the records do not have to be the same length but must be read or written in order (i.e., sequentially).

This section begins by explaining the basics of accessing a random-access file, proceeds through refining these methods, and ends with some programming hints which will make the programs a little easier to write, read, and alter.

EDDIE GERMANO

CHAPTER 4

RANDOM-ACCESS FILES

Terminology is usually the first barrier to someone's pursuing a new subject. This is true in computer science in general and in microcomputer disk technology in particular. But this terminology barrier is also easy to overcome. The glossary in the back of this book contains definitions of many important terms. If you need more information, you'll find several dictionaries of data processing words in libraries and book stores. Also, any dictionary of the English language, particularly a recent one, will contain many terms.

Here are a few terms often used in describing random-access files:

FILE	A section of the disk reserved for the storage of data or programs. On most systems, when a file is set up (the process of setting up a file is called *opening* the file), the computer keeps track of it by a file name. The file name is choosen when the file is opened and then is used to reference the file.
RECORD	A division of a file in which one set of data is stored. For example, in a file of addresses, one record will store one name and address.
BLOCK	The amount of data that in one operation is read from or written to the disk by the computer. The size of the block varies from computer to computer, but most blocks are around 256 bytes long.
BYTE	The basic unit of the computer's memory, a byte is a sequence of bits that represents a single character. It is almost always 8 bits in length (a *bit*, or binary integer, stores a binary value of one or zero. Eight bits store values from 0 to 255).

These definitions are not complete and might leave some unanswered questions, but using them in this chapter should help clear up the questions, because what's missing in the definitions is how these terms relate to each other.

To begin discussing the handling of these files, consider the block and the record to be the same unit. This is a possibility and is not that uncommon. This also is the simplest random-access file. In such a file, you can read or write one single record using the simplest forms of the disk commands listed in the manual.

The difference in the ways that each of the microcomputers is set up to reference the disk presents a problem in discussing the files. The most common method seems to be the use of GET and PUT. I use these words in this book. To determine the equivalent commands on other systems requires some investigation. GET, in the form GETn,m, where n is the file number and m is the record number, reads one record (record number m) from file n. The file number is determined in the program when the file is commanded to OPEN (see OPEN for more explanation—that word should be in the manual for any disk system). PUT is in the same format, and writes record m to file n. In some systems, the variable(s) containing (or to contain) the information must also appear in the statement that is reading or writing. In other systems, this variable or list of variables is set in a FIELD statement. Depending upon the specific system, use the variable B$ (B is for block, as that is, technically, the amount of data being transferred) or use the FIELD statement 255 AS B$.

Data files are commonly used to store names and addresses. To set up such a file, follow these steps:

1. OPEN the file. The OPEN statement should refer to the file as file 1 and name it NAMES. The file number and name can be a variety of other choices, but these will be used in this chapter for the descriptions. If the OPEN statement requires a file length, as some do, restrict it to 100 records, or blocks (sometimes referred to as sectors).
2. If required, FIELD the data with a FIELD statement of 255 AS B$.
3. Set B$ to all blanks (ASCII code 32, base 10, or 20 in base 16—this is equivalent to a space). Set up a FOR/NEXT loop and use PUT to place such a record in blocks 1 through 100. This initializes the file, or sets it to a starting position.
4. End the program, which should include using the CLOSE command.

These steps should initialize the file, which is the first step. In Microsoft BASIC, such a program would look like this:

```
10  CLEAR 600
20  OPEN "R",1,"NAMES"
30  FIELD 1, 255 AS B$
40  B1$ = STRING$(255,32)
50  FOR I = 1 TO 100
60  LSET B$ = B1$
70  PUT 1,I
80  NEXT I
90  CLOSE 1
100 END
```

In the above example, B1$ is used to store the string of blanks to set up the B$ string in the loop. The LSET and RSET commands move the contents of the variable into a special section of the computer's memory set aside to contain one block of information for transfers from and to the disk. To give an example of how this task can differ on different computers, a program written on a WANG 2200 system would look like this:

```
10  DIM B$(4)62
20  INIT(20)B$( )
30  DATASAVE DC OPEN F 102, "NAMES"
40  FOR I = 1 TO 100
50  DATA SAVE DC B$( )
60  NEXT I
70  DATA SAVE DC END
80  END
```

Instead of relying on one linear string variable for storage, the Wang system uses an array for the disk storage. In the OPEN statement, this system requires the file length but does not require the FIELD statement. As this system does not use the file number in the program, it uses the file number zero by default. To make it file number one, you can insert a number one in line 30 between F and 102, and also in line 50 and line 70 immediately following the DC. Also, someone using a Wang system must make a SELECT DISK statement at the beginning of the program so that the computer will know which disk platter to use.

Obviously, the Wang system uses a very different method for accessing the disks based on entirely different storage concepts. Wang also allows other forms for accessing the disk. This is because the Wang system was developed earlier and refined along different lines than most of the methods for microcomputers. Fortunately, most microcomputers use methods similar to the example in Microsoft BASIC.

Once a file has been initialized, it can be used. Writing blank records to each of the records in the file allows the computer to create an internal roadmap that it will use later to find each record.

Any program written to use this file should use the OPEN and FIELD statements in the example. This sets up the file so that the computer will know how to PUT and GET the records correctly. The next problem to solve is how to store the information in the newly established file.

There are many more ways of using the FIELD statement to define how data is stored in the record. This form of defining the entire record as one string allows some flexibility not afforded by other methods. For example, changing the structure of how the data is stored in order to add more information to each record later becomes simpler. Using this form for the FIELD statement leaves the problem of packing the data.

The next step is to determine the fields in the records. Each record should have exactly the same format as all of the other records in the same file so that the computer can read and write them correctly. The basic items for a name and address file are:

1. Name—Restrict this to 20 characters.
2. Address—This can also be 20 characters.
3. City—Generally, this can be restricted to 16 characters.
4. State—Using the postal abbreviations, this requires only two characters.
5. Zip Code—All zip codes in the United States are five digits. For simplicity use five characters.

The above fields and the limits described for each are used in this chapter's random-access file, but the names and lengths of fields could be altered to fit many applications. The zip code, at the time of this writing, was still five digits but was rumored to be increasing to nine in the near future, so that field may be expanded. The field may also be expanded to include Canadian names and addresses.

As each character will be stored in 1 byte, adding the lengths of these items will produce the record length in bytes. Numbers are stored differently, and that topic will be covered later. The length of this record is 63 bytes. On a system where the block length is 255 bytes, a common length in microcomputers, 192 unused bytes remain in each block. These extra bytes will be wasted. While the ways to make use of them will be explained in a later chapter, for now, ignore these extra bytes.

Now choose the variable to store these items while they are in the computer's memory. Use N$, A$, C$, S$, and Z$, in that order. Since B$ is the only string read from or written to the disk, there must be some way of putting these values into and getting these values from B$.

This text features subroutines often used in programs which access the disk as several required operations, such as packing and unpacking records. The subroutines eliminate the need to repeat several different series of statements. If the program text occupies from line 10 up to line 5999, lines 6000 and up may be used exclusively for subroutines. The reasons for splitting the text between program and subroutine will become much clearer in later chapters. With that in mind, use the following two subroutines to pack and unpack the record:

```
6000 STOP
6010 B1$ =STRING$(255,32)
6020 B2$ =STRING$(20,32)
6030 MID$(B1$,1,20) =N$ +B2$
6040 MID$(B1$,21,20) =A$ +B2$
6045 MID$(B1$,41,16) =C$ +B2$
6050 MID$(B1$,57,2) =S$ +B2$
6060 MID$(B1$,59,5) =Z$ +B2$
6070 LSET B$ =B1$
6080 RETURN
6090 N$ =LEFT$(B$,20)
6100 A$ =MID$(B$,21,20)
6110 C$ =MID$(B$,41,16)
6120 S$ =MID$(B$,57,2)
6130 Z$ =MID$(B$,59,5)
6140 RETURN
```

The above text contains two subroutines. The first one starts at line 6010 and packs the five variables containing the data into B1$, then sets up B$ in the form required in the PUT statement. B1$ is initialized to spaces so that the length agrees with the FIELD statement. Add B2$ to all of the variables so that there will be no *null* or meaningless empty spaces in the record, which, if they are ignored, can cause problems on many systems. Line 6090 starts the second routine, which unpacks the record into the five variables. This subroutine can be used immediately following the GET statement.

Although this chapter has presented much information on random-access files, all that has been done so far in the examples is setting up the file on the disk and preparing subroutines to read and write data. The initialization step is important not only to eliminate any "garbage" that may have been on the disk in the area allocated to the file but also, on some computers, to set up an internal roadmap the system will use later to locate the records. The subroutines to read and write the data are required to make using the files easier. Sufficient preparation, although it makes the first steps more difficult, simplifies using the files.

A simple example of using the file can be built around the two subroutines. The following program text will allow you to write a name and address into the file and also to display one name and address at a time on the screen. You should enter the two subroutines first, and then do the following:

```
10  CLEAR1000
20  OPEN"R",1,"NAMES"
30  FIELD1,255ASB$
40  CLS
50  INPUT"ENTER 1 TO WRITE OR 2 TO READ";N
60  IFN = 1THEN100
70  IFN = 2THEN300
80  PRINT"ERROR—PLEASE ENTER 1 OR 2"
90  GOTO40
100  CLS
110  PRINT"WRITE A NEW RECORD TO THE FILE"
120  INPUT"ENTER RECORD NUMBER (1 TO 100)":N
130  IFN > = 1THEN160
140  PRINT"ERROR—RECORD NUMBER MUST BE 1 TO 100"
150  GOTO120
160  IFN > 100THEN140
170  INPUT"NAME";N$
180  INPUT"ADDRESS";A$
190  INPUT"CITY";C$
200  INPUT"STATE";S$
210  INPUT"ZIP CODE";Z$
220  GOSUB6010
230  PUT1,N
240  GOTO40
300  CLS
310  PRINT"READ A RECORD FROM THE FILE"
320  INPUT"ENTER RECORD NUMBER";N
330  IFN > = 1THEN360
340  PRINT"ERROR—RECORD NUMBER MUST BE 1 TO 100"
350  GOTO320
360  IFN > 100THEN340
370  GET1,N
380  GOSUB6090
390  PRINT"NAME : ";N$
400  PRINT"ADDRESS : ";A$
410  PRINT"CITY : ";C$
420  PRINT"STATE : ";S$
430  PRINT"ZIP CODE : ";Z$
440  GOTO50
```

This example shows basically how to access a random-access file. The program is set up to show the disk-access functions and is not intended to be a showpiece on the display screen. If this is to be a frequently used program, the PRINT and INPUT statements could be improved, but these adornments are not needed for the example.

The program is in four sections, not counting the two subroutines. The first section, made up of lines 10 through 30, initializes. Initialization in this program includes the CLEAR statement to set aside room for the string variables and the OPEN and FIELD statements for the file. The second section, lines 40 through 90, requests a decision from the operator as to which of the last two sections should be run. The third section, lines 100 through 240, writes one record to the file. The last section, lines 300 through 440, reads and displays one record.

With the program texts presented so far, a random-access file can be read from and written to by using a number from 1 to 100. This works well but has very limited use. Even printouts of the file would be of limited use if they were in record number order. The solution to this problem is, in part, sorting. The simplest approach, although not the most practical or the most useful, is to sort the entire file directly. When this is done, you can print the file in some useful order. What makes this method inefficient and of limited use is that the record number of any given name and address will probably change in the process of sorting.

All sorting methods have advantages and disadvantages, but you should learn as many as possible and that way learn which methods to use for which applications. You can then learn to combine methods to fit specific circumstances.

In a direct sort, the records are physically placed in some order. For example, if the sort is by name, all of the names which begin with A will be first in the file, followed by the names which begin with B, etc. The example to follow illustrates a push-down or bubble sort. It is one of many different types of sorts used, and may be one of the most common direct sorts because it is very easy to program. To explain the logic of the sort, consider ordering the following five letters alphabetically:

```
1   2   3   4   5
Q   Z   I   S   R
```

Begin with the first two letters, Q and Z. These two are in the correct order, so they are left alone. Go on to the next two letters, Z and I. These are out of order, so swap them. The order is now:

```
1   2   3   4   5
Q   I   Z   S   R
```

Go on to the next two letters, which are now Z and S. These are also out of order, so swap them. The last two letters are now Z and R, which are also out of order, so swap them. This completes the first part or *pass* in the sort. It resulted in the letter Z being *pushed down* to the end of the series, or *bubbled up* to the top, depending on how you look at it. The resulting order is now:

1	2	3	4	5
Q	I	S	R	Z

The next pass stops at letter number four, but follows the same logic as the first pass. First, swap the letters Q and I. The next pair, Q and S, are in the correct order, so leave them alone. The last pair in this pass are the letters S and R. They are out of order, so swap them. This results with the following order:

1	2	3	4	5
I	Q	R	S	Z

The letters are now in the correct order. In this example, the letters were sorted in two passes. For five elements (entries on the list to be sorted), the maximum number of passes is four, or one less than the number of elements. This will occur when the elements are in reverse order before the sort.

You can easily transfer the logic of the bubble sort to the sorting of an array on the computer. The following program will sort five letters into alphabetical order:

```
10  CLEAR100
20  DIMA$(5)
30  PRINT"ENTER THE FIVE LETTERS ONE AT A TIME:"
40  FORI = 1TO5
50  PRINT"ENTER LETTER NO.";I;
60  INPUTA$(I)
70  NEXTI
80  FORI = 1TO4
90  FORJ = 2TO6 - I
100  IFA$(J) > = A$(J - 1)THEN140
110  A$ = A$(J)
120  A$(J) = A$(J - 1)
130  A$(J - 1) = A$
```

```
140 NEXTJ
150 NEXTI
160 FORI = 1TO5
170 PRINTI;A$(I)
180 NEXTI
190 STOP
```

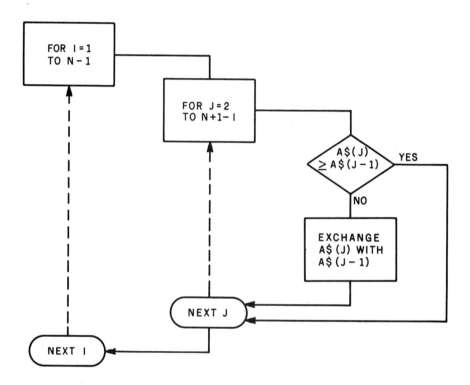

Figure 4.1: *Bubble sort flow chart where* N *is the number of items to be sorted.*

The FOR statements in lines 80 and 90 control the number of passes and length of each pass. In line 80, the variable I will take values from numbers one to four, which is one number less than the number of elements. The index variable I is used only as a counter except in line 90. The index variable here, J, starts at two and so it ends at six minus I and will go from five in the first pass down to two in the last pass. J will be the higher element in each pair examined. This examination takes place at line 100. If the letters are in the correct order, the program will branch to the NEXT J statement. If they are not in the correct order, lines 110 through 130 will swap them. The array A$(5) holds the five letters. The linear string variable A$ is used as a temporary variable, also called a work variable, which is a place to put something for temporary storage and is not needed before or after the process. Note that there is no check for the length of the entries. This program will also sort entire sentences up to the maximum string length for the computer used. Experimenting with different character combinations will show you how the computer sorts words and other longer strings which may include numbers and characters.

To apply this sorting to the random-access file, load the program used to access the random-access file back into the computer. Now add one of two functions to the program—sort or print. You can replace lines 50 through 80 with the lines as indicated on the listing. Add the routines at lines 500 through 650 (these will print the records in order) and at lines 700 through 830 (these will sort the file). If there is no printer, change all of the LPRINT commands to PRINT and add:

```
612 PRINT"PRESS ENTER FOR NEXT NAME AND ADDRESS"
614 W$ =INKEY$:IFW$ =''''THEN614
```

For systems which do not have the equivalent of INKEY$, use an input statement for line 614 that inputs W$.

```
10 CLEAR1000
20 OPEN"R",1,"NAMES:1"
30 FIELD1,255ASB$
40 CLS
50 INPUT"ENTER 1 TO WRITE, 2 TO READ, 3 TO PRINT OR 4 TO
   SORT";N
60 IFN<1THEN80
62 IFN>4THEN80
70 ONNGOTO100,300,500,700
80 PRINT"ERROR—ENTER 1, 2, 3 OR 4"
90 GOTO40
100 CLS
110 PRINT"WRITE A NEW RECORD TO THE FILE"
120 INPUT"ENTER RECORD NUMBER (1 TO 100)";N
130 IFN> =1THEN160
140 PRINT"ERROR—RECORD NUMBER MUST BE 1 TO 100"
150 GOTO120
160 IFN>100THEN140
170 INPUT"NAME";N$
180 INPUT"ADDRESS";A$
190 INPUT"CITY";C$
200 INPUT"STATE";S$
210 INPUT"ZIP CODE";Z$
220 GOSUB6010
```

```
230  PUT1,N
240  GOTO40
300  CLS
310  PRINT"READ A RECORD FROM THE FILE"
320  INPUT"ENTER RECORD NUMBER";N
330  IFN> =1THEN360
340  PRINT"ERROR—RECORD NUMBER MUST BE 1 TO 100"
350  GOTO320
360  IFN>100THEN340
370  GET1,N
380  GOSUB6090
390  PRINT"NAME : ";N$
400  PRINT"ADDRESS : ";A$
410  PRINT"CITY : ";C$
420  PRINT"STATE : ";S$
430  PRINT"ZIP CODE : ";Z$
440  GOTO50
500  INPUT"START AT RECORD NO.";N
510  INPUT"END AT RECORD NO.";N1
520  IFN<1THEN640
530  IFN1<NTHEN640
540  IFN1>100THEN640
550  FORI=NTON1
560  GET1,I
570  GOSUB6090
575  IFLEFT$(B$,1) =" "THEN620
580  LPRINTI;N$
590  LPRINTA$
600  LPRINTC$;",    ";S$;" ";Z$
610  LPRINT" "
620  NEXTI
630  GOTO40
640  PRINT"ERROR—ENTER RECORD NUMBERS CORRECTLY"
650  GOTO500
700  PRINT"SORTING THE FILE"
710  FORI=1TO99
720  GET1,1
730  B1$ =B$
740  FORJ=2TO101 −I
750  GET1,J
752  IFLEFT$(B$,1) =" "THEN800
754  IFLEFT$(B1$,1) =" "THEN770
760  IFB$ > =B1$THEN800
770  PUT1,J − 1
780  LSETB$ =B1$
790  PUT1,J
800  B1$ =B$
```

```
810 NEXTJ
820 NEXTI
830 GOTO40
6000 STOP
6010 B1$=STRING$(255,32)
6020 B2$=STRING$(20,32)
6030 MID$(B1$,1,20)=N$+B2$
6040 MID$(B1$,21,20)=A$+B2$
6045 MID$(B1$,41,16)=C$+B2$
6050 MID$(B1$,57,2)=S$+B2$
6060 MID$(B1$,59,5)=Z$+B2$
6070 LSETB$=B1$
6080 RETURN
6090 N$=LEFT$(B$,20)
6100 A$=MID$(B$,21,20)
6110 C$=MID$(B$,41,16)
6120 S$=MID$(B$,57,2)
6130 Z$=MID$(B$,59,5)
6140 RETURN
```

The sorting routine (lines 700 through 830) is very similar to the short alphabetical sort program. The basic difference is that the equivalent of A$(J − 1) is not available, and B1$ is used to hold the value of the last record. Since the routine that makes one pass always starts with the second record, B1$ is initially set to the value of the first record in the file. The swapping looks very different in this routine. Instead of swapping two variables in memory, this sort uses PUT statements to reorder the disk file.

Notice how long this routine takes to sort the 100-record file. That is a distinct disadvantage to the bubble sort. But the operation can be speeded up—the sorting terminated early—if there are no more swaps in the pass. The initial example was terminated when the user added a simple test to the program to force the sort to end after a successful pass in which no elements were swapped. With the test, files with fewer than 100 records or any files that require fewer passes do not take as long. With the variable SW, the user counts the number of swaps in a pass.

Implementing this counter is simple. Add :SW=0 to line 730 to initialize the counter before each pass. Add line 795 SW=SW+1 to count the number of swaps.

This IF statement will cause the outer loop to terminate after any pass that does not swap any records.

```
815 IF SW=0 THEN I=99
```

And now you have something useful—a routine that will give an alphabetical listing of the file by name. The entire string B$ can be used because the first field in it is the name.

POWER OF
BINARY
MULTIPLES

EDDIE GERMANO

CHAPTER 5

THE BINARY SEARCH

An old story tells of a peasant who saved his king's life. Since it is an old story, in some versions the peasant also saved the entire kingdom. But in any case, how the peasant saved anything varies considerably among versions. How the king rewarded the peasant does not vary, and this is fortunate because the method of reward is the interesting part of the story.

The king was a chess player. When he told the peasant to name any reward he wanted, the peasant took advantage of this by relating the reward to the chessboard. On the first square, the peasant requested one grain of wheat be placed. On the second square, two grains of wheat. On the third square, four grains, and on each square in turn, twice the number was placed as on the previous square until all the squares had been used. The grain would be the reward.

At this request, the king laughed and stated that the grain was too small a reward for the peasant's gallantry, but the peasant insisted and the order was issued. The grain counting began.

It was soon determined that there was not nearly enough grain in the entire kingdom to fill the peasant's request. The total number of grains that would be required would be 18,446,744,073,709,551,615. This is two to the sixty-fourth power, minus one grain.

This story shows something of how the base two numbering system works. The whole system is based on doubling. With it, 64 squares added up to an incredibly high number. The computer is based on this base two (more often called *binary*) number system, and is therefore subject to all of its eccentricities. In their most basic forms, all numbers, letters, characters, and even program statements are stored as ones and zeroes, which are the only two digits in the binary system. Working the analogy of the king and the peasant backwards yields a very efficient method of searching through sorted records, whether in a random-access disk file or in an array in memory. For example, to find a record in a file that has as many records as the number of grains noted in the story, only 64 searches would be required (one search being the operation of looking at one particular record).

Using the binary system approach, searching through sorted records is not much different from looking up a word in the dictionary. The basic difference is that the method used on the computer must be a little more exact and less random. A typical search through the dictionary, say to look up the word "number," may go like this:

First, you open the dictionary somewhere in the middle. The page you turn to starts with "monitor" and ends with "monoacidic." Both of these words are earlier in the alphabet than the word "number," so you turn a few more pages. This next page you read starts with "new" and ends with "next." "Number" is still further ahead, so you turn a few more pages. Now the page goes from "obtain" to "occasional." These words are both later in the alphabet than "number," so you turn back a few pages. You keep repeating this process until you come to the page containing the word "number."

A simple example of a more exact application of this logic can be found in a popular game. Many radio station games and a few electronic games are based on it. The game is a number guessing game, where the player is to guess a number between two given numbers. After each guess, the player is told whether the guess was too high or too low. If the range of numbers is 1 to 1000, the number could be guessed in 10 guesses or less using a searching technique based on the binary system. This technique is commonly called the binary search method. Using the binary search method to guess the number 566 would involve the following set of guesses:

1. The limits are 1 and 1000, so the first guess is the average of 0 and 1001 (the numbers immediately outside the range, because you know that the number to guess is not one of these). Round up the average, which is exactly 500.5, and give 501 as the first guess. This is too low, so move up the lower limit of 0 to 501 because you now know that the number is between 501 and 1001.
2. The next guess is the average of these new limits, or 751. This is too high, so move down the upper limit to 751. Now the limits are 501 and 751.
3. The average of these limits is 626. This is also too high, so the new limits are 501 and 626.
4. This average is 564. This is fairly close, but the only information we can use is that it is too low, so the new limits become 564 and 626.
5. This guess is 595, which is too high, so the upper limit becomes 595. The number is between 564 and 595, which means that it is now one of 30 numbers.
6. This average is 580, which is also too high, so the limits become 564 and 580.
7. This guess is 572, which is also too high. The new limits are 564 and 572.
8. There are only seven possibilities left. This guess is 568, which is too high. The range is now 568 and 564, a range of three numbers.

9. This guess is 566, which is the answer. Nine guesses got this one, but it should be clear that 565 and 567, had one of them been the number, would have required the same steps, but would also have needed one more step.

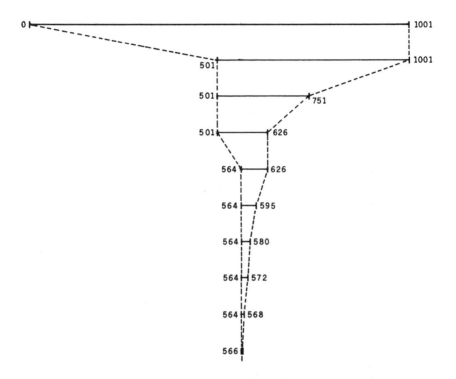

Figure 5.1: *Closing in on a number using a binary search.*

It is obvious that some numbers can be guessed in fewer guesses than others, but if there are only 1000 numbers, never will it require more than 10 guesses. Actually, these are not really guesses at all, but specific points to test.

You can apply this method directly to the file sorted in the last chapter. The only differences are that the file is alphanumeric instead of numeric and that the records are not sequential, as are the numbers, but are in sorted order.

Another example, smaller than the one with 1000 numbers and more similar to working with the dictionary, will show how these differences can be handled. Consider this group of letters, sorted alphabetically:

1	2	3	4	5	6	7	8	9
B	E	G	H	M	O	Q	Y	Z

You can search for one of the letters in this sample file by using the numbers above each letter. With nine records in this file, finding any one of them will not take more than four searches. Note that the binary search method works more efficiently on larger files. The 1000 numbers guessing game required that no more than 10, which is one percent of the total, be tested, but in this small file, four out of nine, almost half, must be tested. Although nine is not a practical size, it is still sufficient to show how the method works.

This search will be for the letter "O." Since there are nine records, the limits will begin at 0 and 10. The first average is five, which corresponds to the letter "M." That is too small (i.e. earlier in the alphabet), so set the lower limit to five. The second guess is the average of five and ten, which is eight (remember—round up). That corresponds to the letter "Y", which is too large. The new limits are five and eight, giving the next guess as seven (the letter "Q"). That is too large, so the next guess, the average of five and seven, is six, which is the correct number as it corresponds with the letter "O." This method works well when the letter being searched is there, but not when the letter is not there, like the letter "J."

The search for the letter "J" is as follows:

GUESS	LIMITS	AVERAGE	LETTER	
1	0-10	5	M	too large
2	0-5	3	G	too small
3	3-5	4	H	too small

Now there is a problem. The letter corresponding to four is too low and the one corresponding to five is too high. Since there is no record between four and five, "J" is not in the file.

There are two ways to determine that the search was not successful. First, make sure that the upper and lower limits are only one number apart and that the upper and lower limits have already been tested or are outside the area to test. Second, check to see that the maximum number of searches for that size file has already been made without finding the record. To use this method you need some way to determine the maximum number of searches for the file.

Since this method is called the binary search method, it seems quite logical that the maximum number of searches is related to the binary system of numbers. It is. This magic number is the power of two which is equal to or just greater than the number of records in the file. Refer to the appendix for the powers of two from 1 to 20. The file has nine records in it. The correct power of two is four. Three would give 8, but that is lower, so four must be used. For the example of 1000 numbers, 10 is the magic number because it corresponds to 1024 and nine corresponds to 512. The table in the appendix gives this magic number for any file with up to a million records. To extend the table further, simply keep doubling the number to get the next power.

Now, to go back to the program from Chapter 4, the binary search method can add the function of looking up a record by name. The program will first need to be altered so that this new function can be called. Alter the following lines to read:

```
50  PRINT"ENTER 1 TO WRITE, 2 TO READ, 3 TO PRINT,"
52  INPUT"4 TO SORT OR 5 TO SEARCH";N
62  IFN>5THEN80
70  ON N GOTO 100,300,500,700,900
```

Note that line 60 does not need to be changed. The only part left is to write the section that performs the search. Since that doesn't look quite as simple as the last change, look at the logic first. The basic steps for this are:

1. Use INPUT to get the name to search. Store this in N1$.
2. Set the limits as L1 and L2. These should be initialized to 0 and 101 for a 100-record file. Set the counter L4 to 0.
3. Set L3 equal to the average $(L3 = INT((L1 + L2)/2 + .5))$ and get record number L3.
4. If the name in this record is greater than N1$, set $L2 = L3$.
5. If the name in this record is less than N1$, set $L1 = L3$.
6. If the name in this record is equal to N1$, end the search—the name was found.
7. Add 1 to L4. If $L4 < 7$, go back to step #3.
8. The search ends without success here.

This logic translates into the code in listing 5.1, lines 900 to 1000. This routine ends when it finds the record by branching into the routine that gets a record by number and displays it. If the record is not found, it displays a message to that effect and gives the number of a record that was close.

In the program that was not in the logic is the part that takes care of the unused records. Statement 930 sets any blank records to a very high value so that a blank record is higher than the name being searched. Also, L5 was added to keep the length of the name entered so that the comparison would only compare the number of characters entered. Otherwise, a short name like "DOE" would always test out higher in the file because it is followed by other information.

```
10 CLEAR1000
20 OPEN"R",1,"NAMES:1"
30 FIELD1,255ASB$
40 CLS
50 PRINT"ENTER 1 TO WRITE, 2 TO READ, 3 TO PRINT,"
52 INPUT"4 TO SORT OR 5 TO SEARCH";N
60 IFN<1THEN80
62 IFN>5THEN80
70 ONNGOTO100,300,500,700,900
80 PRINT"ERROR - ENTER 1, 2, 3 OR 4"
90 GOTO40
100 CLS
110 PRINT"WRITE A NEW RECORD TO THE FILE"
120 INPUT"ENTER RECORD NUMBER (1 TO 100)";N
130 IFN>=1THEN160
140 PRINT"ERROR - RECORD NUMBER MUST BE 1 TO 100"
150 GOTO120
160 IFN>100THEN140
170 INPUT"NAME";N$
180 INPUT"ADDRESS";A$
190 INPUT"CITY";C$
200 INPUT"STATE";S$
210 INPUT"ZIP CODE";Z$
220 GOSUB6010
230 PUT1,N
240 GOTO40
300 CLS
310 PRINT"READ A RECORD FROM THE FILE"
320 INPUT"ENTER RECORD NUMBER";N
330 IFN>=1THEN360
340 PRINT"ERROR - RECORD NUMBER MUST BE 1 TO 100"
350 GOTO320
360 IFN>100THEN340
370 GET1,N
380 GOSUB6090
390 PRINT"NAME : ";N$
400 PRINT"ADDRESS : ";A$
410 PRINT"CITY : ";C$
420 PRINT"STATE : ";S$
430 PRINT"ZIP CODE : ";Z$
440 GOTO50
500 INPUT"START AT RECORD NO.";N
510 INPUT"END AT RECORD NO.";N1
520 IFN<1THEN640
530 IFN1<NTHEN640
540 IFN1>100THEN640
550 FORI=NTON1
560  GET1,I
570  GOSUB6090
575  IFLEFT$(B$,1)=" "THEN620
580  PRINTN$
590  PRINTA$
600  PRINTC$;", ";S$;" ";Z$
610  PRINT" "
612  PRINT"PRESS ENTER FOR NEXT NAME AND ADDRESS"
614  W$=INKEY$:IFW$=""THEN614
620 NEXTI
630 GOTO40
640 PRINT"ERROR - ENTER RECORD NUMBERS CORRECTLY"
650 GOTO500
700 PRINT"SORTING THE FILE"
710 FORI=1TO99
715 SW=0
720  GET1,1
730  B1$=B$
740  FORJ=2TO101-I
750   GET1,J
752   IFLEFT$(B$,1)=" "THEN800
754   IFLEFT$(B1$,1)=" "THEN770
760   IFB$>=B1$THEN800
765   SW=SW+1
770   PUT1,J-1
```

```
780    LSET B$=B1$
790    PUT1,J
800    B1$=B$
810   NEXTJ
815  IFSW=0THENI=99
820  NEXTI
830  GOTO40
900  INPUT"ENTER NAME TO SEARCH";N1$
910  L1=0:L2=101:L4=0:L5=LEN(N1$)
920  L3=INT((L1+L2)/2+.5):GET1,L3
930  IFLEFT$(B$,1)=" "THENLSETB$=STRING$(10,255)
940  IFLEFT$(B$,L5)>N1$THENLETL2=L3
950  IFLEFT$(B$,L5)<N1$THENLETL1=L3
960  IFLEFT$(B$,L5)=N1$THEN380
970  L4=L4+1
980  IFL4<7THEN920
990  PRINT"NAME NOT FOUND - IT IS NEAR RECORD NO.";L3
1000 GOTO50
6000 STOP
6010 B1$=STRING$(255,32)
6020 B2$=STRING$(20,32)
6030 MID$(B1$,1,20)=N$+B2$
6040 MID$(B1$,21,20)=A$+B2$
6045 MID$(B1$,41,16)=C$+B2$
6050 MID$(B1$,57,2)=S$+B2$
6060 MID$(B1$,59,5)=Z$+B2$
6070 LSET B$=B1$
6080 RETURN
6090 N$=LEFT$(B$,20)
6100 A$=MID$(B$,21,20)
6110 C$=MID$(B$,41,16)
6120 S$=MID$(B$,57,2)
6130 Z$=MID$(B$,59,5)
6140 RETURN
```

Listing 5.1

The program as it is set up misses out on one very obvious and important point. Using it will quickly reveal that the program searches and alphabetizes on the first name. If the file were of all company names, this would not be a problem, but if the file were of people's names it would be. People tend to alphabetize by their last names. Listing 5.2 is another variation of the program that adds a key field to the record as the first field. This key field can be the last name or any other value that will specify the record. To use this new program, reinitialize the data file because the new field has reordered where the other fields will be in the records.

```
10  CLEAR1000
20  OPEN"R",1,"NAMES:1"
30  FIELD1,255ASB$
40  CLS
50  PRINT"ENTER 1 TO WRITE, 2 TO READ, 3 TO PRINT,"
52  INPUT"4 TO SORT OR 5 TO SEARCH";N
60  IFN<1THEN80
62  IFN>5THEN80
70  ONNGOTO100,300,500,700,900
80  PRINT"ERROR - ENTER 1, 2, 3 OR 4"
90  GOTO40
100 CLS
110 PRINT"WRITE A NEW RECORD TO THE FILE"
```

```
120 INPUT"ENTER RECORD NUMBER (1 TO 100)";N
130 IFN>=1THEN160
140 PRINT"ERROR - RECORD NUMBER MUST BE 1 TO 100"
150 GOTO120
160 IFN>100THEN140
165 INPUT"KEY";K$
170 INPUT"NAME";N$
180 INPUT"ADDRESS";A$
190 INPUT"CITY";C$
200 INPUT"STATE";S$
210 INPUT"ZIP CODE";Z$
220 GOSUB6010
230 PUT1,N
240 GOTO40
300 CLS
310 PRINT"READ A RECORD FROM THE FILE"
320 INPUT"ENTER RECORD NUMBER";N
330 IFN>=1THEN360
340 PRINT"ERROR - RECORD NUMBER MUST BE 1 TO 100"
350 GOTO320
360 IFN>100THEN340
370 GET1,N
380 GOSUB6090
385 PRINT"KEY : ";K$
390 PRINT"NAME : ";N$
400 PRINT"ADDRESS : ";A$
410 PRINT"CITY : ";C$
420 PRINT"STATE : ";S$
430 PRINT"ZIP CODE : ";Z$
440 GOTO50
500 INPUT"START AT RECORD NO.";N
510 INPUT"END AT RECORD NO.";N1
520 IFN<1THEN640
530 IFN1<NTHEN640
540 IFN1>100THEN640
550 FORI=NTON1
560   GET1,I
570   GOSUB6090
575 PRINTK$
580   PRINTN$
590   PRINTA$
600   PRINTC$;", ";S$;" ";Z$
610   PRINT" "
612   PRINT"PRESS ENTER FOR NEXT NAME AND ADDRESS"
614   W$=INKEY$:IFW$=""THEN614
620 NEXTI
630 GOTO40
640 PRINT"ERROR - ENTER RECORD NUMBERS CORRECTLY"
650 GOTO500
700 PRINT"SORTING THE FILE"
710 FORI=1TO99
715 SW=0
720   GET1,1
730   B1$=B$
740   FORJ=2TO101-I
750     GET1,J
752     IFLEFT$(B$,1)=" "THEN800
754     IFLEFT$(B1$,1)=" "THEN770
760     IFB$>=B1$THEN800
765     SW=SW+1
770     PUT1,J-1
780     LSET B$=B1$
790     PUT1,J
800     B1$=B$
810   NEXTJ
815 IFSW=0THENI=99
820 NEXTI
830 GOTO40
900 INPUT"ENTER KEY TO SEARCH";N1$
910 L1=0:L2=101:L4=0:L5=LEN(N1$)
920 L3=INT((L1+L2)/2+.5):GET1,L3
930 IFLEFT$(B$,1)=" "THENLSETB$=STRING$(10,255)
```

```
940 IFLEFT$(B$,L5)>N1$THENLETL2=L3
950 IFLEFT$(B$,L5)<N1$THENLETL1=L3
960 IFLEFT$(B$,L5)=N1$THEN380
970 L4=L4+1
980 IFL4<7THEN920
990 PRINT"KEY NOT FOUND - IT IS NEAR RECORD NO.";L3
1000 GOTO50
6000 STOP
6010 B1$=STRING$(255,32)
6020 B2$=STRING$(20,32)
6025 MID$(B1$,1,10)=K$+B2$
6030 MID$(B1$,11,20)=N$+B2$
6040 MID$(B1$,31,20)=A$+B2$
6045 MID$(B1$,51,16)=C$+B2$
6050 MID$(B1$,67,2)=S$+B2$
6060 MID$(B1$,69,5)=Z$+B2$
6070 LSET B$=B1$
6080 RETURN
6090 K$=LEFT$(B$,10)
6095 N$=MID$(B$,11,20)
6100 A$=MID$(B$,31,20)
6110 C$=MID$(B$,51,16)
6120 S$=MID$(B$,67,2)
6130 Z$=MID$(B$,69,5)
6140 RETURN
```

Listing 5.2

CHAPTER 6

SUBROUTINES

Usually, when someone writes a book, thesis, or report, that person starts with an outline or the equivalent to organize the presentation. When someone wants to program something, the first thing that person usually does is sit down at the computer. As a result, most books, theses, and reports are in some sort of logical order, and most programs look like cooked spaghetti. This does not have to be. A few simple guidelines would help. The major organizing aid taught for programming is the flow chart, which could be the last step, but certainly not the first step, before programming. Flow charts have their place, but they answer the question of how it works when the first question should ask what does it do. This difference becomes particularly important when the complexities of disk access are added to the program.

Since this subject will be handled in more detail in later chapters, this chapter will deal only with the highlights. This subject is important here because one part of it, subroutine use, needs some discussion before more complex disk techniques can be approached. Organizing a program that uses disk files requires a specific order. The starting point is the organization of the data files, including how the data fit into the records and how these records are loaded, unpacked, packed, and saved. You should handle these functions by subroutines.

One way to help avoid the "spaghetti syndrome" in programming in BASIC is to divide the program by statement numbers between the main program and the subroutines and keep the program split so that the main program is below and the subroutines are above some predetermined line number. On most systems that line number could be 5000 or 6000. The examples given in this book use line 6000. That line is a STOP statement so that the programmer can build and test the program in sections and not risk having it run into the subroutines if an ending point were to be left out of the part being tested. The first subroutine will then start at line 6010.

Subroutines are usually presented as devices to avoid repeating text. A better way to think of a subroutine is as a *macro-statement*. This device is used in assembly language (a means of communicating with a computer at a low level) to eliminate coding a series of statements that do a lot of busy work like converting dates into and out of different formats. The macro-statement is not required in the main part of the program, because it would make the logic harder to read by making the reader wade through the superfluous logic of things like date format conversion. If a statement like "convert this to Julian" were acceptable in the text, it would make for much easier reading. In BASIC, GOSUB 7030 could mean the same thing. A list of the functions of the subroutine set should be available when reading the main program text.

The basic subroutines for disk access should be able to perform the following functions:

- Get a specific record from disk and unpack it.
- Put a specific record on disk after packing it.
- Find (search) a record on the disk.
- Delete a record from the disk.
- Search out the next greater record on disk (see text).

The subroutines presented in Chapter 4 perform the packing and unpacking. The main program handled the getting and putting as well as performing the search. Two more terms, deleting and searching out the next greater record, need to be explained here. Delete simply eliminates a record from the file. Searching the next greater record can be used in a sorted file or in most key files, which will be introduced in the next section, to produce an ordered listing.

Rather than an ironclad set of rules, the above list is simply a set of guidelines to show the things to keep in mind when designing the subroutines. Getting a record and unpacking it, for example, can be two separate subroutines or can be combined with the searching to be all one subroutine. The specific application should be examined to determine the best use of the subroutines.

Another set of subroutines, general input subroutines, can also be quite useful. These subroutines request data from the operator, eliminating a few of the problems of using just the INPUT statement. These routines can perform such things as cursor positioning so that the input can be placed at a specific location on the screen. They can also check the input for things like alphanumerics being within length limits, numerics being within a certain range, and dates being in a valid format.

Parameters are also important to understand when discussing subroutines. These are variables set to certain values before the routine is called from the main program (i.e., before the GOSUB statement). They control the function of the subroutine. For example, a subroutine that gets a record from the disk must have some way to determine which record to get. Some variable must be set equal to the record number (in the main program) before the GOSUB statement is made to this subroutine. That variable is a *parameter*. Parameters can also control more of what a subroutine can do. For example, consider an unpacking subroutine that can unpack almost any type of record. This subroutine may require an entire array of parameters that will instruct the subroutine on how to unpack the record. The parameters will include the length and type of each field in the record as well as how many fields are in the record.

If the proper subroutine set is developed, the main program will look very simple. All that would be required to read it, in addition to the listing, is a list of the subroutines telling what each one does. Assembling a list of subroutines is actually the second step in organizing the effort of programming. The first step is determining what the program is to do.

First, start with the intended output of the program, whether this is in the form of printed reports, screen displays, or other output. The information required for this output is the first clue as to what should be in the data files. Also, this will show if there are to be more files and in what order the files should be. Next, look at the required processing. If the application is one that does some computations on the data, then these computations should be examined to determine if data that do not appear on the output are needed. A list of all data for each file required should be made. When the list or lists are complete, each field should be given length limitations so that the packing and unpacking subroutines can be written.

To get a real example up to this point, consider a simple inventory program. This inventory should keep track of the number of items in stock at all times so that items can be reordered at the correct times. The reports required will include a general list of items, a list of items that should be reordered, and a list of items which are on order but have not yet arrived.

Examining these three reports shows that the following data are required:

- Item number—this is also the order in which the items are to appear on the listing, so this is the "key" field.
- Description—the name of the item.
- Quantity in stock.
- Quantity on order.
- Reorder quantity—if the quantity falls below this, then the item should be reordered.

This inventory needs no processing, so there will be no fields added to this list from that source. There is only one file, which simplifies the program.

The next step is to determine the field lengths. The item number will vary depending upon whose inventory this is and what is being inventoried, but for the example assume eight characters are enough. The description could be restricted to 20 characters. The three quantities will be restricted differently depending upon what is being stored, but assume that there will never be more than 9999 items.

Now the subroutine designing can begin. First, name the variables to use. The item number and description are alphanumeric, so use the strings I$ and D$. The three quantities are numeric and can be integers (the assumption is that they will never be greater than 9999), and can be named S%, O%, and R%, in that order.

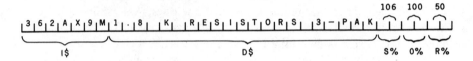

Figure 6.1: *A sample of one packed record.*

The first subroutines required include packing and unpacking, as they did in the first example of the file of names and addresses. These subroutines can start at 6010 (leave a STOP at 6000). They look similar to the name and address set:

```
6000 STOP
6010 B1$ =STRING$(255,32)
6020 B2$ =STRING$(20,32)
6030 MID$(B1$,1,8) =I$ +B2$
6040 MID$(B1$,9,20) =D$ +B2$
6050 MID$(B1$,29,2) =MKI$(S%)
6060 MID$(B1$,31,2) =MKI$(O%)
6070 MID$(B1$,33,2) =MKI$(R%)
6080 LSET B$ =B1$
6090 RETURN
6100 I$ =LEFT$(B$,8)
6110 D$ =MID$(B$,9,20)
6120 S% =CVI(MID$(B$,29,2))
6130 O% =CVI(MID$(B$,31,2))
6140 R% =CVI(MID$(B$,33,2))
6150 RETURN
```

The subroutine starting at 6010 will pack one record given the five variables for the fields and 6090 will unpack B$ to the five variables. To determine what the other subroutines should be requires investigating the structure of the program according to what the person who will operate it should see.

The user will require, in addition to the three reports, some way to enter new items, to change data on any particular item, and to delete items from the file. The user may also want to include some posting routines to allow for entering orders and posting items put into and taken out of the inventory. The list of functions required so far is:

1. Input new items.
2. Change (edit) particular records.
3. Post orders placed and received.
4. Post sales (items taken out of inventory).
5. Make reports (all three).

The functions of deleting and editing items can be combined, and the reports can all be produced using one routine.

With these functions it would be handy to have certain other subroutines. For example, a routine to find a particular item by the item number or key would make looking up an item much simpler. Assuming that the file is sorted, a user could employ a binary search. To write a subroutine that will find the correct record, use the same logic as was used in the binary search in Chapter 5. The subroutine can start at line 6150.

The binary search subroutine will require only one parameter from the main program, which is the key to find. When using this routine, set up I$ in the main program with the value of the key to be found, then state GOSUB 6150. Set up the subroutine so that it will set a variable with that key equal to the record number. Use another variable to act as an indicator to the main program so that it could tell if the search were successful or not.

One subroutine can call another subroutine. This is called *nesting*, and it can be used to simplify programming one more step. The main program really needs to have a subroutine that can take the key for the record, find the record, load it, and unpack it. If the subroutine starting at 6150 ends at 6270, this next subroutine can start at 6280 and would be:

```
6280  GOSUB6150
6290  IF L4 = 1 THEN RETURN
6300  GOTO 6100
```

This subroutine assumes that L4 is returned from the subroutine at 6150 as 1 if the record has not been found or as 0 if it has been found. It first calls the subroutine at 6150, then checks to see if the record were found, then, if the record has been found, branches directly to the unpacking routine. The RETURN statement in that routine will return control to the main program.

Using a program like this one to handle a file will quickly reveal that the method is too awkward and slow to handle larger files. Every time a record is added or deleted, the file must be rearranged in order to compensate for the changes. There is a much better way to do this: a key file. The key file is an index to the file. Using one will eliminate many of the problems with using the disk.

SECTION II

Introduction

Most books, particularly reference books, contain indexes to help in locating particular subjects. A library contains an index of all books in a card catalog. When a new book is brought into the library, three new cards are placed in the card catalog classifying the book by title, subject, and author. The sequential ordering of the entire file, as was done in Section I, is somewhat like the classification system of a library that has no card catalog and keeps all books in alphabetical order by title. Adding a new book on a shelf with no more room can become a large project if all books that have titles falling later in the alphabet have to be moved to make room. In the same way adding a new record to a sorted file is a large project for the computer.

There is a solution to this problem, and that is what is to be covered in this next section. The solution is called a key file and is roughly the equivalent of the library card catalog.

CHAPTER 7

MULTIPLE RECORD BLOCKS

Before we attempt to index all the files, we should discuss one more point. In Section I, the two examples of files both used a relatively small amount of each block, wasting the rest. For the name and address file, after adding the key, the record took up 73 bytes of the 255 available on each block. The rest (182 bytes) were wasted. That was enough for two more names and addresses! Using that file and altering it to store three names and addresses on each block would take one-third the space on disk as did the example in Section I.

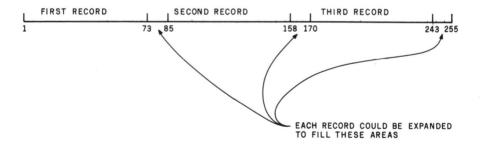

Figure 7.1: *A multiple-record block for an inventory file showing 36 extra bytes.*

You can make subroutines handle all the math and string handling necessary for separating the three records on each block. The first step in organizing this is to determine where each record will be on the block. Dividing 255 by three will give the maximum number of bytes which can be assigned to each record. Assuming there are three records per block, this result is exactly 85. The block can be divided into three records and still allow the record to expand to 85 bytes, or an extra 12 bytes above its original form. This calculates out to the following:

	START	END
FIRST RECORD	1	85
SECOND RECORD	86	170
THIRD RECORD	171	255

In order to find the record still using record numbers, you must first calculate the block number and then a local record number that is the number of the record within the block. Given the record number N, the block number will be $INT((N - 1)/3)$. The block number can be called B, giving the following to be the local record number: $N - B \times 3$.

You can still use B$ to represent the block but must introduce a new variable to contain the record number. This variable will be R$ in our examples.

With some alterations you can use the same program shown in Section I. First, keep the file initialization exactly the same. That initializes the blocks. Also, do not change the block size. But do change the use of B$ and the PUT and GET statements. In the program as it stands, change all occurrences of B$ to R$ (for readability, also change B1$ and B2$ to R1$ and R2$). Remove the LSET command in the pack subroutine. Replace it with the statement R$ = R1$.

Because their functions have become more extensive, PUT and GET must be replaced by subroutines. In listing 7.1, these subroutines are lines 7000 through 7030 for the GET function and 7050 through 7090 for the PUT function.

```
10 CLEAR2000
20 OPEN"R",1,"NAMES:1"
30 FIELD1,255ASB$
40 CLS
50 PRINT"ENTER 1 TO WRITE, 2 TO READ, 3 TO PRINT,"
52 INPUT"4 TO SORT OR 5 TO SEARCH";N
60 IFN<1THEN80
62 IFN>5THEN80
70 ONNGOTO100,300,500,700,900
80 PRINT"ERROR - ENTER 1, 2, 3 OR 4"
90 GOTO40
100 CLS
110 PRINT"WRITE A NEW RECORD TO THE FILE"
120 INPUT"ENTER RECORD NUMBER (1 TO 100)";N
130 IFN>=1THEN160
140 PRINT"ERROR - RECORD NUMBER MUST BE 1 TO 100"
150 GOTO120
160 IFN>100THEN140
165 INPUT"KEY";K$
170 INPUT"NAME";N$
180 INPUT"ADDRESS";A$
190 INPUT"CITY";C$
```

```
200 INPUT"STATE";S$
210 INPUT"ZIP CODE";Z$
220 GOSUB6010
230 GOSUB7040
240 GOTO40
300 CLS
310 PRINT"READ A RECORD FROM THE FILE"
320 INPUT"ENTER RECORD NUMBER";N
330 IFN>=1THEN360
340 PRINT"ERROR - RECORD NUMBER MUST BE 1 TO 100"
350 GOTO320
360 IFN>100THEN340
370 GOSUB7000
380 GOSUB6090
385 PRINT"KEY : ";K$
390 PRINT"NAME : ";N$
400 PRINT"ADDRESS : ";A$
410 PRINT"CITY : ";C$
420 PRINT"STATE : ";S$
430 PRINT"ZIP CODE : ";Z$
440 GOTO50
500 INPUT"START AT RECORD NO.";N
510 INPUT"END AT RECORD NO.";N1
520 IFN<1THEN640
530 IFN1<NTHEN640
540 IFN1>100THEN640
550 FORI=NTON1
560 N=I:GOSUB7000
570  GOSUB6090
575 PRINTK$
580  PRINTN$
590  PRINTA$
600  PRINTC$;", ";S$;" ";Z$
610  PRINT" "
612  PRINT"PRESS ENTER FOR NEXT NAME AND ADDRESS"
614  W$=INKEY$:IFW$=""THEN614
620 NEXTI
630 GOTO40
640 PRINT"ERROR - ENTER RECORD NUMBERS CORRECTLY"
650 GOTO500
700 PRINT"SORTING THE FILE"
710 FORI=1TO99
715 SW=0
720 N=1:GOSUB7000
730 R4$=R$
740  FORJ=2TO101-I
750   N=J:GOSUB7000
752   IFLEFT$(R$,1)=" "THEN800
754   IFLEFT$(R4$,1)=" "THEN765
760   IFR$>=R4$THEN800
765   SW=SW+1
770   N=J-1:GOSUB7040
780   R$=R4$
790   N=J:GOSUB7040
800   R4$=R$
810  NEXTJ
815 IFSW=0THENI=99
820 NEXTI
830 GOTO40
900 INPUT"ENTER KEY TO SEARCH";N1$
910 L1=0:L2=101:L4=0:L5=LEN(N1$)
920 L3=INT((L1+L2)/2+.5):GET1,L3
930 IFLEFT$(R$,1)=" "THENLETR$=STRING$(10,255)
940 IFLEFT$(R$,L5)>N1$THENLETL2=L3
950 IFLEFT$(R$,L5)<N1$THENLETL1=L3
960 IFLEFT$(R$,L5)=N1$THEN380
970 L4=L4+1
980 IFL4<7THEN920
990 PRINT"KEY NOT FOUND - IT IS NEAR RECORD NO.";L3
1000 GOTO50
6000 STOP
6010 R1$=STRING$(255,32)
```

```
6020 R2$=STRING$(20,32)
6025 MID$(R1$,1,10)=K$+R2$
6030 MID$(R1$,11,20)=N$+R2$
6040 MID$(R1$,31,20)=A$+R2$
6045 MID$(R1$,51,16)=C$+R2$
6050 MID$(R1$,67,2)=S$+R2$
6060 MID$(R1$,69,5)=Z$+R2$
6070 R$=R1$
6080 RETURN
6090 K$=LEFT$(R$,10)
6095 N$=MID$(R$,11,20)
6100 A$=MID$(R$,31,20)
6110 C$=MID$(R$,51,16)
6120 S$=MID$(R$,67,2)
6130 Z$=MID$(R$,69,5)
6140 RETURN
7000 B=INT((N-1)/3):R=N-B*3
7005 B=B+1
7010 GET1,B
7020 R$=MID$(B$,R*85-84,85)
7030 RETURN
7040 R1$=R$
7050 GOSUB7000
7060 B1$=B$:R$=R1$
7070 MID$(B1$,R*85-84;85)=R$
7080 LSET B$=B1$
7085 PUT1,B
7090 RETURN
```

Listing 7.1

Replace all PUT statements with a GOSUB 7040 and all GET statements with a GOSUB 7000. Note that the record number must be N, so in the statements such as line 560, the record number must be moved into that variable. Line 560 should be altered to read:

```
560 N=I:GOSUB 7000
```

Because the subroutines use R1$, there is a conflict in the sort routine. Note the changes in lines 730, 754, 760, 780, and 800 using the temporary variable R4$.

One other note concerns the FIELD statement. This refers to the blocks rather than to the records and so should be left as is. There are other forms of FIELD statements that could be employed for multiple record blocks, but this method was chosen because it makes some functions a little easier to program and is also more universal, as almost every computer can use it or something similar.

The formulae used in lines 7000, 7020, and 7070 are the basic formulae required in multiple record blocks. For any number of records per block, the formulae are:

●$B = INT((N-1)/A)$ where B is the block number to load, N is the desired record number, and A is the number of records per block.

●$R = N - B \times A$ where N, B, and A have the same values as above, and R is the local record number.

●$R \times L - (L-1)$ is the expression used to locate the first byte of the desired record. R is the local record number from the second formula. L is the record length.

For the number of records per block and the maximum record lengths allowed for each possibility, using L for the record length and M for the number of records per block, use these formulae:

$M = INT(255/L)$

Maximum $L = 255/M$

There is also the possibility of records being longer than one block. These are called multiple block records and are handled in a manner not too different from the multiple record blocks. The same formulae apply, but some of the constants act differently. A is now a fraction. For two block records, A will equal one-half, for three record blocks, A will equal one-third, etc. The resulting block number will be the first block of the record. You do not need the local record number and the expression to find the first byte of the record on the block.

Note that the formula to calculate the block number begins with block number 0. Since the files on most systems start with block number 1, add 1 to B after using it in the local record number formula. This is reflected in the listing (line 7005). This is also true in the case of a multiple block record file.

Condensing the file by using three records per block has now either reduced the file to one-third the space or increased it to a 300-record file. Listing 7.1 reflects all of the changes presented so far in this chapter. To reduce the disk space to 34 blocks, change the initialization to initialize only 34 blocks. To increase the number of records to 300, change the 101 in lines 740 and 910 to 301 and change the seven (maximum number of searches for a record) to nine.

CHAPTER 8

INDEXES

Once you understand how to access the disk with a random-access file, adding an index to the file is not that complicated. The index is another file that will point to the records in the main file. The index is called the *key file* and contains only the keys and one value called the pointer or locator. This is the record number of the record to which this key is assigned, and, continuing with the library example used in the introduction, is comparable to the number of the book. A book's number tells where to find it in the library, and a key file's locator tells where the record is in the disk file.

Introducing another complete file to locate the records in the first file does not look like a way to simplify things. But speed is a kind of simplicity, and finding the correct record from a key file is usually much faster than using a binary search on the entire file. Inserting a new record using a key file is, also, much faster.

Of the many different methods of keeping the keys in the proper order, three will be discussed in this section. One of them, the hashing method, doesn't keep the keys in alphabetical order at all, but finds them very quickly. Since it does not keep the keys in alphabetical order, it has some limitations, but its advantage is speed. It uses a formula to extract a number from the key that corresponds to a block in the key file. If it is in file, the desired key will be somewhere on that block. To locate any particular record the computer must read two blocks from the disk. The first block is the one containing the key and the pointer or locator, and the second block is the one containing the desired record.

A second type of file is an in-memory method where all of the keys and locators are kept in the computer's memory in a large string array. Sorting them and keeping them in order is much faster than sorting a file on the disk, but if the array of keys is changed, the entire file must be rewritten onto the disk to keep the index permanent. This method's advantage is that it is the easiest to program.

The third type of key file uses a tree-structured method to keep all keys

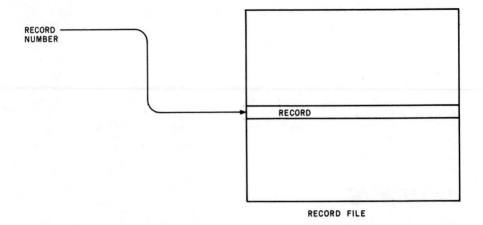

(a)

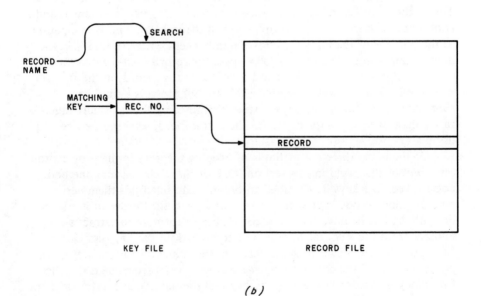

(b)

Figure 8.1a: *Random-access file.* **b:** *Key-file access. Adding the extra step complicates the program but simplifies operation for the user.*

on disk but avoids having to sort the entire key file every time a key is inserted or deleted. The keys are kept in small, sorted groups on the disk and require a kind of roadmap to find any particular key. This roadmap contains information showing in which order the blocks need to be read to be put in alphabetical order.

Computer operating systems often use the hashing method to keep the index of the disk files on a disk platter. It is about the best and simplest method of keeping track of records (or files by name) when an alphabetical listing is not required. The alphabetical-array method is usually used in a limited way to keep track of look-up tables, or files that store a table of values that can be called by name. The type of file most used for the alphabetical file is one where keys are not added, deleted, or changed, as these are the method's weakest points. The tree-structured files seem to be most common for most programming applications. This is the most versatile of the three, but it is also the hardest one to program. This book will present one modification of this method that is restricted to a maximum of 254 blocks of keys. There are some file limitations to it, but it is a lot simpler to program than a full tree-structured file system.

The speed advantage of using a key file over a sorted random-access file stems from the fact that the key is much shorter than the entire record. Although the version of the sorted random-access file presented earlier required one disk reading for each record, it could be altered so that one disk reading could allow up to three records to be loaded at once, as three is the number of records per block. The key file will be between 10 and 21 keys on each block and will allow the system to search more quickly by making the entire block available in memory at once.

Programming key files requires a good working knowledge of random-access files, sorting methods, and the binary search method. All of the logic for accessing the key files will be in the subroutine set except for some operations like opening the file and fielding the data. Once the subroutine set is complete and tested, writing the main program is very simple.

The hashing method requires an algorithm. This algorithm takes the characters in the key and from them determines a number between one and the number of blocks in the key file. Many perform some Boolean operations on the characters. The simplest form converts the characters to numeric first, and then performs some numeric functions on them to get the number. The American Standard Code (ASC) function is available on microcomputers to perform this conversion, although it has different names on some systems. It will take one character from a string and convert it to a number between 0 and 255 depending upon the character.

To develop the algorithm, you first determine the number of characters in the key. In the name and address file, for example, the key was 10 characters long. Next, determine the number of blocks required in the key file. For 100 records, use at least 125 spaces for keys (25 percent more than the number of records). The reason for this extra space will become clear later on. Since the key plus the locator occupy 12 bytes, there can be as many as 21 keys on each block. You need 6 blocks to store the 125 keys.

The next step is developing the algorithm. A very simple algorithm could be to accumulate the ASC values of each of the 10 bytes, then use the remainder of the result divided by the number of blocks. The following segment of text will always produce a number from one to six for any value of K$:

```
7000  K1$ =STRING$(10,32)
7010  K$ =K$ +K1$:N =0
7020  FOR I =1TO10
7030  N =N +ASC(MID$(K$,I,1))
7040  NEXTI
7050  N =N −INT((N −1)/6) ×6
```

The algorithm in that series of statements is a very simple one and may not prove to be the correct one for a particular file. There are many algorithms possible, and each one should be tested with a sampling of keys. Just make sure the sample contains an even distribution of keys. If 36 sample keys are run through the algorithm and about six are assigned to each of the six sectors, then this algorithm is probably a good one. If the distribution is lopsided, then another one should be developed.

Once a block number is determined for a key that is to be added to the file, the locator must be packed into the key. The locator is simply the number of the record to which the key will point. The number may be packed using the MKI$ function on most microcomputers. This function will take an integer and pack it into 2 bytes. The locator should be packed into bytes 11 and 12 of the key. Next, the key block is loaded into memory and the first available space on it is found. The assembled key and locator can be placed in that space and then the block should be resaved. Locating a record that is already in the file consists of loading the block containing the key, finding the key, and unpacking the locator. The unpacking can be done using the CVI function. The locator is the record number corresponding to the key. Deleting a key consists of finding it and writing a blank key over its location on the key block.

The key is a separate and independent file from the record file, but it should be maintained along with it. When a record is deleted, the key must also be deleted. When a record is added, the key must also be added. For this reason, it is usually a good idea to write the subroutines so that one GOSUB will accomplish all of the required steps to perform the function in both files. Adding to the file will require packing and saving the record and packing and saving the key. This could be all one function. The subroutines for accessing a key file should be:

1. Insert a new key and record.

2. Find and load a record, given the key.
3. Find and load the "next greater" key and record.
4. Delete a key and its record.

The disadvantage of the hashing method is that it can not provide the third function on the above list because the keys are not in alphabetical order. To provide this function for the reports and displays, all the keys could be read into one large string array and sorted, but then the result would be the alphabetical-array method.

In the alphabetical-array file, all of the keys are maintained in alphabetical order in a large string array. The keys are stored on disk, usually in a sequential file, so that they would not be lost in the case of a power failure. The key file is read at the beginning of the program and rewritten every time a key is added or deleted.

Of the two types of files described above, one can be used for frequent additions and deletions (the hashing method) and the other can be used to keep the keys in alphabetical order (the alphabetical-array method). The tree-structured method, the third type, is an all-purpose type which keeps the keys in alphabetical order and yet adds and deletes keys very quickly. It is a little slower than the hashing method when locating, adding, and deleting keys, and a little slower than the alphabetical array method in locating the next greater key. It is much faster than the alphabetical-array method in adding and deleting keys. The benefits of this type of file in application programs far outweigh the few drawbacks. One drawback of the tree-structured method is that it is much more complicated to program.

The logic behind a full tree-structured method is more complex than is required for a microcomputer, but there is a simpler variation presented in this section that works quite well. In this variation, a few keys are kept on each block of the file in alphabetical order. A roadmap is used to keep the alphabetical order between the blocks. When one block becomes full as keys are added to it, the system splits the block to put the first half on one block and the second half on a new block. The roadmap is updated to show that the second of these blocks follows the first one alphabetically.

There is also one small problem that will not be covered completely until the next section. That problem is keeping track of which records in the file are occupied and which ones are free. There is a good method presented in the next section, but until the logic of each of these key-file methods has been explained, a simpler one will suffice. In this simpler method, a number is kept that corresponds to the number of records that have been added to the file. When a new record is added, this number is incremented and used as the new record number. But this method has the disadvantage of not considering the spaces left when a record is deleted, so it does not work well on a file that is updated frequently.

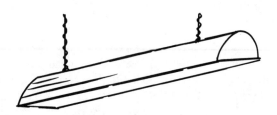
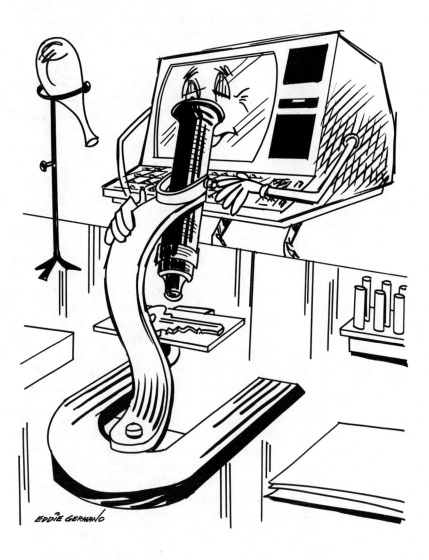

EDDIE GERMANO

CHAPTER 9

KEY-FILE TEST PROGRAM

When learning how to drive a car, you can absorb all of the theories and explanations, but you will never know if you can drive a car until you sit behind the wheel. In the same way, you may think you understand the three types of key files described in the previous chapter, but you won't be sure until you read this chapter. This chapter describes a program that allows access to a subroutine set that controls a key file. It is written so that it can be used with all three methods with little alteration.

The same program can be used with all three methods if the subroutines (which actually define the method used) are written so that the calling lines are the same (i.e., the line numbers used in the GOSUB statements) and the values passed to them and returned from them (the parameters) are all the same. The same program will use the following five subroutines:

* 7000 Put a new key and record into the file.
* 7500 Get a record from the file, given the key.
* 8000 Get the next sequential record from the file, by key.
* 8500 Delete a record from the file, given the key.
* 9000 Resave a record, given the key.

These subroutines will take care of the key file, but you need the subroutines developed earlier for handling the record file. I added one function to the previous list. Replacing a record, which allows data to be changed within a previously saved record, is written so that it verifies that the key is in file before it resaves the record.

The test program should perform the following functions:

1. Initialize new files.
2. Put a new record into the file.
3. Get the record with a certain key.
4. Get the next greater record, given a key.
5. Delete a record and key.
6. Alter and replace a record.

Besides performing the above functions, the main program must OPEN and FIELD the files, set up memory with the appropriate CLEAR and DIM statements, and act as a traffic controller so that the operator can easily select one of the six functions.

The above restrictions will now allow the program to be structured by line number. The following list of statement numbers and the functions they will perform will be used to develop the program:

- 10 - 90 CLEAR, DIM, OPEN and FIELD statements and any other initialization required.
- 100 - 490 List functions and allow operator selection.
- 500 - 690 File initialization.
- 700 - 890 Add new record to file.
- 900 - 1090 Get a record from the file.
- 1100 - 1290 Get next greater record.
- 1300 - 1490 Delete a record from the file.
- 1500 - 1690 Change data and replace the record.
- 6000 - 6990 Subroutines used by key subroutines.
- 7000 - 9990 Key subroutines.

The basic requirement of the test program is to give access to all five of the subroutine functions so that each one can be tested. Listing 9.1 is the test program that is developed in this chapter, and the line numbers will refer to it. The listing is in sections by line number. Lines 10 through 90 make up the program initialization section, which includes the CLEAR statement, the file OPEN and FIELD statements, the DIM statement and any other preliminary operations that are required before and not during the normal program operation. Lines 100 through 490 are reserved as the control section of the program, which is the part that allows access to the functions. The program functions start at line 500, and the five of them will each be assigned 200 line numbers. The first function, file initialization, will be different in each of the functions, so it does not appear on this listing. This function will be developed along with the subroutines for each of the three methods. The subroutines handling the record file, most of which were developed in previous chapters, occupy lines 6000 through 6990, and the key-file-handling subroutines, as described above, can occupy lines 7000 and above.

```
9 REM -- 0010-0090 PROGRAM INITIALIZATION --
10 CLEAR2000
20 REM**THIS STATEMENT RESERVED FOR DIM STATEMENTS **
30 OPEN"R",1,"RECORDS:1"
40 FIELD1,255ASB$
50 OPEN"R",2,"KEY:1"
60 FIELD2,255ASKY$
99 REM -- 0100-0490 CONTROL SECTION --
100 CLS
110 PRINTTAB(20);"KEY FILE TEST"
120 PRINTTAB(10);"1  INITIALIZE FILES"
130 PRINTTAB(10);"2  PUT A NEW RECORD IN FILE"
140 PRINTTAB(10);"3  GET A RECORD, GIVEN THE KEY"
150 PRINTTAB(10);"4  GET NEXT RECORD, GIVEN A KEY"
160 PRINTTAB(10);"5  DELETE A RECORD"
170 PRINTTAB(10);"6  ALTER AND REPLACE A RECORD"
180 PRINT
190 INPUT"  ENTER NUMBER OF SELECTION";N
200 IFN<1THEN220
210 IFN<=6THEN240
220 PRINT"ERROR - PLEASE ENTER A NUMBER FROM 1 TO 6"
230 GOTO190
240 ONNGOTO500,700,900,1100,1300,1500
499 REM -- 0500-0699 INITIALIZE FILES FUNCTION --
699 REM -- 0700-0899 PUT NEW KEY AND RECORD FUNCTION --
700 CLS.
710 PRINTTAB(16);"PUT NEW KEY AND RECORD IN FILE"
720 PRINT
730 INPUT"NEW KEY";K$
740 KN$=K$
750 GOSUB7500
760 IFE=1THEN790
770 PRINT"ERROR - KEY ALREADY IN FILE"
780 GOTO730
790 K$=KN$
795 INPUT"NAME";N$
800 INPUT"ADDRESS";A$
810 INPUT"CITY";C$
820 INPUT"STATE";S$
830 INPUT"ZIP CODE";Z$
840 INPUT"IS THE ABOVE CORRECT (Y OR N)";OK$
850 IFOK$="Y"THEN890
860 IFOK$="N"THEN700
870 PRINT"ERROR - PLEASE ANSWER Y OR N"
880 GOTO840
890 GOSUB7000
895 GOTO100
899 REM -- 0900-1099 GET RECORD GIVEN KEY FUNCTION --
900 CLS
910 PRINTTAB(22);"GET A RECORD GIVEN THE KEY"
920 PRINT
930 INPUT"KEY";K$
940 GOSUB7500
950 IFE=0THEN980
960 PRINT"KEY NOT IN FILE"
970 GOTO930
980 PRINT"NAME : ";N$
990 PRINT"ADDRESS : ";A$
1000 PRINT"CITY, STATE AND ZIP : ";C$;", ";S$;" ";Z$
1010 PRINT
1020 PRINT"PRESS ENTER WHEN FINISHED VIEWING"
1030 W$=INKEY$:IFW$=""THEN1030
1040 GOTO100
1099 REM -- 1100-1299 GET NEXT FUNCTION --
1100 CLS
1110 PRINTTAB(22);"GET NEXT GREATER KEY"
1120 PRINT
1130 INPUT"KEY";K$
1140 GOSUB8000
1150 IFE=0THEN1180
1160 PRINT"END OF FILE.  THERE IS NO GREATER KEY"
1170 GOTO1100
```

```
1180 PRINT"KEY : ";K$
1190 GOTO980
1299 REM -- 1300-1499 DELETE RECORD FUNCTION --
1300 CLS
1310 PRINTTAB(25);"DELETE A RECORD"
1320 PRINT
1330 INPUT"KEY TO DELETE (OR END)";K$
1340 IFK$="END"THEN100
1350 GOSUB8500
1360 IFE=0THEN1390
1370 PRINT"KEY NOT FOUND AND NOT DELETED"
1380 GOTO1400
1390 PRINT"KEY DELETED"
1400 PRINT"PRESS ENTER AFTER READING MESSAGE"
1410 W$=INKEY$:IFW$=""THEN1410
1420 GOTO100
1499 REM -- 1500-1699 ALTER RECORD FUNCTION --
1500 CLS:PRINTTAB(20);"CHANGE DATA IN A RECORD":PRINT
1510 INPUT"KEY";K$
1520 GOSUB7500
1530 IFE=0THEN1560
1540 PRINT"ERROR - KEY NOT FOUND"
1550 GOTO1510
1560 PRINT"1. NAME : ";N$
1570 PRINT"2. ADDRESS : ";A$
1580 PRINT"3. CITY : ";C$
1590 PRINT"4. STATE : ";S$
1600 PRINT"5. ZIP CODE : ";Z$
1610 PRINT
1620 INPUT"ENTER NUMBER OF FIELD TO CHANGE";FN
1630 IFFN<1THEN1650
1640 IFFN<=5THEN1670
1650 PRINT"ERROR - PLEASE ENTER A NUMBER FROM 1 TO 5"
1660 GOTO1620
1670 ONFNGOSUB1680,1685,1690,1695,1700
1675 GOSUB9000
1677 GOTO100
1680 INPUT"NEW NAME";N$
1682 RETURN
1685 INPUT"NEW ADDRESS";A$
1687 RETURN
1690 INPUT"NEW CITY";C$
1692 RETURN
1695 INPUT"NEW STATE";S$
1697 RETURN
1700 INPUT"NEW ZIP CODE";Z$
1702 RETURN
5999 REM -- 6000-6990 RECORD FILE SUBROUTINES --
6000 STOP
6009 REM -- 6010-6080 PACK RECORD --
6010 R1$=STRING$(85,32)
6020 R2$=STRING$(20,32)
6025 MID$(R1$,1,10)=K$+R2$
6030 MID$(R1$,11,20)=N$+R2$
6040 MID$(R1$,31,20)=A$+R2$
6045 MID$(R1$,51,16)=C$+R2$
6050 MID$(R1$,67,2)=S$+R2$
6060 MID$(R1$,69,5)=Z$+R2$
6070 R$=R1$
6080 RETURN
6089 REM -- 6090-6140 UNPACK RECORD --
6090 K$=LEFT$(R$,10)
6095 N$=MID$(R$,11,20)
6100 A$=MID$(R$,31,20)
6110 C$=MID$(R$,51,16)
6120 S$=MID$(R$,67,2)
6130 Z$=MID$(R$,69,5)
6140 RETURN
6149 REM -- 6150-6180 GET RECORD BY NUMBER --
6150 B=INT((N-1)/3):R=N-B*3
6155 B=B+1
6160 GET1,B
```

```
6170 R$=MID$(B$,R*85-84,85)
6180 RETURN
6189 REM -- 6190-6240 PUT RECORD BY NUMBER --
6190 R1$=R$
6200 GOSUB6150
6210 B1$=B$
6220 MID$(B1$,R*85-84,85)=R1$
6230 LSET B$=B1$
6235 PUT1,B
6240 RETURN
6249 REM -- 6250-6305 GET NEXT AVAILABLE RECORD NUMBER --
6250 GET1,1
6260 B1$=B$
6270 FR=CVI(LEFT$(B1$,2))+1
6280 MKI$(LEFT$(B1$,2))=FR
6290 LSET B$=B1$
6300 PUT1,1
6305 RETURN
6999 REM -- 7000-7499 PUT NEW RECORD AND KEY --
7499 REM -- 7500-7999 GET RECORD --
7999 REM -- 8000-8499 GET NEXT --
8499 REM -- 8500-8999 DELETE KEY AND RECORD --
8999 REM -- 9000-9499 RESAVE RECORD --
```

Listing 9.1

The program is written in these sections. The program initialization section (lines 10 through 90—not to be confused with the file initialization, which is a different type of function) actually only uses lines 10 through 60. There will be some use later for the lines not yet used, and line 20, which is now a REM statement, will be used to dimension the array used in the alphabetical-array method. Note that the record file is fielded like the record file in the random-access method descriptions, and the key file is also fielded using the new variable KY$, the key-file buffer.

Lines 100 through 490 are reserved for the control section, which in this program clears the screen, lists all of the options, and allows the operator to choose one from the list. When each of the functions is completed, it is written to return to line 100. The options are made to PRINT to the screen in lines 110 through 180, then the selection is requested in line 190 and checked for validity in lines 200 through 230. If it is valid, the ON...GOTO statement in line 240 will select the indicated function.

Before proceeding to the functions, pay some attention to the subroutine set. You have to consider how to handle unsuccessful operations. For example, what happens when the get key subroutine is called with a key that is not in the file? Unless there is some communication from the subroutine to the main program, there is no way to deal with this. The listing as shown assumes that, on return from one of the subroutines, the variable E is set to zero if all went well, or to one if there were a problem. For most of the subroutines, there is only one problem. For getting a key, replacing a record after some data has been changed, or for deleting a key, the only problem is that the key is not in file. For getting the next sequential key, the only problem is that the key given was the last one in the file (i.e., there are no greater keys). Putting a new key in file will be a problem if there is a duplicate key already there (duplicate keys should not be allowed in a single-key system—the section explaining multiple-key files will deal with this in more detail). Putting a new key in the file may also present another problem. If there is no more room in the file, the key will not be stored. In this particular case, E will have the value of two.

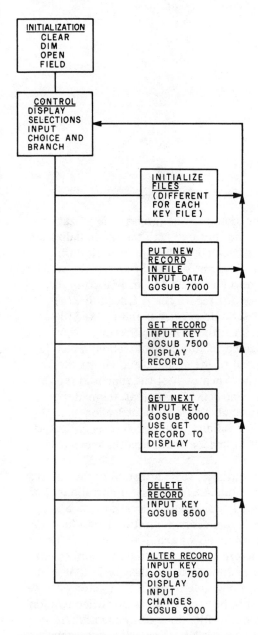

Figure 9.1: *Simplified flow chart of key-file test program.*

How this error code works can be seen in the second function (the first function, initializing new files, is not written until the key-file method that uses the file is written), which begins at line 700. The screen is set up in lines 700 through 730, which includes inputting the key to be put into the file. Line 740 places the value into KN$ so that the key value will not be lost in the next step, which is searching for the key in the file. Line 750 calls the subroutine that searches for the key K$. If this subroutine is successful, E will be returned as zero, and this indicates that the key is already in the file. In this case, the IF statement in line 760 will not branch, and the screen will display the message in line 770 and go back to request a new key. This logic avoids the possibility of trying to save duplicate keys. Using this type of logic could destroy the contents of K$, depending upon how the get key routine is written, so the temporary variable KN$ is used to avoid this. K$ is restored in line 790.

Lines 795 through 830 allow entry of the record. Lines 840 through 880 allow verification before it is saved. The saving operation is accomplished by calling the subroutine at line 7000 (the GOSUB in line 890). This function ends by branching back to line 100 by the GOTO in line 895.

Getting a record, given the key, is a much simpler function. Lines 900 through 930 set up the screen and allow input of the key. The verification in lines 940 through 970 is the same as with the put routine except the checking of the error code in E. This time the desired result is a successful search, which means E will be zero. If this is the case, the function proceeds with lines 980 through 1010, which display the record on the screen. Lines 1020 and 1030 wait for the operator to finish viewing the record by using the INKEY$ function. This function accepts any key, although the message indicates the ENTER key. You could replace these two lines with an INPUT statement to wait for the ENTER key without any problem. The return to the control section is in line 1040. Lines 1050 through 1090 are not required.

The next function, getting the record with the next greater key, borrows some lines from that last function. Lines 1100 through 1170 perform the same functions as lines 900 through 970, except that you use a different subroutine and the messages are different. When a next greater key is found, line 1180 displays it, then branches into the section of the last function to display the record on the screen, which will include the wait routine in lines 1020 and 1030 and the return to the control section. This is the simplest of the functions, once the GET KEY function is programmed.

Delete is also a simple function, although the subroutine it uses is one of the more complicated ones. Lines 1300 through 1380 look very much like the start of the other functions. The subroutine called will delete the key if it is there, so line 1380 branches to another waiting section and line 1390 prints another message and uses the same waiting section. If the key is not found, the message will be the text in lines 1370 and 1400. If the key is found and deleted, the message will be the text in lines 1390 and 1400. The same wait scheme is used as in the GET KEY function and could also be replaced with an INPUT if that is desired. The return to the control section is again the last line in the function, line 1420.

The most complicated function used more lines than it was allocated, but it is the last function on the list, so there is no problem. This function usually does require more space than other functions. To change data in a record requires displaying the record first (lines 1500 through 1610), allowing the selection of one of the fields in the record (lines 1620 through 1670), requesting the new value for the appropriate field (lines 1680 through 1702), and resaving the record (line 1675).

The purpose of the programming in this chapter is to form a shell that can be used to develop the key-file subroutines, so there is one more section to work on. The key-file subroutines will require the record-handling routines in lines 6000 to 6990. All of those line numbers will not be required, so there is plenty of room for the required subroutines.

The first two subroutines to write may be copied from the random-access file program developed earlier. Lines 6000 is the STOP statement that begins the subroutine area. Lines 6010 through 6080 pack the record and lines 6090 through 6140 unpack it. For the more efficient multiple-record blocks to be used in the record file, the appropriate routine can be renumbered to fit into lines 6150 through 6240.

The next record-handling subroutine will take care of assigning new record numbers when records are added. The subroutine in lines 6250 through 6305 uses the first record in the file to store the number of records used in the file. When this routine is called, it gets this value (lines 6250 through 6270) and adds one to it (appended to line 6270). It then resaves this new value (lines 6280 through 6300) and returns to the calling subroutine with the variable FR equaling the next available record number. This record number can then be used to save the new record. When the files are initialized, the first record must be in the correct form and have the number one packed in it to show that this record is occupied, and the first available record for storing data is record number two.

This program shell can now be saved on disk. The short utility program (listing 9.2) can be used if the program is saved in the ASCII format to list the REM statements. This list (listing 9.3) will give a table on where all of the functions and subroutines are, which will be very useful in writing the key-file routines. Such a list should always be a part of the documentation of a program.

```
10 CLEAR1000
20 INPUT"PROGRAM NAME";PN$
30 OPEN"I",1,PN$
40 LINEINPUT#1,A$
50 AA=EOF(1)
60 A=0
70 A=A+1:IFA>LEN(A$)THEN200
80 C=ASC(MID$(A$,A,1))
90 IFC<58ANDC>47THEN70
100 A=A+1
110 IFMID$(A$,A,3)<>"REM"THEN200
120 A=A+3:B=LEN(A$)
```

```
130 LPRINTMID$(A$,A,B-A)
200 IFAA=OTHEN40:ELSE STOP
```

Listing 9.2

```
 -- 0010-0090 PROGRAM INITIALIZATION -
**THIS STATEMENT RESERVED FOR DIM STATEMENTS *
 -- 0100-0490 CONTROL SECTION -
 -- 0500-0699 INITIALIZE FILES SECTION -
 -- 0700-0899 PUT NEW KEY AND RECORD FUNCTION -
 -- 0900-1099 GET RECORD GIVEN KEY FUNCTION -
 -- 1100-1299 GET NEXT FUNCTION -
 -- 1300-1499 DELETE RECORD FUNCTION -
 -- 1500-1699 ALTER RECORD FUNCTION -
 -- 6000-6990 RECORD FILE SUBROUTINES -
 -- 6010-6080 PACK RECORD -
 -- 6090-6140 UNPACK RECORD -
 -- 6150-6180 GET RECORD BY NUMBER -
 -- 6190-6240 PUT RECORD BY NUMBER -
 -- 6250-6305 GET NEXT AVAILABLE RECORD NUMBER -
 -- 7000-7499 PUT NEW RECORD AND KEY -
 -- 7500-7999 GET RECORD -
 -- 8000-8499 GET NEXT -
 -- 8500-8999 DELETE KEY AND RECORD -
 -- 9000-9499 RESAVE RECORD -
```

Listing 9.3

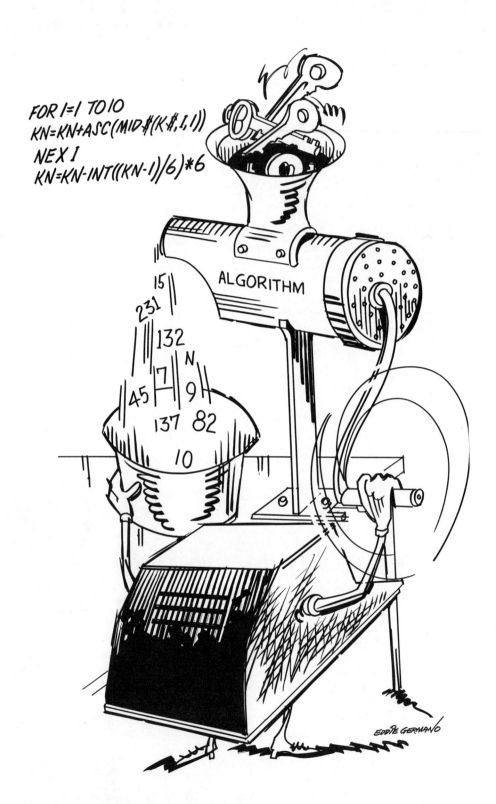

CHAPTER 10

THE HASHING METHOD

This is the simplest, but not the most practical of the three methods. It cannot perform what might be called the *get next* function, but it can insert, locate, and delete. The first statement in the get next subroutine and the first statement to add to the program shell created in the last chapter is statement 8000. Load that program into the memory and type in:

```
8000 STOP
```

Executing the get next function would make the system stop when the subroutine was called. That function should never be tried, so statement 8000 should never be executed.

The first real concern, then, is file initialization. The key file, as calculated in previous chapters, should contain six blocks. These must be initialized to the value for *blank* keys, that is, keys with all bits turned on, or the ASCII character 255. Next, the record file should be initialized to be blank records. After this initialization, record number one should be changed to contain the record counter. This is initialized to one so that the first record used will be record number two. Listing 10.1 is a complete listing of the hashing method program, including the shell developed in the previous chapter. The initialization function starts at line 500 and ends at line 650 (with plenty of space—its allocated space goes to line 699).

```
9 REM -- 0010-0090 PROGRAM INITIALIZATION --
10 CLEAR2000
20 REM**THIS STATEMENT RESERVED FOR DIM STATEMENTS **
30 OPEN"R",1,"RECORDS:1"
40 FIELD1,255ASB$
50 OPEN"R",2,"KEY:1"
```

```
60 FIELD2,255ASKY$
99 REM -- 0100-0490 CONTROL SECTION --
100 CLS
110 PRINTTAB(20);"KEY FILE TEST"
120 PRINTTAB(10);"1  INITIALIZE FILES"
130 PRINTTAB(10);"2  PUT A NEW RECORD IN FILE"
140 PRINTTAB(10);"3  GET A RECORD, GIVEN THE KEY"
150 PRINTTAB(10);"4  GET NEXT RECORD, GIVEN A KEY"
160 PRINTTAB(10);"5  DELETE A RECORD"
170 PRINTTAB(10);"6  ALTER AND REPLACE A RECORD"
180 PRINT
190 INPUT"  ENTER NUMBER OF SELECTION";N
200 IFN<1THEN220
210 IFN<=6THEN240
220 PRINT"ERROR - PLEASE ENTER A NUMBER FROM 1 TO 6"
230 GOTO190
240 ONNGOTO500,700,900,1100,1300,1500
499 REM -- 0500-0699 INITIALIZE FILES SECTION --
500 K1$=STRING$(255,255)
510 FORI=1TO6
520 LSET KY$=K1$
530 PUT2,I
540 NEXTI
550 B1$=STRING$(255,32)
560 FORI=1TO34
570 LSET B$=B1$
580 PUT1,I
590 NEXTI
600 GET1,1
610 B1$=B$
620 MID$(B1$,1,2)=MKI$(1)
630 LSET B$=B1$
640 PUT1,1
650 GOTO100
699 REM -- 0700-0899 PUT NEW KEY AND RECORD IN FILE FUNCTION --
700 CLS
710 PRINTTAB(16);"PUT NEW KEY AND RECORD IN FILE"
720 PRINT
730 INPUT"NEW KEY";K$
740 KN$=K$
750 GOSUB7500
760 IFE=1THEN790
770 PRINT"ERROR - KEY ALREADY IN FILE"
780 GOTO730
790 K$=KN$
795 INPUT"NAME";N$
800 INPUT"ADDRESS";A$
810 INPUT"CITY";C$
820 INPUT"STATE";S$
830 INPUT"ZIP CODE";Z$
840 INPUT"IS THE ABOVE CORRECT (Y OR N)";OK$
850 IFOK$="Y"THEN890
860 IFOK$="N"THEN700
870 PRINT"ERROR - PLEASE ANSWER Y OR N"
880 GOTO840
890 GOSUB7000
892 STOP
895 GOTO100
899 REM -- 0900-1099 GET RECORD GIVEN KEY FUNCTION --
900 CLS
910 PRINTTAB(22);"GET A RECORD GIVEN THE KEY"
920 PRINT
930 INPUT"KEY";K$
940 GOSUB7500
950 IFE=0THEN980
960 PRINT"KEY NOT IN FILE"
970 GOTO930
980 PRINT"NAME : ";N$
990 PRINT"ADDRESS : ";A$
1000 PRINT"CITY, STATE AND ZIP : ";C$;", ";S$;" ";Z$
1010 PRINT
1020 PRINT"PRESS ENTER WHEN FINISHED VIEWING"
```

```
1030 W$=INKEY$:IFW$=""THEN1030
1040 GOTO100
1099 REM -- 1100-1299 GET NEXT FUNCTION --
1100 CLS
1110 PRINTTAB(22);"GET NEXT GREATER KEY"
1120 PRINT
1130 INPUT"KEY";K$
1140 GOSUB8000
1150 IFE=0THEN1180
1160 PRINT"END OF FILE.   THERE IS NO GREATER KEY"
1170 GOTO1100
1180 PRINT"KEY : ";K$
1190 GOTO980
1299 REM -- 1300-1499 DELETE RECORD FUNCTION --
1300 CLS
1310 PRINTTAB(25);"DELETE A RECORD"
1320 PRINT
1330 INPUT"KEY TO DELETE  (OR END)";K$
1340 IFK$="END"THEN100
1350 GOSUB8500
1360 IFE=0THEN1390
1370 PRINT"KEY NOT FOUND AND NOT DELETED"
1380 GOTO1400
1390 PRINT"KEY DELETED"
1400 PRINT"PRESS ENTER AFTER READING MESSAGE"
1410 W$=INKEY$:IFW$=""THEN1410
1420 GOTO100
1499 REM -- 1500-1699 ALTER RECORD FUNCTION --
1500 CLS:PRINTTAB(20);"CHANGE DATA IN A RECORD":PRINT
1510 INPUT"KEY";K$
1520 GOSUB7500
1530 IFE=0THEN1560
1540 PRINT"ERROR - KEY NOT FOUND"
1550 GOTO1510
1560 PRINT"1. NAME : ";N$
1570 PRINT"2. ADDRESS : ";A$
1580 PRINT"3. CITY : ";C$
1590 PRINT"4. STATE : ";S$
1600 PRINT"5. ZIP CODE : ";Z$
1610 PRINT
1620 INPUT"ENTER NUMBER OF FIELD TO CHANGE";NF
1630 IFNF<1THEN1650
1640 IFNF<=5THEN1670
1650 PRINT"ERROR - PLEASE ENTER A NUMBER FROM 1 TO 5"
1660 GOTO1620
1670 ONNFGOSUB1680,1685,1690,1695,1700
1675 GOSUB9000
1677 GOTO100
1680 INPUT"NEW NAME";N$
1682 RETURN
1685 INPUT"NEW ADDRESS";A$
1687 RETURN
1690 INPUT"NEW CITY";C$
1692 RETURN
1695 INPUT"NEW STATE";S$
1697 RETURN
1700 INPUT"NEW ZIP CODE";Z$
1702 RETURN
5999 REM -- 6000-6990 RECORD FILE SUBROUTINES --
6000 STOP
6009 REM -- 6010-6080 PACK RECORD --
6010 R1$=STRING$(85,32)
6020 R2$=STRING$(20,32)
6025 MID$(R1$,1,10)=K$+R2$
6030 MID$(R1$,11,20)=N$+R2$
6040 MID$(R1$,31,20)=A$+R2$
6045 MID$(R1$,51,16)=C$+R2$
6050 MID$(R1$,67,2)=S$+R2$
6060 MID$(R1$,69,5)=Z$+R2$
6070 R$=R1$
6080 RETURN
6089 REM -- 6090-6140 UNPACK RECORD --
```

```
6090 K$=LEFT$(R$,10)
6095 N$=MID$(R$,11,20)
6100 A$=MID$(R$,31,20)
6110 C$=MID$(R$,51,16)
6120 S$=MID$(R$,67,2)
6130 Z$=MID$(R$,69,5)
6140 RETURN
6149 REM -- 6150-6180 GET RECORD BY NUMBER --
6150 B=INT((N-1)/3):R=N-B*3
6155 B=B+1
6160 GET1,B
6170 R$=MID$(B$,R*85-84,85)
6180 RETURN
6189 REM -- 6190-6240 PUT RECORD BY NUMBER --
6190 R1$=R$
6200 GOSUB6150
6210 B1$=B$
6220 MID$(B1$,R*85-84,85)=R1$
6230 LSET B$=B1$
6235 PUT1,B
6240 RETURN
6249 REM -- 6250-6305 GET NEXT AVAILABLE RECORD NUMBER --
6250 GET1,1
6260 B1$=B$
6270 FR=CVI(LEFT$(B1$,2))+1
6280 MID$(B1$,1,2)=MKI$(FR)
6290 LSET B$=B1$
6300 PUT1,1
6305 RETURN
6309 REM -- 6310-6510 SEARCH FOR KEY --
6310 K1$=STRING$(10,32)
6320 K$=K$+K1$:KN=0
6330 FORI=1TO10
6340   KN=KN+ASC(MID$(K$,I,1))
6350 NEXTI
6360 KN=KN-INT((KN-1)/6)*6
6370 GET2,KN
6380 FORI=1TO21
6390   K1$=MID$(KY$,I*12-11,12)
6400   IFLEFT$(K1$,10)=LEFT$(K$,10)THEN6500
6410 NEXTI
6420 K1$=STRING$(10,255)
6430 FORI=1TO21
6440   IFLEFT$(K1$,10)=MID$(KY$,I*12-11,10)THEN6480
6450 NEXTI
6460 E=2
6470 RETURN
6480 E=1
6490 RETURN
6500 E=0
6510 RETURN
6999 REM -- 7000-7499 PUT NEW RECORD AND KEY --
7000 GOSUB6310
7010 IFE=2THENRETURN
7020 IFE=1THEN7040
7030 E=1:RETURN
7040 GOSUB6250
7050 K$=LEFT$(K$,10)+MKI$(FR)
7060 KZ$=KY$
7070 MID$(KZ$,I*12-11,12)=K$
7080 LSET KY$=KZ$
7090 PUT2,KN
7100 GOSUB6010
7110 N=FR:GOSUB6190
7120 E=0
7130 RETURN
7499 REM -- 7500-7999 GET RECORD --
7500 GOSUB6310
7510 IFE=0THEN7540
7520 E=1
7530 RETURN
7540 N=CVI(MID$(K1$,11,2))
```

```
7550 GOSUB6150
7560 GOSUB6090
7570 E=0
7580 RETURN
7999 REM -- 8000-8499 GET NEXT --
8000 E=1:RETURN
8499 REM -- 8500-8999 DELETE KEY AND RECORD --
8500 GOSUB6310
8510 IFE=0THEN8540
8520 E=1
8530 RETURN
8540 KZ$=KY$
8550 MID$(KZ$,I*12-11,12)=STRING$(255,12)
8560 LSET KY$=KZ$
8570 PUT2,KN
8580 E=0
8590 RETURN
8999 REM -- 9000-9499 RESAVE RECORD --
9000 GOSUB6310
9010 IFE=0THEN9040
9020 E=1
9030 RETURN
9040 N=CVI(MID$(K1$,11,2))
9050 GOSUB6010
9060 GOSUB6190
9070 E=0
9080 RETURN
```

Listing 10.1

There is also one more subroutine to add to the 6000 series subroutines. This is not a record-handling subroutine, but it is a subroutine that will be used by the subroutines above line 7000 and not directly by the main program. The subroutine begins at line 6310 and is meant to locate a key in the key file. The reason that this subroutine is not part of the subroutines above line 7000 is that several of them use this subroutine. Its location here is a matter of convenience—it is among the other subroutines used by the main key-file subroutines.

This new subroutine will look for the key. In this method, it must first *hash* the key (i.e., extract the number from it that corresponds to the key-file block). The hashing is done in statements 6310 through 6360 and statement 6370 loads into memory the block number that results. The FOR/NEXT loop in lines 6380 through 6410 searches the block for the key. If it is found, the IF statement in line 6400 branches to line 6500, which sets E equal to zero (to indicate that the search was successful) and then returns to the calling routine. If it is not found, the FOR/NEXT loop in lines 6430 through 6450 is executed. This loop searches for a blank key (the compared value is set in line 6420). If it finds one, line 6440 branches to line 6480, which sets E equal to one (indicating that the key was not found, but room to insert it was found), then returns RETURN to the calling routine. If a blank spot cannot even be found, the FOR/NEXT loop terminates and line 6460 sets E equal to two (indicating that the key-file block is full), then again returns to the calling routine.

Now you can write all of the key-file subroutines. The first one, which starts at line 7000, puts a new key and record into the file. It must also check to make sure it is not a duplicate key and that there is room to put it on the proper block. Line 7000 calls the new subroutine at line 6310 to first hash the key and load the key block. The error code E being equal to two indicates that there is no more room, so if the subroutine at 6310 returns this code, all you need to do is return to the main program. The main program will then get the message that the key cannot be inserted because there is no room. If the error code returned is one, then the key can be inserted and there is no duplicate. Line 7020 checks this condition. If the subroutine at 6310 returns E equal to zero, these IF statements do not branch. This means that a key with that value has been located. Line 7030 sets E equal to one and returns to the main program, indicating that there is a duplicate key. If all of the conditions are tested and it is found that the key does not exist and there is room to put it, the subroutine will continue at line 7040.

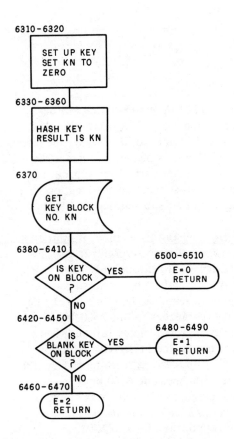

Figure 10.1: *Functional diagram of hashing subroutine (listing 10.1).*

Line 7040 calls the subroutine at line 6250, which gets the next available record number. Lines 7050 through 7090 pack this number into bytes 11 and 12 of the key, then they insert the key into the block and save it on disk. Line 7100 calls the packing subroutine and line 7110 sets the record number (N) equal to the new record number (FR), then calls the routine that saves the record. Lines 7120 and 7130 set E equal to zero to indicate that the operation was successful, then return to the main program.

Note that subroutine called as many as four other subroutines in order to insert the key and the record. It may make it a little less complex if the list of REM statements is updated and changed slightly. To do that, first place a REM statement at line 6309 to describe the new subroutine at lines 6310 through 6510, then save this program (ASCII format) under another name (e.g., "HASH"). Next, load in the REM printing program and add an LPRINT" " or two between lines 130 and 200. This will leave some room on the list of REM statements to add some comments on how the subroutines work, like what parameters are required and what is returned, including the values of E for the various possible errors.

The next subroutine is a little easier. All it does is get the record with the given key. Line 7500 is the same as the first subroutine. The first four lines of the subroutines at 7500, 8500, and 9000 are all the same, using the routine at 6310 to hash and load the key, then check the error code. If the key is not in the file, all three of these routines must return E equal to one. The get-record routine logic continues at line 7540 by unpacking the record number from the key. Next, it calls the load-record routine and the unpack-record routine (the GOSUB statements at lines 7550 and 7560), sets E equal to zero and returns.

The routine at line 8000 is not valid for the hashing method (this is the get next function), so the delete routine at line 8500 is the next one to program. Lines 8500 through 8530 are the same as the get key routine. Line 8540 transfers the key buffer (KY$) into a program variable, then 8550 writes the blank key code over the position where the key was found. 8560 and 8570 replace the key block in the proper place in the key file using the variable KN, which was established as the key block in the routine at line 6310. All that is left is to set E equal to zero and return (lines 8580 and 8590).

The last subroutine to program is the one that will update an existing record to reflect some changes in the data. It will not handle a change in the key. To change the key will require deleting the record and reentering it with the new key. The put-key and record subroutine needs the duplicate key check and cannot be used to resave a key in order to prevent accidentally eliminating a previously saved record when a new record is entered with the same key. This resave routine is almost identical to the get-record routine. It follows the same logic except that it does not load and unpack a record. Instead, it packs and saves the record where the key indicated it to be. Note that the two subroutines are identical except for the two subroutine calls (lines 9050 and 9060 as compared to 7550 and 7560).

In many of the routines in this book, the disk buffer is placed into another variable in order to alter the contents before resaving it. Different systems will have different rules pertaining to how these buffers can be used in memory. This method of transferring it to a variable that is not defined to be a buffer should work on all of the systems, although it will not be required on some.

Now that the hashing method subroutines are in place, save them in their own file on disk, then test them. The test should be first to initialize the files, then to use the put function to place some sample records in the file. Once this is done, test the other routines. If a program error is discovered and corrected, be prepared to reinitialize the files in case some invalid records remain because of the error, for these invalid records might prevent the now-valid routines from functioning properly. Spend some time in this testing. The error correction is the best method available for learning.

EDDIE GERMANO

CHAPTER 11

THE ALPHABETICAL-ARRAY METHOD

This is a relatively simple method of keeping the keys in alphabetical order. Finding a specific key with this method will take a little longer than it did with the hashing method, and inserting or deleting keys will take much longer. But this method affords you the luxury of being able to extract the keys from the file in alphabetical order. Combining this method with the hashing method will provide both functions (the quick insert and delete and the ability to extract the keys in alphabetical order), but combining them does require a lengthy sort.

To do this all you do is add one extra step to the hashing method. First, add a function that will load (GET) each block in the key file and store each of the keys in a large string array, one key per array element, then sort the array. Then write the subroutine at 8000 (get next key) to use this new array. This would be a useful function to add to the hashing method for a system where the reports are required in key order. If the reports require other orders, the function that assembles the array could use the other field to do it, as long as the locator is packed in the proper place so that the proper record can be located.

A full alphabetical-array system can use many of the routines developed in the hashing method, with some alteration. Starting with the hashing method program (load that into memory first), delete the routine that performs the hashing (lines 6310 through 6510). This will later be replaced with another routine. Also, delete lines 50 and 60, as the key file will not be a random-access file but a sequential file. More string space will be needed for the array, so increase the CLEAR to 4000. Now make statement 20

20 DIM KY$(100)

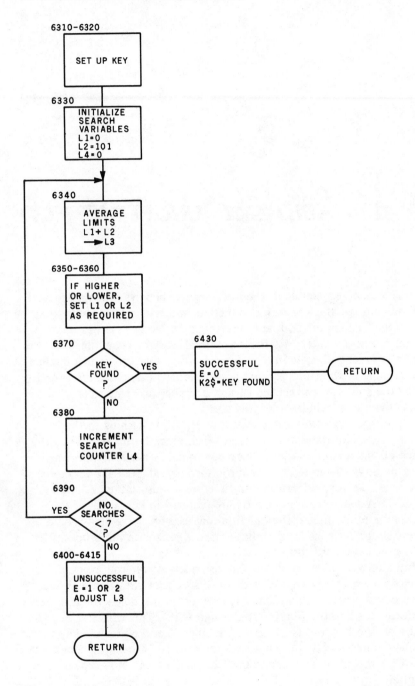

Figure 11.1: *Functional diagram of alphabetical-array search subroutine (listing 11.1).*

THE ALPHABETICAL-ARRAY METHOD **81**

Of the key subroutines, two require no changes. These are the ones at 7500 (read a record given a key) and at 9000 (replace a record after changes have been made). The changes will be first in the subroutine starting at line 6310, and then in the other key-access subroutines. The subroutine at 6310 was the hashing algorithm. To find the key for the alphabetical-array method, you need to use a binary search method. The error codes (the variable E) need some alteration. For the *no error* condition (E equals zero), instead of returning the local key number, the subscript of the next higher key in the array will be returned. It will return E is equal to two only when there is no more room in the array and the key has not been found. Refer to listing 11.1 for the new code for this subroutine, which will be in line numbers 6310 through 6440.

Lines 6310 through 6330 initialize all of the variables that will be required for the binary search of the array. The searching, which should look familiar, is in lines 6340 through 6390. Lines 6400 through 6420 handle the condition that the key was not found. Line 6400 sets E equal to two if the last key in the file—KY$(100)—contains a valid key, or E equal to one if it is blank. Line 6410 protects against the possible condition of the last key tested in the unsuccessful search being lower than the key being searched. The return condition specifies that it is to be the next higher. The way the search works, the key that it last tested could be the one either immediately above or immediately below the value searched. If it is the one immediately below, this statement simply adds one. Lines 6430 and 6440 handle the condition where the correct key is found. K1$ will be given the value of the key entry to make the code a little shorter in the other subroutines (by using a linear variable instead of one with a subscript).

Adding a new key to the file requires some different logic in the subroutine (starting line 7000). The first few statements will be the same, but the actual insertion of the key requires some more work. The last few statements also can be the same. The only ones that are changed are lines 7050 through 7090. First, make room to insert the key in the FOR/NEXT loop in lines 7050 through 7070, and then pack and insert the key, in one step, in line 7080. Line 6450 will start another subroutine (yet to be written) that will resave the keys in the sequential file.

The subroutine at line 8500 is the next to change. Again, much of the logic is still valid. The changes occur in lines 8540 through 8570. Delete must condense the array, which is done in the FOR/NEXT loop in lines 8540 through 8560. This will write over the key that is to be deleted. In case the array is full, which will mean that the last key (subscript #100) will now be equal to the next-to-last key (subscript #99), line 8565 sets the last key in the file to the blank key characters. Line 8570 reuses the subroutine starting at 6450, which is still to be written, to resave the sequential key file.

You now have only two subroutines left for this conversion before you can look at the main program again. Both of these subroutines are new. The first is the get next routine that starts at line 8000. The easiest way to write this routine, given the other subroutines in the system, is to use the routine at 6310 to return the value of the current key. If the key is found, increase the subscript by one. Otherwise, the subscript returned is the next greater key or the end of file. Lines 8000 through 8020 take care of getting the key and increasing the subscript if the key is found. Lines 8030 and 8040 take care of the end-of-file conditions, which could be due to the subscript going over 100 (line 8030) or the key being a blank key (which, in a sorted array, indicates that there are no more keys). The rest of the subroutine is like the end of the get-key routine.

The other new subroutine begins at line 6450. All it does is write all of the keys back into the sequential file. This is required when keys are added and deleted. The logic to handle this may be very simple or very complicated, depending upon the computer system used. On many systems, if only one key were written to the file during each PRINT# statement, the file would require 100 blocks. Fortunately, most of the microcomputers do not have this problem. If you PRINT# an entire block's worth of keys at once, only six blocks would be required. Another consideration is that on most microcomputers that will PRINT# more than one key per block (even when they are done one at a time), you must use a comma between each key so that they can be read back correctly. This will allow only 19 keys per block, because each key will now occupy 13 bytes instead of 12. One simple way to eliminate the possible eccentricities of a particular computer system is to pack the keys, 20 to a block, then save them. The routine in lines 6450 through 6540 does this. It opens the file as an output file (sequential), then uses nested FOR/NEXT loops to pack and save each of the key blocks. Finally, the CLOSE statement will cause any computer system that saves the blocks only after they are full (these are the systems that allow one key at a time to be saved but still store more than one on a block) to save the final block in the file (it holds the blocks in memory until they are full). Also, if this routine is used again, the CLOSE statement avoids an error when a user attempts to open the file again at line 6450.

Next, in the main program, comes the file initialization routine. The part that initializes the records can stay, because the record file did not change. The part that needs to be changed is lines 500 through 530. Delete line 540. Fewer statements are needed, although the initialization is a little more involved, because the subroutine at line 6450 is used. Because the keys must be read into memory at the beginning of the program, and they can not be read in until they are initialized for the first time, RUN the program and select the initialization now. Use the break key to end it after initialization. Now enter the routine in lines 50 through 94. This reads the keys into the memory in the form that they were written in the subroutine starting at line 6450.

```
10 CLEAR4000
20 DIMKY$(100)
30 OPEN"R",1,"RECORDS:1"
40 FIELD1,255ASB$
50 OPEN"I",2,"KEY:1"
60 FORI=0TO99STEP20
```

```
70 LINEINPUT#2,K3$
80 FORJ=I+1TOI+20
90 KY$(J)=MID$(K3$,(J-I)*12-11,12)
92 NEXTJ:NEXTI
94 CLOSE2
100 CLS
110 PRINTTAB(20);"KEY FILE TEST"
120 PRINTTAB(10);"1  INITIALIZE FILES"
130 PRINTTAB(10);"2  PUT A NEW RECORD IN FILE"
140 PRINTTAB(10);"3  GET A RECORD, GIVEN THE KEY"
150 PRINTTAB(10);"4  GET NEXT RECORD, GIVEN A KEY"
160 PRINTTAB(10);"5  DELETE A RECORD"
170 PRINTTAB(10);"6  ALTER AND REPLACE A RECORD"
180 PRINT
190 INPUT"  ENTER NUMBER OF SELECTION";N
200 IFN<1THEN220
210 IFN<=6THEN240
220 PRINT"ERROR - PLEASE ENTER A NUMBER FROM 1 TO 6"
230 GOTO190
240 ONNGOTO500,700,900,1100,1300,1500
500 FORI=1TO100
510 KY$(I)=STRING$(12,255)
520 NEXTI
530 GOSUB6450
550 B1$=STRING$(255,32)
560 FORI=1TO34
570 LSET B$=B1$
580 PUT1,I
590 NEXTI
600 GET1,1
610 B1$=B$
620 MID$(B1$,1,2)=MKI$(1)
630 LSET B$=B1$
640 PUT1,1
650 GOTO100
700 CLS
710 PRINTTAB(16);"PUT NEW KEY AND RECORD IN FILE"
720 PRINT
730 INPUT"NEW KEY";K$
740 KN$=K$
750 GOSUB7500
760 IFE=1THEN790
770 PRINT"ERROR - KEY ALREADY IN FILE"
780 GOTO730
790 K$=KN$
795 INPUT"NAME";N$
800 INPUT"ADDRESS";A$
810 INPUT"CITY";C$
820 INPUT"STATE";S$
830 INPUT"ZIP CODE";Z$
840 INPUT"IS THE ABOVE CORRECT (Y OR N)";OK$
850 IFOK$="Y"THEN890
860 IFOK$="N"THEN700
870 PRINT"ERROR - PLEASE ANSWER Y OR N"
880 GOTO840
890 GOSUB7000
895 GOTO100
900 CLS
910 PRINTTAB(22);"GET A RECORD GIVEN THE KEY"
920 PRINT
930 INPUT"KEY";K$
940 GOSUB7500
950 IFE=0THEN980
960 PRINT"KEY NOT IN FILE"
970 GOTO930
980 PRINT"NAME : ";N$
990 PRINT"ADDRESS : ";A$
1000 PRINT"CITY, STATE AND ZIP : ";C$;", ";S$;" ";Z$
1010 PRINT
1020 PRINT"PRESS ENTER WHEN FINISHED VIEWING"
1030 W$=INKEY$:IFW$=""THEN1030
1040 GOTO100
```

```
1100 CLS
1110 PRINTTAB(22);"GET NEXT GREATER KEY"
1120 PRINT
1130 INPUT"KEY";K$
1140 GOSUB8000
1150 IFE=0THEN1180
1160 PRINT"END OF FILE.   THERE IS NO GREATER KEY"
1170 GOTO1100
1180 PRINT"KEY : ";K$
1190 GOTO980
1300 CLS
1310 PRINTTAB(25);"DELETE A RECORD"
1320 PRINT
1330 INPUT"KEY TO DELETE (OR END)";K$
1340 IFK$="END"THEN100
1350 GOSUB8500
1360 IFE=0THEN1390
1370 PRINT"KEY NOT FOUND AND NOT DELETED"
1380 GOTO1400
1390 PRINT"KEY DELETED"
1400 PRINT"PRESS ENTER AFTER READING MESSAGE"
1410 W$=INKEY$:IFW$=""THEN1410
1420 GOTO100
1500 CLS:PRINTTAB(20);"CHANGE DATA IN A RECORD":PRINT
1510 INPUT"KEY";K$
1520 GOSUB7500
1530 IFE=0THEN1560
1540 PRINT"ERROR - KEY NOT FOUND"
1550 GOTO1510
1560 PRINT"1. NAME : ";N$
1570 PRINT"2. ADDRESS : ";A$
1580 PRINT"3. CITY : ";C$
1590 PRINT"4. STATE : ";S$
1600 PRINT"5. ZIP CODE : ";Z$
1610 PRINT
1620 INPUT"ENTER NUMBER OF FIELD TO CHANGE";NF
1630 IFNF<1THEN1650
1640 IFNF<=5THEN1670
1650 PRINT"ERROR - PLEASE ENTER A NUMBER FROM 1 TO 5"
1660 GOTO1620
1670 ONNFGOSUB1680,1685,1690,1695,1700
1675 GOSUB9000
1677 GOTO100
1680 INPUT"NEW NAME";N$
1682 RETURN
1685 INPUT"NEW ADDRESS";A$
1687 RETURN
1690 INPUT"NEW CITY";C$
1692 RETURN
1695 INPUT"NEW STATE";S$
1697 RETURN
1700 INPUT"NEW ZIP CODE";Z$
1702 RETURN
6000 STOP
6010 R1$=STRING$(85,32)
6020 R2$=STRING$(20,32)
6025 MID$(R1$,1,10)=K$+R2$
6030 MID$(R1$,11,20)=N$+R2$
6040 MID$(R1$,31,20)=A$+R2$
6045 MID$(R1$,51,16)=C$+R2$
6050 MID$(R1$,67,2)=S$+R2$
6060 MID$(R1$,69,5)=Z$+R2$
6070 R$=R1$
6080 RETURN
6090 K$=LEFT$(R$,10)
6095 N$=MID$(R$,11,20)
6100 A$=MID$(R$,31,20)
6110 C$=MID$(R$,51,16)
6120 S$=MID$(R$,67,2)
6130 Z$=MID$(R$,69,5)
6140 RETURN
6150 B=INT((N-1)/3):R=N-B*3
```

```
6155 B=B+1
6160 GET1,B
6170 R$=MID$(B$,R*85-84,85)
6180 RETURN
6190 R1$=R$
6200 GOSUB6150
6210 B1$=B$
6220 MID$(B1$,R*85-84,85)=R1$
6230 LSET B$=B1$
6235 PUT1,B
6240 RETURN
6250 GET1,1
6260 B1$=B$
6270 FR=CVI(LEFT$(B1$,2))+1
6280 MID$(B1$,1,2)=MKI$(FR)
6290 LSET B$=B1$
6300 PUT1,1
6305 RETURN
6310 K1$=STRING$(10,32)
6320 K$=K$+K1$:KN=0
6330 L1=0:L2=101:L4=0
6340 L3=INT((L1+L2)/2)
6350 IFLEFT$(K$,10)<LEFT$(KY$(L3),10)THEN LET L2=L3
6360 IFLEFT$(K$,10)>LEFT$(KY$(L3),10)THEN LET L1=L3
6370 IFLEFT$(K$,10)=LEFT$(KY$(L3),10)THEN 6430
6380 L4=L4+1
6390 IFL4<7THEN6340
6400 E=2:IFKY$(100)=STRING$(12,255)THENLETE=1
6410 IFLEFT$(K$,10)>LEFT$(KY$(L3),10)THENLETL3=L3+1
6415 IFL3=0THENL3=1
6420 RETURN
6430 E=0:K1$=KY$(L3)
6440 RETURN
6450 OPEN"O",2,"KEY:1"
6460 FORI=0TO99STEP20
6470 K3$=""
6480 FORJ=I+1TOI+20
6490 K3$=K3$+KY$(J)
6500 NEXTJ
6510 PRINT#2,K3$
6520 NEXTI
6530 CLOSE2
6540 RETURN
7000 GOSUB6310
7010 IFE=2THENRETURN
7020 IFE=1THEN7040
7030 E=1:RETURN
7040 GOSUB6250
7050 FORI=99TOL3STEP-1
7060 KY$(I+1)=KY$(I)
7070 NEXTI
7080 KY$(L3)=LEFT$(K$,10)+MKI$(FR)
7090 GOSUB6450
7100 GOSUB6010
7110 N=FR:GOSUB6190
7120 E=0 ·
7130 RETURN
7500 GOSUB6310
7510 IFE=0THEN7540
7520 E=1
7530 RETURN
7540 N=CVI(MID$(K1$,11,2))
7550 GOSUB6150
7560 GOSUB6090
7570 E=0
7580 RETURN
8000 GOSUB6310
8010 IFE=1THEN8030
8020 L3=L3+1
8030 IFL3<100THEN8060
8040 IFKY$(L3)<STRING$(12,255)THEN8060
8050 E=1:RETURN
```

```
8060 N=CVI(MID$(KY$(L3),11,2))
8070 GOSUB6150
8080 GOSUB6090
8090 E=0
8100 RETURN
8500 GOSUB6310
8510 IFE=0THEN8540
8520 E=1
8530 RETURN
8540 FORI=L3TO99
8550 KY$(I)=KY$(I+1)
8560 NEXTI
8565 KY$(100)=STRING$(12,255)
8570 GOSUB6450
8580 E=0
8590 RETURN
9000 GOSUB6310
9010 IFE=0THEN9040
9020 E=1
9030 RETURN
9040 N=CVI(MID$(K1$,11,2))
9050 GOSUB6010
9060 GOSUB6190
9070 E=0
9080 RETURN
```

Listing 11.1

You may now save this program on the disk in its own program file. Test it in the same way you did the hashing program. Also, check the new routine that gets the next greater key. Note that the insert and delete functions take lots of time. This is partially due to the fact that the entire key array must be resaved on disk every time a key is added or deleted. This can be limited by eliminating the GOSUB 6450 calls in the two subroutines and adding a function that resaves the keys before the program is ended so that the operator may decide when the keys are to be saved. Since the keys are not read from disk during the run, they are written only to make them permanent. However, even with this alteration, the routines to add and delete may still run a little slower than the hashing method routines. This depends upon the internal speed of the computer and the efficiency of the BASIC interpreter. If the computer is internally fast and has a good interpreter, the binary searching could be faster than the extra disk search required by the hashing method. Generally, in-memory routines will be faster than disk operations, but a binary search uses many statements to find the key.

CHAPTER 12

THE TREE-STRUCTURED METHOD

Although a diagram of the easy-to-program version of the tree-structured method presented in this chapter does not closely resemble a tree, the version it is derived from does. That original actually does branch out in different directions to search for the key. You might say that with a smaller key file, our simpler tree-structured method resembles a seedling.

This version will handle a maximum of 254 blocks of keys. Since most microcomputers use minifloppy disks which contain only about 350 blocks, this is not that much of a limitation. Consider, also, that the record file will be even larger. The maximum number of blocks required for a file can be estimated. Using this method, there is no way to determine the exact number of blocks the key file requires, because it depends on the order in which the keys are entered. The worst case is when the keys are entered in alphabetical order. This may seem odd, but the method works best when the keys are entered in a random order. The minimum and ideal number of blocks is the number of keys divided by the number that one block can contain. From the hashing method calculations, this number should be 21. Because of the way that the tree-structured method works, one key per block will be wasted, so the number of keys per block becomes 20. For a 100-key file, this means at least five blocks. More likely, there will be between five and ten blocks. Twice the calculated number (i.e., 10 blocks) is the worst case, which will happen if all of the keys are entered in alphabetical order. Chances are that there will be seven or eight blocks in the key file.

When this file is in use, place the first 20 keys on the first block in the key file. When the next key is entered, it will be placed there, then another routine will be triggered by the presence of the last key. The routine will divide the block in half, leaving the first half in place and starting a new block with the remaining keys. Then it will update the roadmap to show that, alphabetically, the second block follows the first. When one of these blocks becomes full, the routine will split that block and create the third block. The roadmap is then updated again to show that the new order is blocks one, two, then three, if the second block is split, or one, three, then two if the first block is split. The roadmap itself actually occupies the first block of the key file, so the first block, as indicated above, is actually the second block in the file.

The roadmap is actually a series of bytes the value of which indicates the block by its numerical equivalent. This number is between 1 and 254, which is one reason that the number of key blocks is limited to 254. 255 is used to indicate that a block is not occupied. Zero is not used because some systems have problems with a null byte in the middle of a string variable. Searching for a key is done by employing a binary search on the blocks.

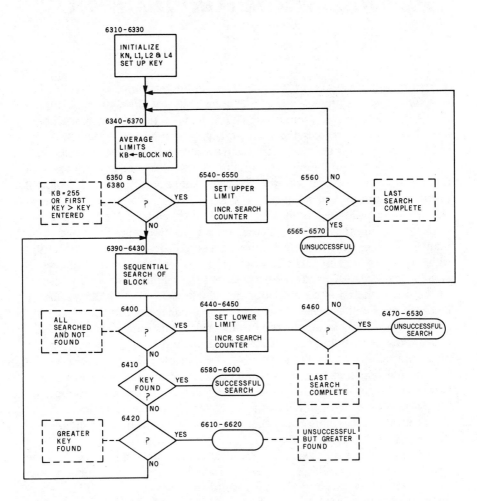

Figure 12.1: *Generalized flow of modified tree-structured search routine (listing 12.1).*

Using the bytes in the roadmap, each block is located by the number selected in the binary search, and the block indicated is searched for the key. The limits are changed if it is not the correct block, and a new block is read by the number from the indicated place in the roadmap. In the method presented in this chapter, the search in the block is a sequential search, which is not that slow since the average number of keys on the block is about 15. Also, the block will be searched only in the case where the first key on the block is lower than the key being searched. If it is higher, then the entire block is higher, so no block search is required to satisfy the binary search's condition.

In the initialization, an extra key is inserted as the first position of the first key block. This is required in order to make the logic a little easier to program, in that inserting the first key on the first block would require some extra coding. This first key is made up of spaces (ASCII code is decimal 32) which should be lower than any key entered.

You can alter the alphabetical-array method to code this method. Load it into the computer's memory. Then replace the DIM in line 20 with the original REM statement, since it is no longer needed. Next, replace lines 50 and 60 with the OPEN and FIELD statements that the hashing method used. Now delete lines 70 through 94. They will be replaced later with other coding that will read in the roadmap, but, like the alphabetical-array method, this cannot be done before the file is first initialized. Also delete the searching and resaving routines from lines 6310 through 6540. A new search routine must be written for this method. To do it refer to listing 12.1, the finished program. Do not put routines into place out of the order that the text in this chapter dictates.

```
9 REM -- 0010-0090 PROGRAM INITIALIZATION --
10 CLEAR4000
20 REM**THIS STATEMENT RESERVED FOR DIM STATEMENTS **
30 OPEN"R",1,"RECORDS:1"
40 FIELD1,255ASB$
50 OPEN"R",2,"KEY:1"
60 FIELD2,255ASKY$
70 GET2,1
80 RM$=KY$
99 REM -- 0100-0490 CONTROL SECTION --
100 CLS
110 PRINTTAB(20);"KEY FILE TEST"
120 PRINTTAB(10);"1  INITIALIZE FILES"
130 PRINTTAB(10);"2  PUT A NEW RECORD IN FILE"
140 PRINTTAB(10);"3  GET A RECORD, GIVEN THE KEY"
150 PRINTTAB(10);"4  GET NEXT RECORD, GIVEN A KEY"
160 PRINTTAB(10);"5  DELETE A RECORD"
170 PRINTTAB(10);"6  ALTER AND REPLACE A RECORD"
180 PRINT
190 INPUT"  ENTER NUMBER OF SELECTION";N
200 IFN<1THEN220
210 IFN<=6THEN240
220 PRINT"ERROR - PLEASE ENTER A NUMBER FROM 1 TO 6"
230 GOTO190
240 ONNGOTO500,700,900,1100,1300,1500
499 REM -- 0500-0699 INITIALIZE FILES SECTION --
500 RM$=CHR$(1)+STRING$(9,255)
```

```
505 LSET KY$=RM$
510 PUT2,1
512 K1$=STRING$(12,32)+STRING$(243,255)
514 LSET KY$=K1$
516 PUT2,2
550 B1$=STRING$(255,32)
560 FORI=1TO34
570 LSET B$=B1$
580 PUT1,I
590 NEXTI
600 GET1,1
610 B1$=B$
620 MID$(B1$,1,2)=MKI$(1)
630 LSET B$=B1$
640 PUT1,1
650 GOTO100
699 REM -- 0700-0899 PUT NEW KEY AND RECORD IN FILE FUNCTION --
700 CLS
710 PRINTTAB(16);"PUT NEW KEY AND RECORD IN FILE"
720 PRINT
730 INPUT"NEW KEY";K$
740 KN$=K$
750 GOSUB7500
760 IFE=1THEN790
770 PRINT"ERROR - KEY ALREADY IN FILE"
780 GOTO730
790 K$=KN$
795 INPUT"NAME";N$
800 INPUT"ADDRESS";A$
810 INPUT"CITY";C$
820 INPUT"STATE";S$
830 INPUT"ZIP CODE";Z$
840 INPUT"IS THE ABOVE CORRECT (Y OR N)";OK$
850 IFOK$="Y"THEN890
860 IFOK$="N"THEN700
870 PRINT"ERROR - PLEASE ANSWER Y OR N"
880 GOTO840
890 GOSUB7000
895 GOTO100
899 REM -- 0900-1099 GET RECORD GIVEN KEY FUNCTION --
900 CLS
910 PRINTTAB(22);"GET A RECORD GIVEN THE KEY"
920 PRINT
930 INPUT"KEY";K$
940 GOSUB7500
950 IFE=0THEN980
960 PRINT"KEY NOT IN FILE"
970 GOTO930
980 PRINT"NAME : ";N$
990 PRINT"ADDRESS : ";A$
1000 PRINT"CITY, STATE AND ZIP : ";C$;", ";S$;" ";Z$
1010 PRINT
1020 PRINT"PRESS ENTER WHEN FINISHED VIEWING"
1030 W$=INKEY$:IFW$=""THEN1030
1040 GOTO100
1099 REM -- 1100-1299 GET NEXT FUNCTION --
1100 CLS
1110 PRINTTAB(22);"GET NEXT GREATER KEY"
1120 PRINT
1130 INPUT"KEY";K$
1140 GOSUB8000
1150 IFE=0THEN1180
1160 PRINT"END OF FILE.   THERE IS NO GREATER KEY"
1170 GOTO1100
1180 PRINT"KEY : ";K$
1190 GOTO980
1299 REM -- 1300-1499 DELETE RECORD FUNCTION --
1300 CLS
1310 PRINTTAB(25);"DELETE A RECORD"
1320 PRINT
1330 INPUT"KEY TO DELETE (OR END)";K$
1340 IFK$="END"THEN100
```

```
1350 GOSUB8500
1360 IFE=0THEN1390
1370 PRINT"KEY NOT FOUND AND NOT DELETED"
1380 GOTO1400
1390 PRINT"KEY DELETED"
1400 PRINT"PRESS ENTER AFTER READING MESSAGE"
1410 W$=INKEY$:IFW$=""THEN1410
1420 GOTO100
1499 REM -- 1500-1699 ALTER RECORD FUNCTION --
1500 CLS:PRINTTAB(20);"CHANGE DATA IN A RECORD":PRINT
1510 INPUT"KEY";K$
1520 GOSUB7500
1530 IFE=0THEN1560
1540 PRINT"ERROR - KEY NOT FOUND"
1550 GOTO1510
1560 PRINT"1. NAME : ";N$
1570 PRINT"2. ADDRESS : ";A$
1580 PRINT"3. CITY : ";C$
1590 PRINT"4. STATE : ";S$
1600 PRINT"5. ZIP CODE : ";Z$
1610 PRINT
1620 INPUT"ENTER NUMBER OF FIELD TO CHANGE";NF
1630 IFNF<1THEN1650
1640 IFNF<=5THEN1670
1650 PRINT"ERROR - PLEASE ENTER A NUMBER FROM 1 TO 5"
1660 GOTO1620
1670 ONNFGOSUB1680,1685,1690,1695,1700
1675 GOSUB9000
1677 GOTO100
1680 INPUT"NEW NAME";N$
1682 RETURN
1685 INPUT"NEW ADDRESS";A$
1687 RETURN
1690 INPUT"NEW CITY";C$
1692 RETURN
1695 INPUT"NEW STATE";S$
1697 RETURN
1700 INPUT"NEW ZIP CODE";Z$
1702 RETURN
5999 REM -- 6000-6990 RECORD FILE SUBROUTINES --
6000 STOP
6009 REM -- 6010-6080 PACK RECORD --
6010 R1$=STRING$(85,32)
6020 R2$=STRING$(20,32)
6025 MID$(R1$,1,10)=K$+R2$
6030 MID$(R1$,11,20)=N$+R2$
6040 MID$(R1$,31,20)=A$+R2$
6045 MID$(R1$,51,16)=C$+R2$
6050 MID$(R1$,67,2)=S$+R2$
6060 MID$(R1$,69,5)=Z$+R2$
6070 R$=R1$
6080 RETURN
6089 REM -- 6090-6140 UNPACK RECORD --
6090 K$=LEFT$(R$,10)
6095 N$=MID$(R$,11,20)
6100 A$=MID$(R$,31,20)
6110 C$=MID$(R$,51,16)
6120 S$=MID$(R$,67,2)
6130 Z$=MID$(R$,69,5)
6140 RETURN
6149 REM -- 6150-6180 GET RECORD BY NUMBER --
6150 B=INT((N-1)/3):R=N-B*3
6155 B=B+1
6160 GET1,B
6170 R$=MID$(B$,R*85-84,85)
6180 RETURN
6189 REM -- 6190-6240 PUT RECORD BY NUMBER --
6190 R1$=R$
6200 GOSUB6150
6210 B1$=B$
6220 MID$(B1$,R*85-84,85)=R1$
6230 LSET B$=B1$
```

```
6235 PUT1,B
6240 RETURN
6249 REM -- 6250-6305 GET NEXT AVAILABLE RECORD NUMBER --
6250 GET1,1
6260 B1$=B$
6270 FR=CVI(LEFT$(B1$,2))+1
6280 MID$(B1$,1,2)=MKI$(FR)
6290 LSET B$=B1$
6300 PUT1,1
6305 RETURN
6309 REM -- 6310-6510 SEARCH FOR KEY --
6310 K1$=STRING$(10,32)
6320 K$=K$+K1$:KN=0
6330 L1=0:L2=10:L4=0
6340 L3=INT((L1+L2)/2)
6350 IFMID$(RM$,L3,1)=CHR$(255)THEN6540
6360 KB=ASC(MID$(RM$,L3,1))
6370 GET2,KB+1
6380 IFLEFT$(KY$,10)>LEFT$(K$,10)THEN6540
6390 KN=0
6400 KN=KN+1:IFKN=21THEN6440
6410 IFLEFT$(K$,10)=MID$(KY$,KN*12-11,10)THEN6580
6420 IFLEFT$(K$,10)<MID$(KY$,KN*12-11,10)THEN6610
6430 GOTO6400
6440 L1=L3
6450 L4=L4+1
6460 IFL4<4THEN6340
6470 E=1
6480 L3=L3+1
6490 KB=ASC(MID$(RM$,L3,1))
6500 K1$=STRING$(12,255):IFKB=255THENRETURN
6510 GET2,KB+1
6520 K1$=LEFT$(KY$,12)
6530 RETURN
6540 L2=L3
6550 L4=L4+1
6560 IFL4<4THEN6340
6565 E=1:IFL1>0THEN6500
6570 PRINT"KEY FILE INITIALIZATION ERROR !!":STOP
6580 E=0
6590 K1$=MID$(KY$,KN*12-11,12)
6600 RETURN
6610 E=1
6620 GOTO6590
6999 REM -- 7000-7499 PUT NEW RECORD AND KEY --
7000 GOSUB6310
7020 IFE=1THEN7040
7030 E=1:RETURN
7040 GOSUB6250
7045 KZ$=KY$
7050 IFKB=255THEN7180
7060 IFLEFT$(K$,10)<LEFT$(KZ$,10)THENKN=1
7070 FORI=21TOKNSTEP-1:MID$(KZ$,I*12-11,12)=MID$(KZ$,(I-1)*12-11,12)
7072 NEXTI
7074 MID$(KZ$,KN*12-11,12)=LEFT$(K$,10)+MKI$(FR)
7080 LSET KY$=KZ$
7090 PUT2,KB+1
7100 GOSUB6010
7110 N=FR:GOSUB6190
7120 E=0
7130 IFMID$(KY$,241,12)=STRING$(12,255)THENRETURN
7140 L4=0:FORI=1TO10:IFASC(MID$(RM$,I,1))=255THEN7144
7142 IFASC(MID$(RM$,I,1))>L4THEN L4=ASC(MID$(RM$,I,1))
7144 NEXTI
7146 I=0
7148 I=I+1:IFASC(MID$(RM$,I,1))<>KBTHEN7148
7150 J=10
7152 J=J-1:MID$(RM$,J+1,1)=MID$(RM$,J,1):IFJ>ITHEN7152
7156 MID$(RM$,I+1,1)=MKI$(L4+1)
7158 KZ$=KY$:KX$=MID$(KY$,121,134)+STRING$(120,255)
7160 MID$(KZ$,121,134)=STRING$(134,255)
7162 LSET KY$=KZ$:PUT2,KB+1
```

```
7164 LSET KY$=KX$:PUT2,L4+2
7166 LSET KY$=RM$:PUT2,1
7170 E=0:RETURN
7180 L4=0
7182 L4=L4+1:IFL4<=10THEN7184:ELSESTOP
7184 IFASC(MID$(RM$,L4+1,1))<255THEN7182
7186 KB=ASC(MID$(RM$,L4,1)):GET2,KB+1
7188 KN=0
7190 KN=KN+1:IFMID$(KY$,KN*12-11,12)<STRING$(12,255)THEN7190
7192 GOTO7050
7499 REM -- 7500-7999 GET RECORD --
7500 GOSUB6310
7510 IFE=0THEN7540
7520 E=1
7530 RETURN
7540 N=CVI(MID$(K1$,11,2))
7550 GOSUB6150
7560 GOSUB6090
7570 E=0
7580 RETURN
7999 REM -- 8000-8499 GET NEXT --
8000 K$=K$+STRING$(10,32):E=ASC(MID$(K$,10,1))+1
8010 MID$(K$,10,1)=CHR$(E)
8020 GOSUB6310
8030 IFE=0THEN7540
8040 IFMID$(K1$,1,10)<STRING$(10,255)THEN8060
8050 E=1:RETURN
8060 E=0:GOTO7540
8070 GOSUB6150
8080 GOSUB6090
8090 E=0
8100 RETURN
8499 REM -- 8500-8999 DELETE KEY AND RECORD --
8500 GOSUB6310
8510 IFE=0THEN8540
8520 E=1
8530 RETURN
8540 KZ$=KY$
8550 FORI=KNTO20
8555 MID$(KZ$,I*12-11,12)=MID$(KZ$,(I+1)*12-11,12)
8557 NEXTI
8560 MID$(KZ$,229,12)=STRING$(12,255)
8565 LSET KY$=KZ$
8570 PUT2,KB+1
8580 E=0
8590 RETURN
8999 REM -- 9000-9499 RESAVE RECORD --
9000 GOSUB6310
9010 IFE=0THEN9040
9020 E=1
9030 RETURN
9040 N=CVI(MID$(K1$,11,2))
9050 GOSUB6010
9060 GOSUB6190
9070 E=0
9080 RETURN
```

Listing 12.1

The search routine in this method is much longer than in either of the other two methods. It starts at line 6310 and ends at line 6620. Using the same returned values as were used in the alphabetical-array method will require fewer changes in the other subroutines. The get-key routine will not need alteration. The return error code of E equals two will not be either required or possible, because the key file will not run out of room unless the disk itself is full, which is neither likely nor tested.

Initialization of the variables required in the binary search takes place in lines 6310 through 6330. Line 6340 should look as familiar as 6310 through 6330. This is the first statement in the search and calculates the value of the test element, which is now a whole block instead of one element in an array. Line 6350 tests to see if the block is in use. If it isn't, the roadmap byte that corresponds to it is all CHR$(255) values. Only the first one is tested. If there is no block yet assigned to that position, then the search location must be higher. The routine at line 6540 will take care of that condition. Lines 6360 and 6370 load into memory the key block. Line 6380 tests to see if the first key on the block is higher than the one being searched. If it is, then the whole block is too high and there is a branch again to the routine that handles that. The sequential search of the block is in lines 6390 (which initializes the counter) to 6430. If one is found that is equal, the routine branches to line 6580, which handles this "found" condition. If a higher one is encountered, then the routine starting at line 6610 will handle the "next available" logic.

Line 6440 is the start of the routine that handles the condition where the block had no keys on it that are equal to or greater than the keys on the one being searched. The block is too low, so the lower limit (L1) is set equal to this block number. L4 is the search counter. It is incremented in line 6450 and checked in line 6460. If the number of searches is less than the "magic number" for the maximum number of blocks (there may be as many as 10 blocks, so the magic number is four), then line 6460 branches back to the beginning of the search. If this logic falls through, then the key is not in the file and the lines below this will return E equals one and either the first key on the next higher (alphabetically higher) block or, if there are no higher blocks, a key equal to a string of CHR$(255) and KB, which is the block number, equal to 255. Either of these can be checked with the calling routine.

The next condition starts at line 6540. In this condition where the block is too high, the upper limit is set equal to the block position searched. The routine then increments and checks the number of the searches. If the key file is not initialized properly or if somehow a key lower than one with all spaces is searched, the IF statement in line 6565 falls through and the error message in line 6570 is displayed. If the program is operated properly, this will not happen, unless there is a program error. The coding at lines 6580 through 6600 takes care of the successful search, returning E equals zero and K1$ equal to the key and locator. Lines 6610 and 6620 take care of the condition where the key is not found, but its place is somewhere on the block in memory.

Now the hardest part is over. The searching is the most complicated of the routines required in this method. Running a close second, however, is the put-key routine, which begins at line 7000. The first part of the logic remains the same. The changes begin at line 7045. The new text here runs from line 7045 through line 7090, then another routine is added that runs from 7130 through 7192. The addition of the key starts with moving the buffer into another variable in line 7045. Line 7050 checks for the condition where the key is not found but will be the highest one in the file. That will be taken into consideration in the last part of the subroutine, beginning at line 7180. Lines 7060 through 7072 find the correct position on the block to insert the key and then make room for it. Lines 7074 through 7090 put the key into the string and then save the block back into the key file. Lines 7130 through 7170 take care of the instance when the block is full. In this case, the block must be split and the roadmap must be updated.

Line 7130 checks to see if key number 21 is used or blank. If it is still blank after the key is inserted, then there is no more work to do, and it returns to the calling function. Lines 7140 through 7144 find the next available block position for storing the new block. Lines 7150 through 7154 make room in the roadmap to store the position indicator. Line 7156 inserts the new value into the roadmap. Lines 7158 and 7160 set up the two key blocks created from the split. Lines 7162 through 7170 resave the blocks and the roadmap, and then return to the calling function.

The only routine left in this subroutine is the one that handles the condition of the new keys being higher than any key now in file. This condition can only happen if the highest block (alphabetically) is full. If the last block is not full, the key will be inserted onto the last block. The loop in lines 7182 through 7186 locates the next available block, then lines 7188 through 7190 insert the new key. The last line allows this routine to borrow the statements that insert the key under normal conditions.

The routine to get a given key needs no alteration, but the get-next routine does. This starts at line 8000. To find the next higher key, this routine adds a binary one to the last byte of the key (excluding the locator), then searches for it. If the newly assembled key is found, then it is the next higher key. If it isn't found, the search routine at line 6310 will return the next higher key. Line 7540 begins the part of the get key routine that gets and unpacks the record, so this routine borrows that coding when the next greater key is found. Line 8030 branches directly to it when the next higher key is the one assembled. Lines 8040 and 8050 return E equals one when the key is higher than any in file and line 8060 returns the next higher key when the key is not the one that was assembled but is in the file.

Delete is the next subroutine that requires some alteration. It is similar in logic to the alphabetical-array method's delete subroutine but works with only one block of keys. Instead of having to move a maximum of 100 keys, therefore, this routine has to move a maximum of 21 keys. The logic of this subroutine (lines 8500 through 8590) can be followed by using the logic of the same routine for the alphabetical-array method.

The last subroutine (replace a record after changes) also requires no alteration, so you can now write the initialization routine.

Initialization is the routine in lines 500 through 650. Lines 500 through 510 initialize the roadmap. Lines 512 through 516 initialize the first key block. Only one key block needs to be initialized, for the additional blocks are intialized as they are required (when the blocks are split). Lines 550 through 590 initialize the record blocks and the remaining lines set up the value in record number one that keeps track of the number of records used in the file.

Now run the program and initialize the files. As in the alphabetical-array method, the files must be initialized before a routine may be added to the beginning of the program. When the initialization is complete, end the program by hitting the BREAK key. Lines 70 and 80 may then be added. These read in the roadmap when the program is started. The program may now be saved, then tested in the same way as the alphabetical-array method.

Note that this method is very much a cross between the hashing method and the alphabetical-array method. Like the hashing method, when the file has enough records in it, there are a few keys on each of several key-file blocks. Like the alphabetical-array method, the keys are in alphabetical order. The keys will take a little longer to add and delete than they did in the hashing method, but considerably less time than they did in the alphabetical array method. The get next function is also available for the reports, as it was in the alphabetical array method.

This example is an alteration of the full tree-structured method. The full method requires far more coding but does operate a little faster and has no restriction on the file size. It also requires more blocks in the key file. The full method does not use a roadmap. Instead, it has levels of blocks that are used to locate other blocks. The highest level block contains a list of the first keys on the next lower level blocks. These blocks also contain the first keys on the next lower level blocks. The lowest level of blocks contains the same information as the key blocks in the method presented here.

The example in listing 12.1 is specifically written for a 100-record file with keys that are 10 bytes long. There are ways to make the subroutines usable in controlling files with different numbers of records and longer or shorter keys. There are also ways of using the records that are abandoned when a record is deleted. The next section will explain how this program can be altered with these possibilities.

SECTION III

INTRODUCTION

In the preceding section, we didn't pay much attention to keeping track of records available in the main file. The methods used simply took the next sequentially available record number and used it. This works fairly well until you delete a number of records from the file, leaving behind unused space. But a method called file reorganization, which rearranges the records to condense the file, makes it possible to recover this unused space. It also alters the locators on the keys so that they show the new locations of the records.

There is another method, the free-record index method, which constantly reuses records left by deletions and does not require file reorganization.

This section also brings new meaning to the word "parameter," for the parameters introduced here control the entire file operation. These parameters are used to define the key length, record length, and other values that control the files and allow the same subroutine set to become more adaptable to other files and to access more than one file in each program.

Other variations that are possible are key-only files, which contain keys but no records, and multiple-key files, which use more than one key file for one record file. The key-only file is sometimes used to sort large arrays on disk. The multiple-key file is used when the records are to be accessed by more than one possible field.

All of the above enhancements are variations of the basic programs and are useful ways to apply the key-file methods. Although all three of the methods can handle these enhancements, this section deals with the most flexible one, the tree-structured method, and the alterations will be on the subroutine set developed for it.

TRACKING
FREE
RECORDS

EDDIE GERMANO

CHAPTER 13

TRACKING FREE RECORDS

In all of the key-file routines presented in the last section, a very primitive method of keeping track of the next available record in the file was used. With this method you had no way to recover the records left by deletions except by writing another program to reorganize the file. And although several methods are available for tracking these records, many key-file systems still require file reorganization.

Of the key-file systems that do not require any file reorganization, all add another index in the files. One uses a method that is commonly used in machine language programming to keep track of things like the location to return to when a subroutine is finished. In this method, the index is a stack of numbers. When the file is initialized, the stack is filled with all of the numbers of all of the records in the file. All of them are blank, so this stack could be called a *free record list*. When a record is to be inserted into the file, one of these numbers is popped off the stack and used as the record number. When a record is deleted, its record number is freed by pushing it onto the stack.

These stacks of numbers are not moved on the disk. Instead, two numbers are used to access them. One number is the pointer, which tells where the bottom of the list is, and the other is the head, which tells where the top of the list is. To explain how stacks work, consider the following list of locations:

```
1  2  3  4  5  6  7  8
A  G  M  N  U  V  X  Z
```

The lists could contain anything. The above list uses letters only as a matter of convenience for the explanation. The elements could just as easily be record numbers.

The head, to start, will be at element number 8 and the pointer at element number 1. Popping the stack gives the letter "A" and moves the pointer up one element to 2. Popping again gives the letter "G" and moves the pointer to element 3. Pushing the letter "B" onto the stack moves the pointer back to 2 and inserts B where G was before. Using these rules for movement will allow an overflow condition to be defined as the pointer already being at position one when something is pushed onto the stack. This is an overflow error, and because of it the element will not be added to the stack. The stack can also empty out when the pointer position is one element higher than the head-of-stack position.

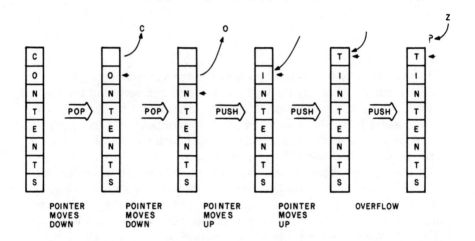

Figure 13.1: *LIFO stack overflow occurs when trying to push onto a full stack.*

The reason for two pointers is not that evident when the above logic is used. The head of the stack never moves. The above stack is called a LIFO (last in—first out) buffer. The head of the stack becomes more important in a FIFO (first in—first out) buffer. In that kind of stack, the elements are pushed in the same way, but must be popped from the other end of the stack. Popping one element from the FIFO stack takes the letter "Z" off the stack and moves the head of the stack one element down to position number seven. A letter can now be pushed onto the stack, as there is room. Since the pointer is now at position one, subtracting one from the position will run it off the end of the stack. When this happens, set the pointer equal to the actual end of the stack. The stack can now be thought of as a circle instead of a line because, when the pointer (or head) of the stack runs out of elements, it is reset to the other end of the stack. There are other checks which must be done to differentiate a completely full stack from a completely empty one.

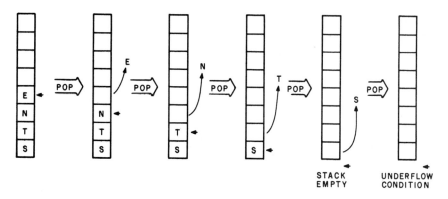

Figure 13.2: *LIFO stack underflow occurs when trying to pop an empty stack.*

The LIFO buffer is the one most easily adapted to use as a free-record index. The stack would be initialized as a series of sequential numbers from one to the number of records in the file. As records are added, the values are popped off the stack for the record numbers. If one is deleted, its record number is pushed onto the stack. In this way, if another record is added right after the deletion, the new record would be assigned the same record number as the one deleted before. A FIFO buffer could also be used for this list, but programming it would be a little more difficult. It would have the one advantage that deleted records would not be immediately wiped out by overwriting a new record and might be recovered with a little extra programming. It is one hedge against accidental deletions, but it's hardly worth the effort.

Another method of keeping track of the unused records in the file is by positioning bits corresponding to each record into a string array. Using entire bytes is also possible (and a little easier to program), but using the bits allows for a smaller index. The bit index will be one-eighth the size of one using bytes. The coding for the bits states that a bit is off when a record is free (binary zero) and on when the record is in use (binary one). For anyone using a computer that cannot handle a null byte in the middle of a string, selecting two different codes that can be used in the bytes will accomplish the same goal, but will use more space.

Using the bit method will allow the index to be stored on one block for any file with up to 2040 records (this is 255 bytes per block times 8 bits per byte). Implementing this method (or the LIFO method) requires the alteration of two subroutines from the key-file examples in the last section. Since the tree-structured method is the most flexible, all of the examples will use it. Load into memory the program saved from Chapter 12 (listing 12.1).

Decimal Values →							
255	255	247	223	192	0	0	0
1	1	1	1	1	0	0	0
1	1	1	1	1	0	0	0
1	1	1	0	0	0	0	0
1	1	1	1	0	0	0	0
1	1	0	1	0	0	0	0
1	1	1	1	0	0	0	0
1	1	1	1	0	0	0	0
1	1	1	1	0	0	0	0

Records → Indicated: 1-8 9-16 17-24 25-32 33-40 41-48 49-56 57-64

record 21 is free   record 27 is free   records 33 and 34 are in use

Table 13.1: *Bit method for tracking free records.*

Begin by writing the subroutine that gets the next available free record from the list. The examples will use the bit method explained above. The subroutine, as it exists now, occupies lines 6250 and 6305. The new method will require more line numbers than that one did, but instead of rearranging the next subroutine, use a line increment of 2 instead of 10.

For this 100-record file, there will be one-eighth of 100, or 13, bytes in the free-record index. These can be placed where the original free-record counter was placed, which was on record number one. This method can also protect itself by declaring that record number one is occupied. The text for this routine is:

```
6250  GET1,1:FB=0
6252  FB=FB+1:IFFB>13THEN6268
6254  IFMID$(B$,FB,1)=CHR$(255)THEN6252
6256  FA=ASC(MID$(B$,FB,1)):FR=FB*8-8:FD=0
6258  FD=FD+1:FC=INT(2 ↑ (8-FD)+.5):FA=FA-FC:
      IFFA>=0THEN6258
6260  FR=FR+FD:FA=ASC(MID$(B$,FB,1))+FC
6262  B1$=B$:MID$(B1$,FB,1)=CHR$(FA)
6264  LSET B$=B1$:PUT1,1
6266  RETURN
6268  FR=101:RETURN
```

To keep track of itself, that routine introduces some extra variables. FB is the counter of the number of bytes in the list. Line 6250 gets the record and initializes this counter to zero. The loop starts at line 6252, where this variable is incremented and checked. If there are no free records in any of the eight locations in that byte number, then the byte has all bits on, which is expressed as CHR$(255). In this condition, the routine goes back to increment the counter and try the next byte.

When a byte is encountered that does not equal CHR$(255), this means that there is at least one free record indicated in it by an off bit. Line 6256 extracts the ASCII equivalent of the byte, initializes the free record indicator FR (this is used the same way as before) to equal the record number immediately preceeding this byte, and then initializes the counter FD. Line 6258 searches for the zero bit. It increments the bit counter FD, then gets the decimal equivalent of this bit. The statement $FA = FA - FC$ is negative if the bit is originally off and positive if it is on. This condition is checked in the last statement on that line.

At line 6260, the bit has been located. The value, which is in the variable FD, is added to the free record indicator FR, which now holds the number of the free record. The next task is to set the bit found to the on position so that it will indicate the record is in use. The value is calculated into the variable FA, then the buffer B$ is placed in the local variable B1$ so that the bit can be set. This is also done in statement 6262. The buffer is moved back to B$ and resaved on disk in line 6264. Line 6268 handles the condition of a full file by setting the record number equal to one greater than the number of records in the file.

The above routine handles only half of the task. The first method presented, using only a counter, does not replace the record to the free status once it has been deleted. This one does, but to do this, part of the delete routine must be added. It can be added as a subroutine within that subroutine by adding a GOSUB statement to line 8540:

```
8540  KZ$ = KY$:GOSUB8600
```

This is the part of the delete routine in which the record has been located and the key is to be deleted. The record number can be extracted from the key, which can be used to calculate the position of the corresponding bit in the free-record index. This new subroutine is:

```
8600  FR = CVI(MID$(K1$,11,2))
8610  FB = INT((FR − 1)/8):FA = FR − FB * 8
8620  GET1,1:B1$ = B$:FB = FB + 1
8630  FC = ASC(MID$(B1$,FB,1))
8640  FC = FC − INT(2 ↑ (8 − FA) + .5)
8650  MID$(B1$,FB,1) = CHR$(FC)
8660  LSET B$ = B1$:PUT1,1
8670  RETURN
```

This routine uses the same basic calculations as the last one did. Line 8600 extracts from the key the record number that is to be deleted. Line 8610 calculates the byte and bit numbers of it. The free-record index is loaded into memory and placed in B1$ in line 8620, and FB is adjusted (the formula that calculated it gives a value of 0 to 12 instead of 1 to 13). Lines 8630 through 8650 turn off the bit in the appropriate byte, and then line 8660 resaves the index onto the disk.

To use the test program developed in the previous section to access these subroutines, alter the initialize-files function to initialize the first record file block to use this new method. This alteration is in line 620. Instead of that statement, set the first 13 bytes of B1$ to 0, then set the first one equal to CHR$(128), which has the bit pattern 1000 0000, showing the first record in the file to be occupied.

You can't use the bit method on computers that can't handle the null bytes. The byte method is similar, but requires more space. For a 100-record file with 85-byte records, you use two records. The bytes can be set to the alphanumeric 1 and 0 (CHR$(49) and CHR$(48), in that order). The subroutines to handle that are in the same locations as the ones shown above and are much simpler to program. Simply search through the bytes until you have the value of CHR$(48), which is the indication of a free record. To reset a deleted record, set it to CHR$(48).

If you use the FIFO method (or LIFO method), store on this first block the required stack plus the pointers. Using the MDI$(and CVI(functions to access the stack will require two bytes for each of the records on the list, and the list must contain 100 record numbers. Adding the pointer to it requires 202 bytes. The head of stack does not need to be stored for the LIFO method, as it never moves, and it can be written into the text as a constant. The head of stack must be stored for the FIFO method, and another indicator should also be kept for sensing overflow and empty-list conditions. This could be one number that is a count of the number of items on the stack. This brings the total bytes required to 206, which will require three records of room, the entire first block.

The chapter that follows will use the bit method for the subroutine set. Any of the above methods or the method that was presented in the last section may be used, but all of the examples will use the one programmed in this chapter. This is not to sell it as the best method (one of the stack methods could prove to be faster on a particular system, although this is unlikely as the file fills) but because it is the most abbreviated method and takes up very little room.

EDDIE GERMANO

CHAPTER 14

PARAMETERS

Perhaps when I explained parameters earlier and gave examples of simple parameter use, these concepts did not seem very earth-shattering to you. But this is because you're accustomed to the structure of BASIC—to the easy access to subroutines that BASIC and parameters provide. Before BASIC came into such widespread use, compiler-based languages were the dominant languages, as they still are on the larger systems. In these languages, GOSUB is not available, much less parameters. In FORTRAN, the statement to call a subroutine is CALL. All of the subroutines have to be named and every variable that is to be passed to the subroutine has to be declared in the CALL statement.

In the FORTRAN compiler, the subroutine is actually more of an independent routine in that all of the variables in the subroutine are separate, and variables with the same name in the subroutine, in the main program, or in other subroutines do not interfere with each other. The line numbers are also kept separately.

As you can see from the structure of the earlier versions of the compiler-based languages, parameters were no simple invention. In some of the earlier versions, it was possible to transfer parameters from the main program to the subroutine but not from the subroutine back to the main program. Today, however, the way that BASIC handles parameters is much simpler.

The compiler-based languages also had one more complication. Since the variables of the subroutines could have the same or different names from the ones in the other routines and in the main program, the COMMON statement was invented to establish more effective communication (note that some BASIC languages have an equivalent command called COM). This set aside an area that contained the variables on this COMMON list. These variables had to be declared in every program and subroutine in the system. They could have had the same or different names, but the COMMON area had to be the same or else some variables could be lost. Variables that were not in this COMMON area were called local variables, as they had meaning only in the routines where they appeared.

Some BASIC languages took more of the logic from these compiler-based languages than others did. Although most of the microcomputer BASIC languages do not, there are some that have COM statements (equivalent to COMMON) and have subroutines that can accept lists of parameters. Wang Laboratories, Inc. has developed a BASIC that makes very good use of these two capabilities. On their systems, programs can be written so that, if the COM area is assigned properly, partial programs can be read into memory to overlay a section of the original program. The COM area can be used to pass values from one program to the next. Also on their system, the marked subroutines, which it has in addition to the GOSUB available on most microcomputers, can pass a list of parameters. This is done with a GOSUB' for the calling statement and a DEFFN' for the *label* statement (the first statement in the subroutine). An example of this is:

```
100  GOSUB'128(A,A1$,W,5,"STOP")
        .
        .
        .
6520  DEFFN'128(M,M$,M1,M2,M1$)
```

Statement 100 calls the subroutine marked 128 (the marks can be any number from 0 to 255) and passes the variables in the list. When the computer encounters the GOSUB' statement, it looks up a matching DEFFN' statement. Then, the variables in the list in the DEFFN' statement are set equal, in the same order, to the list in the GOSUB' statement. The subroutine following line 6520, where the DEFFN' was found, is then executed.

Even on the Wang system, there is only one set of variables in use, so all are local according to the way that word was used in the compiler-based languages—except when you get to the time-sharing systems. Wang, to continue the example, has a system that will handle multiple users with a global partition that is accessible to all users in addition to their local partition. A master subroutine set can be stored in this global partition so that all users who select that global partition may access the same subroutines independently of the other partitions on the system. That system incorporates a local and a global set of variables in the programs. The global system is also a little more sophisticated than the microcomputer's, but that is the direction that microcomputers are headed.

The parameters passed in BASIC will all be local variables. When a subroutine changes the value stored by a variable, it is also changes it for that variable in the main program and vice versa. In some ways that makes it easier to program, but in other ways it makes it more difficult. Usually, the main program requires more variables, which are reused in the subroutines because the subroutines don't have their own, independent list of variables.

Another function of parameters is helping to make the key file more flexible. The way it is now written, if the file were changed to allow for a longer key, longer record, more records, or a different record format, the entire key-file subroutine set would have to be rewritten. There is another way to do this.

There are only a few differences between the key-file subroutines now written and ones that would control a file with different keys and records. These numbers include the key length, the record length, the number of records, the keys per block, and the number of records in the file. If these numbers were to be set up in an array and the elements in the array used in the subroutine instead of constants, then the initialization of the array would change the file that the subroutine set would control. Listing 14.1 shows how the subroutine set could be altered to use the array CA(to contain this list of variables. The pack and unpack routines are not included on this listing. Such routines could also be parameter-driven, but this is another subject.

Listing 14.1 does not include all of the elements dimensioned for the array CA(. This listing comes from a key-file-based system that is a part of a program in use. The other elements are used to drive other subroutines that do not appear on the listing. Some of them will be described later, as they work with packing and unpacking records in parameter-driven routines.

```
6149 REM -- 6150-6180 GET RECORD BY NUMBER --
6150 B=INT((N-1)/CA(3)):R=N-B*CA(3)
6155 B=B+CA(4)
6160 GET 1,B
6170 R$=MID$(B$,CA(1)*(R-1)+1,CA(1))
6180 RETURN
6189 REM -- 6190-6240 PUT RECORD BY NUMBER --
6190 R1$=R$
6200 GOSUB 6150
6210 B1$=B$
6220 MID$(B1$,CA(1)*(R-1)+1,CA(1))=R1$
6230 LSET B$=B1$
6235 PUT1,B
6240 RETURN
6249 REM -- 6250-6305 GET NEXT AVAILABLE RECORD NUMBER --
6250 GET1,1:FB=0
6252 FB=FB+1:IFFB>CA(5)THEN6268
6254 IFMID$(B$,FB,1)=CHR$(255)THEN6252
6256 FA=ASC(MID$(B$,FB,1)):FR=FB*8-8:FD=0
6258 FD=FD+1:FC=INT(2[(8-FD)+.5):FA=FA-FC:IFFA>=0THEN6258
6260 FR=FR+FD:FA=ASC(MID$(B$,FB,1))+FC
6262 B1$=B$:MID$(B1$,FB,1)=CHR$(FA)
6264 LSET B$=B1$:PUT1,1
6266 RETURN
6268 FR=CA(6):E=0:RETURN
6309 REM -- 6310-6510 SEARCH FOR KEY --
```

```
6310 K1$=STRING$(CA(7),32)
6320 K$=K$+K1$:KN=0
6330 L1=0:L2=CA(15):L4=0
6340 L3=INT((L1+L2)/2+.5)
6350 IF MID$(RM$,L3,1)=CHR$(255)THEN6540
6360 KB=ASC(MID$(RM$,L3,1))
6370 GET2,KB+1
6380 IFMID$(KY$,1,CA(9))>MID$(K$,1,CA(9))THEN6540
6390 KN=0
6400 KN=KN+1:IFKN=CA(10)THEN6440
6410 IFMID$(K$,1,CA(9))=MID$(KY$,CA(7)*(KN-1)+1,CA(9))THEN6580
6415 IFMID$(KY$,CA(7)*(KN-1)+1,CA(9))=STRING$(CA(9),255)THEN6440
6420 IFMID$(K$,1,CA(9))<MID$(KY$,CA(7)*(KN-1)+1,CA(9))THEN6610
6430 GOTO 6400
6440 L1=L3
6450 L4=L4+1
6460 IFL4<CA(11)THEN6340
6470 E=1
6480 L3=L3+1
6490 KB=ASC(MID$(RM$,L3,1))
6500 K1$=STRING$(CA(7),255):IFKB=255THENRETURN
6510 GET 2,KB+1
6520 K1$=LEFT$(KY$,CA(7))
6530 RETURN
6540 L2=L3
6550 L4=L4+1
6560 IFL4<CA(11)THEN6340
6565 E=1:GOTO6490
6580 E=0
6590 K1$=MID$(KY$,CA(7)*(KN-1)+1,CA(7))
6600 RETURN
6610 E=1
6620 GOTO6590
6999 REM -- 7000-7499 PUT NEW RECORD AND KEY --
7000 GOSUB6310
7010 IFE=2THENRETURN
7020 IFE=1THEN7040
7030 E=1:RETURN
7040 GOSUB6250
7045 KZ$=KY$
7050 IFKB=255THEN7180
7060 IFLEFT$(K$,CA(7))<LEFT$(KY$,CA(7))THENKN=1
7070 FORI=CA(10)TOKN+1STEP-1:MID$(KZ$,CA(7)*(I-1)+1,CA(7))=MID$(KZ$,CA(7)
*(I-2)+1,CA(7))
7072 NEXTI
7074 MID$(KZ$,CA(7)*(KN-1)+1,CA(7))=MID$(K$,1,CA(9))+MKI$(FR)
7080 LSET KY$=KZ$
7090 PUT2,KB+1
7100 GOSUB6010
7110 N=FR:GOSUB6190
7120 E=0
7130 IFMID$(KY$,(CA(10)-1)*CA(7)+1,CA(7))=STRING$(CA(7),255)THENRETURN
7140 L4=0:FORI=1TO254:IFASC(MID$(RM$,I,1))=255THEN7144
7142 IFASC(MID$(RM$,I,1))>L4THEN L4=ASC(MID$(RM$,I,1))
7144 NEXTI
7146 I=0
7148 I=I+1:IFASC(MID$(RM$,I,1))<>KBTHEN7148
7150 J=CA(15)
7152 J=J-1:MID$(RM$,J+1,1)=MID$(RM$,J,1):IFJ>ITHEN7152
7156 MID$(RM$,I+1,1)=MKI$(L4+1)
7158 KZ$=KY$:KX$=MID$(KY$,CA(13),CA(12))+STRING$(CA(14),255)
7160 MID$(KZ$,CA(13),CA(12))=STRING$(CA(12),255)
7162 LSET KY$=KZ$:PUT2,KB+1
7164 LSET KY$=KX$:PUT2,L4+2
7166 LSET KY$=RM$:PUT2,1
7170 E=0:RETURN
7180 L4=0
7182 L4=L4+1:IFL4<=250THEN7184:ELSE STOP
7184 IFASC(MID$(RM$,L4+1,1))<255THEN7182
7186 KB=ASC(MID$(RM$,L4,1)):GET2,KB+1
7188 KN=0
7190 KN=KN+1:IFMID$(KY$,CA(7)*(KN-1)+1,CA(7))<STRING$(CA(7),255)THEN7190
```

```
7192  GOTO7050
7499  REM -- 7500-7999 GET RECORD --
7500 .GOSUB6310
7510  IFE=0THEN7540
7520  E=1
7530  RETURN
7540  N=CVI(MID$(K1$,CA(7)-1,2))
7550  GOSUB6150
7560  GOSUB6090
7570  E=0
7580  RETURN
7999  REM -- 8000-8499 GET NEXT --
8000  K$=K$+STRING$(CA(9),32):E=ASC(MID$(K$,CA(9),1))+1
8010  MID$(K$,CA(9),1)=MKI$(E)
8020  GOSUB6310
8030  IF E=0THEN7540
8040  IF MID$(K1$,1,CA(9))<>STRING$(CA(9),255)THEN8060
8050  E=1:RETURN
8060  K$=K1$:E=0:GOTO7540
8499  REM -- 8500-8999 DELETE KEY AND RECORD --
8500  GOSUB6310
8510  IFE=0THEN8540
8520  E=1
8530  RETURN
8540  KZ$=KY$:GOSUB8600
8550  FORI=KN TO CA(10)-1
8555  MID$(KZ$,CA(7)*(I-1)+1,CA(7))=MID$(KZ$,CA(7)*I+1,CA(7))
8557  NEXTI
8560  LSET KY$=KZ$
8570  PUT2,KB+1
8580  E=0
8590  RETURN
8600  FR=CVI(MID$(K1$,CA(9)+1,2))
8610  FB=INT((FR-1)/8):FA=FR-FB*8
8620  GET1,1:B1$=B$:FB=FB+1
8630  FA=ASC(MID$(B1$,FB,1))
8640  FA=FA-INT(2[(8-FA)+.5)
8650  MID$(B1$,FB,1)=CHR$(FA)
8660  LSET B$=B1$:PUT1,1
8670  RETURN
8999  REM -- 9000-9499 RESAVE RECORD --
9000  GOSUB6310
9010  IFE=0THEN9040
9020  E=1
9030  RETURN
9040  N=CVI(MID$(K1$,CA(9)+1,2))
9050  GOSUB6010
9060  GOSUB6190
9070  E=0
9080  RETURN
```

Listing 14.1

When you compare listing 14.1 with listing 12.1, taking into account the changes introduced in Chapter 13, the values for the array are:

Subscript	Value	Description
1	85	Record length
2	—	(not used)
3	3	Number of records per block
4	1	First block in record file

5	13	Number of bytes in free record list
6	101	Maximum number of records of file + 1
7	12	Key length plus locator length
8	—	(not used)
9	10	Key length (not including locator)
10	21	Maximum number of keys on one block
11	4	Number of searches on the key file
12	134	Block-splitting constant
13	121	Block-splitting constant
14	120	Block-splitting constant
15	10	Maximum number of key-file blocks

Array elements numbered 12 through 14 are the values of the byte numbers of the keys at the place in the key block where the splitting will occur. Since there are 20 keys on a block (21 triggers the splitting), 10 will remain and 11 will create the new block. CA(13) contains the byte number of the first byte in the key that is to become the first key on the new block, which is the eleventh key on this block. CA(14) is the last byte of the last key that will remain. This is always CA(13)-1. CA(12) is the number of bytes that are to be written to the new block. This is always 255-CA(13).

In the initialization part of the main program, a DIM statement is required to establish the array CA(with 15 elements. After the files are opened and fielded, the values for this array may be defined. This can be done by using READ and DATA, a series of LET statements, or reading them from a special file on disk. The easiest method to maintain uses READ and DATA to establish the array. With this method, all of the elements are lined up in one DATA statement where they may be easily read and altered.

Now that the parameters are defined and set into the subroutine, the subroutine may be stored on disk. When a program is to be developed that requires a key file, this subroutine set may be read into memory and the program may be built below it. As Section IV will show, the best way to design a good program requiring disk files is to design the files first, so all of the data required to define the elements of the array CA(is defined. Simply name the files after this and you've written the first section of the program.

The parameter-driven subroutine set developed in this chapter will work well with any one-key-per-record file system, as long as the keys are reasonably short (at least eight keys per block) and the record length will fit on one block. It does have the limits of the maximum of 254 key blocks and the limit of 2040 records, because of the free record index. You may increase the maximum number of records by altering the two routines developed in the preceding chapter, perhaps by being able to use more than one block for the index because of some additional logic. But increasing the number of keys is a little more difficult. The limit on the keys is the roadmap.

Although the limits imposed on the system by this key-file subroutine set as it now stands would be too tight for larger computer systems, they are adequate for most microcomputer applications. Since this book is for applications on microcomputers, it doesn't explore more sophisticated systems for handling larger files. If there is a need for larger files, the method will become slower as the file size increases. This slowing down is due, in part, to the sequential search of the key blocks. The speed does not become important in the file sizes that are specified as the maximums for this set, but would be very important if the file size were increased substantially. Overcoming this problem would require a slightly different approach to the key-handling routines. The full tree-structured method described in Chapter 12 is a system that is faster in a larger file. The method presented here could be made to run faster by implementing a more efficient technique for searching for a key on a block. You would need more coding to do this, but you could gain much speed. One more area to investigate would be how to limit the number of blocks that must be loaded into memory in search of a key. For the file sizes indicated for this file, the number of blocks for the maximum key file is only eight, which is not incredibly fast, but still requires only about three or four seconds at most.

The subroutine set developed here can undergo more alterations that make it more flexible and more powerful. The areas to be investigated in the remainder of this section include key-only files, multiple-key files and the use of more than one key file in one program. The logic developed so far can be very simply extended to perform all three of these functions. More parameter drivers will be added so that one subroutine set can be developed to handle all of these functions with no program alteration (no program alteration, that is, once the full subroutine set is developed).

CHAPTER 15

KEY-ONLY FILES

The key-file subroutine set developed so far can handle any file with one key for each record, within the limits of 2040 records and 254 key-file blocks. It will not handle other uses for key files. In this chapter, the subroutine set will be modified to handle a *key-only file*, which is a file consisting of the index (i.e., the keys), but no records. This type of file is used in various applications, including disk sorts for arrays that are too large to hold in memory. These sorts can also be set up, on systems that can handle more than one key file at a time, to sort the file on a field other than the key field. Such a key-file system is developed in a later chapter.

This key-only file subroutine set can be formed very simply from the subroutine set that has been developed up to this point. Listing 15.1 shows a quick method of converting the subroutines and also gives a short test program so that the conversion can be checked.

The first part of the conversion concerns the record file, which is no longer needed. All of the subroutines have been deleted and a RETURN statement has been placed in each of the calling line numbers. This is done so that the other subroutines can still call the subroutines that handled the records to avoid their needing alteration, but the record subroutines will do nothing. To convert to a dedicated key-only subroutine set would involve deleting all of the GOSUB statements in the subroutines. I don't do that here, because later chapters will introduce other parameters to convert the subroutine set into one that will have the option of handling records or not.

All of the subroutines that handle the record file are in lines 6000 through 6305. A user can delete all of these if he or she replaces the calling lines will RETURN statements. In the listing (15.1), the REM statements were also left to indicate what subroutines were there.

```
10 CLEAR4000
20 DIMCA(15)
30 OPEN"R",2,"KEYFIL:0"
40 FIELD 2, 255 AS KY$
50 RESTORE
60 FORI=1TO15:READCA(I):NEXTI
70 DATA 0,0,0,0,13,0,12,0,10,21,4,134,121,120,10
100 CLS:PRINT"INITIALIZING THE KEY ONLY FILE"
110 B1$=CHR$(1)+STRING$(254,255)
115 RM$=B1$
120 LSETKY$=B1$
130 PUT2,1
140 MID$(B1$,1,12)=STRING$(12,32)
150 LSETKY$=B1$
160 PUT2,2
200 CLS
210 PRINT"KEY ONLY FILE INPUT AND DISPLAY PROGRAM":PRINT
220 INPUT"ENTER 0 TO END, 1 FOR ENTRY OF KEYS OR 2 TO LIST";N
230 IFN=1THEN300
240 IFN=2THEN500
250 IFN=0THENSTOP
260 PRINT"ERROR - PLEASE ENTER 0, 1 OR 2"
270 GOTO220
300 CLS
310 PRINT"KEY ENTRY"
320 K$=""
330 INPUT"ENTER KEY OR END";K$
340 IFK$="END"THEN200
350 IFLEN(K$)<=10THEN380
360 PRINT"KEY IS TOO LONG - MUST BE NOT MORE THAN 10 CHARACTERS"
370 GOTO330
380 GOSUB7000
390 IFE=0THEN330
400 PRINT"KEY NOT ENTERED - DUPLICATE"
410 GOTO330
500 CLS
510 PRINT"DISPLAY OF KEYS IN FILE":PRINT
520 K$=" "
530 GOSUB8000
535 IFE=1THEN560
540 PRINTK$,
550 GOTO530
560 PRINT
570 INPUT"PRESS ENTER WHEN FINISHED VIEWING";N
580 GOTO200
5999 REM -- 6000-6990 RECORD FILE SUBROUTINES --
6000 STOP
6009 REM -- 6010-6080 PACK RECORD --
6010 RETURN
6089 REM -- 6090-6140 UNPACK RECORD --
6090 RETURN
6149 REM -- 6150-6180 GET RECORD BY NUMBER --
6150 RETURN
6189 REM -- 6190-6240 PUT RECORD BY NUMBER --
6190 RETURN
6249 REM -- 6250-6305 GET NEXT AVAILABLE RECORD NUMBER --
6250 RETURN
6309 REM -- 6310-6510 SEARCH FOR KEY --
6310 K1$=STRING$(CA(7),32)
6320 K$=K$+K1$:KN=0
6330 L1=0:L2=CA(15):L4=0
6340 L3=INT((L1+L2)/2+.5)
6350 IF MID$(RM$,L3,1)=CHR$(255)THEN6540
6360 KB=ASC(MID$(RM$,L3,1))
6370 GET2,KB+1
6380 IFMID$(KY$,1,CA(9))>MID$(K$,1,CA(9))THEN6540
6390 KN=0
6400 KN=KN+1:IFKN=CA(10)THEN6440
6410 IFMID$(K$,1,CA(9))=MID$(KY$,CA(7)*(KN-1)+1,CA(9))THEN6580
6415 IFMID$(KY$,CA(7)*(KN-1)+1,CA(9))=STRING$(CA(9),255)THEN6440
6420 IFMID$(K$,1,CA(9))<MID$(KY$,CA(7)*(KN-1)+1,CA(9))THEN6610
6430 GOTO 6400
```

```
6440 L1=L3
6450 L4=L4+1
6460 IFL4<CA(11)THEN6340
6470 E=1
6480 L3=L3+1
6490 KB=ASC(MID$(RM$,L3,1))
6500 K1$=STRING$(CA(7),255):IFKB=255THENRETURN
6510 GET 2,KB+1
6520 K1$=LEFT$(KY$,CA(7))
6530 RETURN
6540 L2=L3
6550 L4=L4+1
6560 IFL4<CA(11)THEN6340
6565 E=1:GOTO6490
6580 E=0
6590 K1$=MID$(KY$,CA(7)*(KN-1)+1,CA(7))
6600 RETURN
6610 E=1
6620 GOTO6590
6999 REM -- 7000-7499 PUT NEW RECORD AND KEY --
7000 GOSUB6310
7010 IFE=2THENRETURN
7020 IFE=1THEN7040
7030 E=1:RETURN
7040 GOSUB6250
7045 KZ$=KY$
7050 IFKB=255THEN7180
7060 IFLEFT$(K$,CA(7))<LEFT$(KY$,CA(7))THENKN=1
7070 FORI=CA(10)TOKN+1STEP-1:MID$(KZ$,CA(7)*(I-1)+1,CA(7))=MID$(KZ$,CA(7)
*(I-2)+1,CA(7))
7072 NEXTI
7074 MID$(KZ$,CA(7)*(KN-1)+1,CA(7))=MID$(K$,1,CA(9))+MKI$(FR)
7080 LSET KY$=KZ$
7090 PUT2,KB+1
7100 GOSUB6010
7110 N=FR:GOSUB6190
7120 E=0
7130 IFMID$(KY$,(CA(10)-1)*CA(7)+1,CA(7))=STRING$(CA(7),255)THENRETURN
7140 L4=0:FORI=1TO254:IFASC(MID$(RM$,I,1))=255THEN7144
7142 IFASC(MID$(RM$,I,1))>L4THEN L4=ASC(MID$(RM$,I,1))
7144 NEXTI
7146 I=0
7148 I=I+1:IFASC(MID$(RM$,I,1))<>KBTHEN7148
7150 J=CA(15)
7152 J=J-1:MID$(RM$,J+1,1)=MID$(RM$,J,1):IFJ>ITHEN7152
7156 MID$(RM$,I+1,1)=MKI$(L4+1)
7158 KZ$=KY$:KX$=MID$(KY$,CA(13),CA(12))+STRING$(CA(14),255)
7160 MID$(KZ$,CA(13),CA(12))=STRING$(CA(12),255)
7162 LSET KY$=KZ$:PUT2,KB+1
7164 LSET KY$=KX$:PUT2,L4+2
7166 LSET KY$=RM$:PUT2,1
7170 E=0:RETURN
7180 L4=0
7182 L4=L4+1:IFL4<=254THEN7184:ELSE STOP
7184 IFASC(MID$(RM$,L4+1,1))<255THEN7182
7186 KB=ASC(MID$(RM$,L4,1)):GET2,KB+1
7188 KN=0
7190 KN=KN+1:IFMID$(KY$,CA(7)*(KN-1)+1,CA(7))<STRING$(CA(7),255)THEN7190
7192 GOTO7050
7499 REM -- 7500-7999 GET RECORD --
7500 GOSUB6310
7510 IFE=0THEN7540
7520 E=1
7530 RETURN
7540 N=CVI(MID$(K1$,CA(7)-1,2))
7550 GOSUB6150
7560 GOSUB6090
7570 E=0
7580 RETURN
7999 REM -- 8000-8499 GET NEXT --
8000 K$=K$+STRING$(CA(9),32):E=ASC(MID$(K$,CA(9),1))+1
8010 MID$(K$,CA(9),1)=MKI$(E)
```

```
8020 GOSUB6310
8030 IF E=0THEN7540
8040 IF MID$(K1$,1,CA(9))<>STRING$(CA(9),255)THEN8060
8050 E=1:RETURN
8060 K$=K1$:E=0:GOTO7540
8499 REM -- 8500-8999 DELETE KEY AND RECORD --
8500 GOSUB6310
8510 IFE=0THEN8540
8520 E=1
8530 RETURN
8540 KZ$=KY$
8550 FORI=KN TO CA(10)-1
8555 MID$(KZ$,CA(7)*(I-1)+1,CA(7))=MID$(KZ$,CA(7)*I+1,CA(7))
8557 NEXTI
8560 LSET KY$=KZ$
8570 PUT2,KB+1
8580 E=0
8590 RETURN
8999 REM -- 9000-9499 RESAVE RECORD --
9000 GOSUB6310
9010 IFE=0THEN9040
9020 E=1
9030 RETURN
9040 N=CVI(MID$(K1$,CA(9)+1,2))
9050 GOSUB6010
9060 GOSUB6190
9070 E=0
9080 RETURN
```

Listing 15.1

There are no changes above line 6305. These subroutines all deal with the key file only. The only dealings with the record file are GOSUBs that called the newly deleted subroutines.

The main program has five sections, which are program initialization, file initialization, control, insert key, and display keys. The program initialization declares the string space (line 10), dimensions the parameter array (line 20), opens and fields the key file (lines 30 and 40), then reads the parameters from the DATA list (lines 50 through 70). The file initialization sets up the roadmap block and the first key block, then initializes the road-map variable RM$. This is in lines 100-160.

Line 200 is the control section, which allows the options of adding or listing the keys or of ending the program. Other functions like delete and print could be added too. That subroutine replacing a record after the contents are edited is useless. The reason is that when the subroutines call to save the record, they get the already eliminated subroutines, so this can only verify that the key is in file.

Keys are added in the routine in lines 300 through 410 as a list of entries. Because of the way the key file works, they are being sorted as they are entered. The file is set up so that up to 100 keys may be entered. It could probably handle about 150, but there could be a problem if the number of key blocks exceeds 10. This is not checked in the program at all.

The display routine is very simple. All it does is start with a blank key (one with all spaces), then keeps getting the next higher key until the end of file is encountered. The keys are listed in alphabetical order.

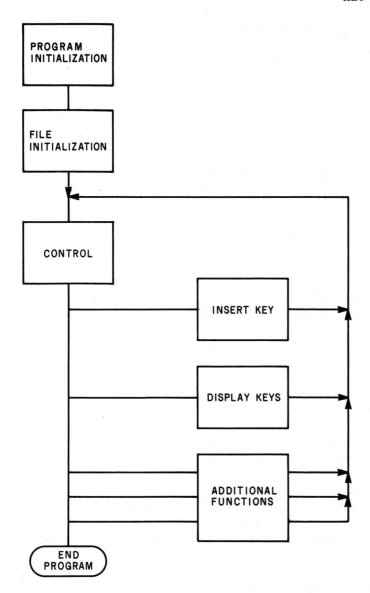

Figure 15.1: *Key-only file test program block flow diagram (listing 15.1).*

A print function could be added as a separate routine or it could replace the display function. The logic is exactly the same, except the PRINTK$, statement should be replaced with LPRINTK$ with or without the comma. Line counting could also be added so that the keys would be paged, if there are more than one page's worth of keys to list.

There is one more use for key-only files that this program could be employed to perform. In files that have very short records, the entire record could be packed in the key. One good example of this is a look-up table, or cross-reference list. This could be a good addition to an inventory program.

Every manufacturer seems to have its own number for a product. To stock every manufacturer's part would require one form of extensive duplication because some other manufacturer would be making an equivalent one. Thus the need for cross referencing came into being.

To restructure the program in listing 15.1 into a cross-reference table requires a little rearranging of the main program (i.e., the program below line 6000). The initialization section will remain about the same. The name of the key file may be different and the DATA statement will later be changed to reflect a different size key. The rest of the program will need so much rearranging and alteration that it is best deleted. Delete lines 100 through 580.

For the example, form a cross-reference table of an imaginary product. Widgets are about the most common imaginary product, so the table will cross reference widgets. Your inventory stocks widgets made by Manufacturer Number One, so your stock numbers agree with that manufacturer's part numbers. The main competition comes from Manufacturer Number Two, who uses an entirely different numbering system for the same parts. What you need is some way to enter the table with the part number from Manufacturer Number Two and come up with the part number from Manufacturer Number One. You can do it with a key-only file.

In this file, the key is the only thing saved on disk. If the file saved records, it would be possible to store the part number from Manufacturer Number One as the record and have the part number from Manufacturer Number Two as the key. There is a simpler way to do this. The key could be the two part numbers packed in a string so that the part number from Manufacturer Number One follows the part number from Manufacturer Number Two.

To put numbers on this, say the part numbers from the competition (Manufacturer Number Two) are seven characters long and the part numbers you use are eight characters long. The key can be composed of the seven character part number followed by the eight character part number. This gives a key that is 15 characters long.

Next, you can define the parameter array. If there are 100 parts in the inventory (there more probably would be more, but this is only an example), and each key is 15 characters plus a two-digit locator (the locator is not actually used, but is still in the program logic and will still take up space), then the number of keys on one key block can be 255 divided by 17, which is 15. There can be as few as the number of keys (100) divided by this number (15), or seven key blocks. Double this for the parameter array. Fourteen blocks will require four searches. The blocks should be split between keys seven and eight, so the block-splitting constants will be 133, 120, and 119.

The control section should give the options of adding a key to the file, deleting a key from the file, looking up one of the part numbers, and printing the list. Also in the program should be a way of initializing the file.

This is required only once, so an unused area of the program can be used to contain a subroutine that can be called from line 80. After the first run, the subroutine can be deleted and the GOSUB in line 80 can be changed to read the roadmap into memory.

You can write the program using the guidelines presented in the previous chapters (particularly Chapter 9). To look up a part number, request the competitor's part number, put this in K$, then use the get next subroutine. Check first to make sure that the end of file has not been encountered, then check to see if the first seven bytes of the key found are the same as the seven bytes of the key entered. If both these tests are successful, the key returned has your part number in bytes 8 through 15.

Listing 15.2 presents the program just described. A few changes in the parameters, the PRINT and INPUT statements, and the parts that pack and unpack the keys will transform this program into almost any look-up or cross-reference table.

```
10 CLEAR4000
20 DIMCA(15)
30 OPEN"R",2,"WIDGETS:0"
40 FIELD 2, 255 AS KY$
50 RESTORE
60 FORI=1TO15:READCA(I):NEXTI
70 DATA 0,0,0,0,0,0,17,0,15,15,4,133,120,119,14
80 GOSUB1100
100 CLS
110 PRINT"          WIDGET CROSS-REFERENCE"
120 PRINT
130 PRINT"    1. ADD ENTRY TO LIST"
140 PRINT"    2. DELETE ENTRY"
150 PRINT"    3. LOOK-UP"
170 PRINT
180 INPUT"  ENTER SELECTION FROM LIST (0 TO END)";N
190 IFN=0THENSTOP
200 IFN>0ANDN<4THEN230
210 PRINT"ERROR - PLEASE ENTER A NUMBER FROM 0 TO 3"
220 GOTO180
230 ONNGOTO300,500,700,900
300 INPUT"YOUR PART NUMBER";YN$
310 INPUT"IS EQUIVALENT TO PART NUMBER";EN$
320 K$=EN$+STRING$(15,32)
330 MID$(K$,8,8)=YN$+STRING$(8,32)
340 GOSUB7000
350 IFE=0THEN100
360 PRINT"ERROR - ENTRY ALREADY IN FILE"
370 INPUT"PRESS ENTER AFTER READING MESSAGE";N
380 GOTO100
500 INPUT"ENTER EQUIVALENT PART NUMBER TO DELETE";K$
510 GOSUB8000
520 IFE=0THEN550
530 PRINT"ERROR - NOT IN FILE"
540 GOTO370
550 PRINT"EQUIVALENT NUMBER = ";MID$(K$,1,7)
560 PRINT"YOUR NUMBER = ";MID$(K$,8,8)
570 INPUT"IS THIS THE ONE TO DELETE (Y OR N)";Q$
580 IFQ$="N"THEN100
590 IFQ$="Y"THEN620
600 PRINT"ERROR - PLEASE ANSWER Y OR N"
610 GOTO570
620 GOSUB8500
630 GOTO100
700 INPUT"ENTER NUMBER TO LOOK UP";EN$
710 K$=EN$
```

Listing 15.2

Listing 15.2 continued

```
720 GOSUB8000
730 IFE=0THEN760
740 PRINT"ENTRY IS NOT IN FILE"
750 GOTO370
760 EN$=EN$+STRING$(7,32)
770 IFMID$(EN$,1,7)<>MID$(K$,1,7)THEN740
780 PRINT"PART NUMBER ";MID$(K$,1,7);" IS EQUIVALENT TO ";MID$(K$,8,8)
790 GOTO370
1100 B$=STRING$(255,255)
1110 MID$(B$,1,1)=CHR$(1)
1120 LSET KY$=B$
1130 PUT2,1
1135 RM$=B$
1140 MID$(B$,1,17)=STRING$(17,32)
1150 LSET KY$=B$
1160 PUT2,2
1170 RETURN
5999 REM -- 6000-6990 RECORD FILE SUBROUTINES --
6000 STOP
6009 REM -- 6010-6080 PACK RECORD --
6010 RETURN
6089 REM -- 6090-6140 UNPACK RECORD --
6090 RETURN
6149 REM -- 6150-6180 GET RECORD BY NUMBER --
6150 RETURN
6189 REM -- 6190-6240 PUT RECORD BY NUMBER --
6190 RETURN
6249 REM -- 6250-6305 GET NEXT AVAILABLE RECORD NUMBER --
6250 RETURN
6309 REM -- 6310-6510 SEARCH FOR KEY --
6310 K1$=STRING$(CA(7),32)
6320 K$=K$+K1$:KN=0
6330 L1=0:L2=CA(15):L4=0
6340 L3=INT((L1+L2)/2+.5)
6350 IF MID$(RM$,L3,1)=CHR$(255)THEN6540
6360 KB=ASC(MID$(RM$,L3,1))
6370 GET2,KB+1
6380 IFMID$(KY$,1,CA(9))>MID$(K$,1,CA(9))THEN6540
6390 KN=0
6400 KN=KN+1:IFKN=CA(10)THEN6440
6410 IFMID$(K$,1,CA(9))=MID$(KY$,CA(7)*(KN-1)+1,CA(9))THEN6580
6415 IFMID$(KY$,CA(7)*(KN-1)+1,CA(9))=STRING$(CA(9),255)THEN6440
6420 IFMID$(K$,1,CA(9))<MID$(KY$,CA(7)*(KN-1)+1,CA(9))THEN6610
6430 GOTO 6400
6440 L1=L3
6450 L4=L4+1
6460 IFL4<CA(11)THEN6340
6470 E=1
6480 L3=L3+1
6490 KB=ASC(MID$(RM$,L3,1))
6500 K1$=STRING$(CA(7),255):IFKB=255THENRETURN
6510 GET 2,KB+1
6520 K1$=LEFT$(KY$,CA(7))
6530 RETURN
6540 L2=L3
6550 L4=L4+1
6560 IFL4<CA(11)THEN6340
6565 E=1:GOTO6490
6580 E=0
6590 K1$=MID$(KY$,CA(7)*(KN-1)+1,CA(7))
6600 RETURN
6610 E=1
6620 GOTO6590
6999 REM -- 7000-7499 PUT NEW RECORD AND KEY --
7000 GOSUB6310
7010 IFE=2THENRETURN
7020 IFE=1THEN7040
7030 E=1:RETURN
7040 GOSUB6250
7045 KZ$=KY$
7050 IFKB=255THEN7180
7060 IFLEFT$(K$,CA(7))<LEFT$(KY$,CA(7))THENKN=1
```

```
7070 FORI=CA(10)TOKN+1STEP-1:MID$(KZ$,CA(7)*(I-1)+1,CA(7))=MID$(KZ$,CA(7)
*(I-2)+1,CA(7))
7072 NEXTI
7074 MID$(KZ$,CA(7)*(KN-1)+1,CA(7))=MID$(K$,1,CA(9))+MKI$(FR)
7080 LSET KY$=KZ$
7090 PUT2,KB+1
7100 GOSUB6010
7110 N=FR:GOSUB6190
7120 E=0
7130 IFMID$(KY$,(CA(10)-1)*CA(7)+1,CA(7))=STRING$(CA(7),255)THENRETURN
7140 L4=0:FORI=1TO254:IFASC(MID$(RM$,I,1))=255THEN7144
7142 IFASC(MID$(RM$,I,1))>L4THEN L4=ASC(MID$(RM$,I,1))
7144 NEXTI
7146 I=0
7148 I=I+1:IFASC(MID$(RM$,I,1))<>KBTHEN7148
7150 J=CA(15)
7152 J=J-1:MID$(RM$,J+1,1)=MID$(RM$,J,1):IFJ>ITHEN7152
7156 MID$(RM$,I+1,1)=MKI$(L4+1)
7158 KZ$=KY$:KX$=MID$(KY$,CA(13),CA(12))+STRING$(CA(14),255)
7160 MID$(KZ$,CA(13),CA(12))=STRING$(CA(12),255)
7162 LSET KY$=KZ$:PUT2,KB+1
7164 LSET KY$=KX$:PUT2,L4+2
7166 LSET KY$=RM$:PUT2,1
7170 E=0:RETURN
7180 L4=0
7182 L4=L4+1:IFL4<=254THEN7184:ELSE STOP
7184 IFASC(MID$(RM$,L4+1,1))<255THEN7182
7186 KB=ASC(MID$(RM$,L4,1)):GET2,KB+1
7188 KN=0
7190 KN=KN+1:IFMID$(KY$,CA(7)*(KN-1)+1,CA(7))<STRING$(CA(7),255)THEN7190
7192 GOTO7050
7499 REM -- 7500-7999 GET RECORD --
7500 GOSUB6310
7510 IFE=0THEN7540
7520 E=1
7530 RETURN
7540 N=CVI(MID$(K1$,CA(7)-1,2))
7550 GOSUB6150
7560 GOSUB6090
7570 E=0
7580 RETURN
7999 REM -- 8000-8499 GET NEXT --
8000 K$=K$+STRING$(CA(9),32):E=ASC(MID$(K$,CA(9),1))+1
8010 MID$(K$,CA(9),1)=MKI$(E)
8020 GOSUB6310
8030 IF E=0THEN7540
8040 IF MID$(K1$,1,CA(9))<>STRING$(CA(9),255)THEN8060
8050 E=1:RETURN
8060 K$=K1$:E=0:GOTO7540
8499 REM -- 8500-8999 DELETE KEY AND RECORD --
8500 GOSUB6310
8510 IFE=0THEN8540
8520 E=1
8530 RETURN
8540 KZ$=KY$
8550 FORI=KN TO CA(10)-1
8555 MID$(KZ$,CA(7)*(I-1)+1,CA(7))=MID$(KZ$,CA(7)*I+1,CA(7))
8557 NEXTI
8560 LSET KY$=KZ$
8570 PUT2,KB+1
8580 E=0
8590 RETURN
8999 REM -- 9000-9499 RESAVE RECORD --
9000 GOSUB6310
9010 IFE=0THEN9040
9020 E=1
9030 RETURN
9040 N=CVI(MID$(K1$,CA(9)+1,2))
9050 GOSUB6010
9060 GOSUB6190
9070 E=0
9080 RETURN
```

Listing 15.2 continued

This program could be tailored further to become a more specialized key-only subroutine set by eliminating unused parts of the subroutine set and eliminating the locator to pack the keys in a smaller space. Instead of doing that, the next chapter will deal with another use of the key-file subroutine set, then the chapter following that will show you how to combine all of the functions into one parameter-driven subroutine set.

EDDIE GERMANO

CHAPTER 16

USING MORE THAN ONE KEY FILE

Up until now, all of the key-file routines were designed to access only one file set per program. But uses for systems that will access more than one file at a time include such programs as invoicing, which must access the inventory file, the customer file, and a file to store the prepared invoices. Storing the prepared invoices can be done in a sequential or in a random-access file, but the inventory and customer files will most probably be key files. Storing the prepared invoices can also be done in a key file, which would make them easier to edit. That can be done by building the key from the order number plus a line counter. Incrementing the line counter by 10 or 100 will make adding to the file easier.

This system would require two or three key files. It would be very impractical to use two or three complete subroutine sets, all in memory at the same time. Instead, there are much better ways to do this.

The method shown in this chapter is not the best way to accomplish this task, but it is fairly easy to implement and will serve as a good instructional exercise. The routines and logic presented for it will introduce some of the concepts that will be detailed in Chapter 17.

The subroutine set that was developed in Chapter 14 can serve as the base for this program. In it, all of the parameters may be stored in an array. The files require more than one set of parameters. There will be one set for every key file (which is actually two physical files—one for the records and one for the keys). There is also the problem of all of the PUT and GET statements referring to file number one for the records and file number two for the keys.

The problems are solved by not opening the files in the program initialization section. They will be opened later, as they are needed. Both the files must be initialized before the program is written. This will eliminate the need for a separate initialization function for each file within the program. Listing 16.1 is a general file initialization program that may be run to initialize the files for any key files used by the subroutine set.

The program initialization section should contain only the CLEAR statement and any DIM and REM statements that are needed. No OPEN or FIELD statements for the key files should be in this section, but the OPEN and FIELD statement for any other random-access file or the OPEN for any sequential file can be placed in it. The file numbers for the non-key files must not be one or two, as these will be used for the key files.

The control section should give the options of adding keys and records to each of the files as well as deleting and performing the other standard functions. These functions should usually use only one of the files each. There will be some functions that will access both of the files (or all three or four—however many there are).

```
10 CLEAR 2000:DEFINT C:DIM CA(15)
20 CLS
30 PRINT"GENERAL FILE INITIALIZATION PROGRAM"
40 PRINT
99 REM ** REQUEST ALL DATA **
100 INPUT "NAME OF RECORD FILE";F1$
110 INPUT "NAME OF KEY FILE";F2$
120 INPUT "INITIALIZE ON DRIVE NO.";FD%
130 IF FD%>=0 AND FD%<4 THEN 160
140 PRINT"ERROR - DRIVES ARE 0, 1, 2 OR 3"
150 GOTO 120
160 INPUT "WHAT IS THE RECORD LENGTH";CA(1)
170 PRINT "ENTER THE KEY LENGTH **WITHOUT**"
180 INPUT "THE LOCATOR";CA(9)
190 INPUT "WHAT IS THE MAXIMUM NUMBER OF RECORDS";CA(6)
200 INPUT "IS ALL OF THAT INFORMATION CORRECT (Y/N)";OK$
210 IF OK$="Y" THEN 300
220 IF OK$="N" THEN 250
230 PRINT "ERROR - PLEASE ANSWER Y OR N"
240 GOTO 200
250 PRINT:PRINT"**** ENTER ALL INFORMATION AGAIN ****"
260 FOR I=1 TO 1000
270 NEXT I
280 GOTO 20
299 REM ** COMPUTE AND DISPLAY CA() **
300 CA(3)=255/CA(1)
310 CA(4)=1
320 CA(5)=CA(6)/CA(3)+2
330 CA(7)=CA(9)+2
340 CA(8)=1
350 CA(10)=255/CA(7)
360 I=0
370 I=I+1
380 IF 2[I<CA(6) THEN 370
390 CA(11)=I
400 CA(12)=CA(7)*INT((CA(10)-1)/2)
410 CA(13)=255-CA(12)
420 CA(14)=CA(13)+1
430 CA(15)=2*CA(6)/CA(10)+2
440 PRINT "THE FILE CONSTANTS ARE:"
450 FOR I=1 TO 15
460 PRINT CA(I);
470 NEXT I
480 PRINT
499 REM ** VERIFY IF READY TO INITIALIZE **
500 INPUT "ENTER Y TO INITIALIZE OR N TO ABORT";OK$
510 IF OK$="Y" THEN 600
520 IF OK$="N" THEN 550
530 PRINT "ERROR - PLEASE ENTER Y OR N"
540 GOTO 500
550 PRINT "** INITIALIZATION ABORTED **"
```

```
560 END
599 REM ** INITIALIZE FILES **
600 PRINT"INSERT PROPER DISKETTE IN DRIVE";FD%;
610 INPUT " (ENTER)";OK$
620 F$=STR$(FD%)
630 MID$(F$,1,1)=":"
640 F1$=F1$+F$
650 F2$=F2$+F$
660 OPEN "R",1,F1$
670 FIELD 1, 255 AS B$
680 OPEN "R",2,F2$
690 FIELD 2, 255 AS KY$
700 K$=CHR$(1)+STRING$(254,255)
710 LSET KY$=K$
720 PUT2,1
730 MID$(K$,1,CA(7))=STRING$(CA(7),32)
740 LSET KY$=K$
750 PUT 2,2
760 K$=STRING$(255,255)
770 MID$(K$,1,CA(5))=STRING$(CA(5),0)
780 I=(CA(5)/CA(1))/8+1
790 MID$(K$,1,I)=STRING$(I,255)
800 LSET B$=K$
810 PUT 1,1
820 K$=STRING$(255,32)
830 FOR I=2 TO CA(5)
840 LSET B$=K$
850 PUT 1,I
860 NEXT I
870 PRINT "**** INITIALIZATION COMPLETE ****"
880 CLOSE1
890 CLOSE2
900 END
```

Listing 16.1

You also need a way to select the file to access. Since there were no OPEN and FIELD statements in the program initialization section, there must be a set elsewhere. The tactic here is to open and field the files just before they are used, reading in the parameter array at the same time. This can be done by a subroutine. Lines 5000 through 5999 are not in use yet. They can be used for some of the subroutines that will be required.

Starting at line 5000 can be the routine that selects one of the files. Use a variable like FD to hold the file number to be selected. This file number will be a different designator than the file number used in the OPEN and FIELD statements. Call this one the file designator. It will be a number between one and the number of files that the program is using. It will be used in various places to determine which of the files is selected. The subroutine at 5000 should open and field as well as read in the control array for the file whose designator is FD. This can be done by using ON. . .GOTO with a series of statements for each of the files in use. The series of statements should open and field the record file as file one and the key file as file two, then branch to a routine that will read in the parameters. The parameter reading routine can be nested FOR/NEXT loops. Assuming that they start at line 5200, they would be:

```
5200  RESTORE
5210  FOR J = 1 TO FD
5220  FOR I = 1 TO 15
5230  READ CA(I)
5240  NEXTI
5250  NEXTJ
5260  RETURN
```

Lines 5270 and up should contain the DATA statements. Line 5270 will be a DATA statement for the file designated one, line 5280 for the file designated two, etc. Remember also that the file names for each of the key and record files must all be different because the computer cannot have two files with identical names.

In the functions that use only one of the key files, a GOSUB 5000 could be the first statement after the LET statement that sets FD equal to the file number. Select the file, and all GOSUBs to the key file subroutines will refer to that selected file. For routines that use more than one file, you should select files just before the GOSUB statements. The subroutine that starts at line 5000 can limit how often the files are opened. Use one more variable, FE, initialized to zero somewhere in the program initialization section. At the beginning of the subroutine at line 5000, check the value of FE against the file designator FD. If they are equal, the files are open. If they are not equal, then continue with the OPEN, FIELD, and FOR/NEXT routines. Somewhere in this section of the subroutine, possibly just before the FOR/NEXT loop, the statement FE = FD should appear to set FE to the file that is being opened.

Accessing any non-key file used in the system will not require any special selection routine. These files, if they are to exist in the program, should be opened (and fielded, if they are random-access) in the program initialization section. One exception would be a sequential file that is to be used in a way that would not allow for opening it here. For example, a sequential file may be used to store a list of data that will be read later. The user must open the file as an output file for writing, then close it and again open it, this time as an input file for reading. In that case, the OPEN statements will be within the text of the appropriate functions.

Using multiple files in this manner can be very awkward in certain applications. This method can be used for applications that keep one file open for a length of time before the other file is required, so that there is no excessive file opening and closing.

One additional note for the subroutine at line 5000 is that you must close the files before the new OPEN statement. After you compare the variables FE and FD, the statement CLOSE1,2 should appear. If closing a file that is not open causes an error on your particular computer, use the statement IF FE < > 0 THEN CLOSE 1,2. The LET statement that sets FE equal to FD must be later in that subroutine. Because a listing is not given for the file described, here is the order that subroutine should follow:

1. Compare FE and FD. If they are equal, RETURN.
2. CLOSE files 1 and 2 (or IF FE< >0 THEN CLOSE 1,2).
3. Use ON. . .GOTO to select the proper OPEN and FIELD statements.
Each set should be:
   a. OPEN "R",1,"(record file name)"
   b. FIELD 1,255 AS B$
   c. OPEN "R",2,"(key file name)"
   d. FIELD 2,255 AS KY$
   e. GOTO beginning of parameter reading
4. (Parameter reading) First set FE = FD.
5. Follow the text for reading the parameters.
6. RETURN.
7. The DATA statements containing the parameters.

Packing and unpacking the records must also be done for each file separately. This can be accomplished by again using the ON FD GOTO statement at the line numbers assigned to the calling statements for the pack and unpack subroutines. The list in the ON. . .GOTO statements in each should refer to where the pack and unpack routines are written. In the 5000 series, they may start immediately after the select subroutine's DATA statements. There must be one subroutine for packing and one subroutine for unpacking for each file designated.

The other subroutines do not need alteration unless one of the files is a key-only file. If this is the case, the first statement of the subroutines starting at lines 6150 and 6190 could be moved down one line, to lines 6152 and 6192, respectively. Replace lines 6150 and 6190 with IF CA(1) = 0 THEN RETURN [CA(1) is the record length—if it is zero, then it must be a key-only file]. For unpacking, the corresponding statement numbers in the ON. . .GOTO lists in lines 6010 and 6090 for all of the key-only files should point to a RETURN statement.

There is no real need to list an example of this method. Experimentation would be the best teacher in this case. Moreover, the method described in the next chapter is more efficient for files that need to be accessed back and forth often. The description for this next method will build on the information presented in this chapter.

CHAPTER 17

SUMMARY

This chapter is a summary of all the information presented in Sections I, II, and III and will produce the final and most flexible form of the subroutine set.

Section I started out by defining the random-access file. But after having looked at the key-file methods, the random-access file looks rather simple. Still, it has its place as a method to hold data. There are many uses for a file of records that are stored by a sequential number. There are also some other variations, not as yet presented, that will make the random-access file a viable alternative in certain applications.

One such variation is the linked-record file. In such a file, each record has one or two pointers, like the pointers in the key file. One pointer is required. The two-pointer system adds a few extra functions. The idea behind the linked records is that the pointer of each record indicates the next one to follow in some predetermined (usually alphabetical by a selected field) order. The second pointer points in the other direction so that the file may be scanned in either direction. This method works well within its limitations. Searching for a specific record is not that easy. Unless other aids are programmed into it, a sequential search through the file is required. The aid that makes it easier is setting up a pointer array in memory. When the program starts, read the entire file, storing each record location in the order indicated by the pointers in one element in the array. Then use the binary search method to locate a specific record. This pointer method could be used for the invoicing application mentioned in Chapter 16. Adding a record, once its position is located, is not difficult. Deleting a record is also as easy. The file should be initialized so that the first record is all spaces and the key is the lowest in the file (similar in concept to the first key in the tree-structured method being all spaces). The logically last record in the chain may be the second record in the file. This should be initialized to all CHR$(255) characters. The pointers, initially, will simply point between the two records. Inserting a record consists of adding it as the next available record and altering the pointers of the other records surrounding it (*surrounding* meaning the next higher and the next lower records in the order of the file as read by the pointers).

The subroutines controlling the file access are acting very much as an interpreter. In an interpreter such as the BASIC interpreter, a command is read in and decoded. The decoded result points to a routine that will carry out the functions indicated by the command. The subroutines are the equivalent of the routine that carries out these functions. The main program, in addition to other logic in BASIC, interprets commands entered by the operator by calling the subroutines in the manner dictated by the main program. In a way, the program with the subroutines is the equivalent of a very high level, specialized interpreter.

Section II gives the fundamentals of key files and presents three basic methods. The multiple record blocks and the indexing chapters lay the groundwork for establishing key files. I explained the three files along with their advantages and disadvantages so that, given an application, you would know the best method or combination of methods to use. The alphabetical-array method can be used in conjunction with a tree-structured method or a hashing method key file to order the records for a report. The hashing method does not order the records at all, so some sorting is required to put a report in any particular order. The tree-structured method, using a single key, puts the records in only one order, the one dictated by the keys. You can form the alphabetical-array by reading all of the records and placing the field plus the record pointer in an array to be sorted. This would be the best method for a fairly small file. If a larger file is to be printed in a different order than the keys, establish a key-only file as described in Chapter 15.

Chapter 16 presents an admittedly awkward method of handling multiple files within one program. There is a much better method that can be used if the program is to go back and forth between the files frequently. This method calls for altering the parameter array slightly. In Chapter 16, when selecting a file other than the one currently open, the open file had to be closed, then the other one was opened and all of the paramters were read in. With this better method, all of the files may be open at the same time. This can be done by first adding another subscript to the array CA(. This second subscript is equal in magnitude to the total number of key files that will be used. Then, define one of the elements described as "not used" as the number of the record file. Next, open the files in such a way as to have the number of the key file one greater than the number of the record file.

For an example of this file numbering system, if the files are the inventory files mentioned in Chapter 16, there will be the inventory item file and the customer file. There could also be the billing or invoicing file as one of the key files. The files are opened and fielded using an array for the buffer:

```
10  CLEAR 5000
20  DIM CA(15,3),B$(3),KY$(3)
30  OPEN "R",1,"ITEMREC"
40  FIELD 1, 255 AS B$(1)
50  OPEN "R",2,"ITEMKEY"
60  FIELD 2, 255 AS KY$(1)
70  OPEN "R",3,"CUSTREC"
80  FIELD 3, 255 AS B$(2)
90  OPEN "R",4,"CUSTKEY"
100  FIELD 4, 255 AS KY$(2)
110  OPEN "R",5,"BILLREC"
120  FIELD 5, 255 AS B$(3)
130  OPEN "R",6,"BILLKEY"
140  FIELD 6, 255 AS KY$(3)
150  RESTORE
160  FOR J = 1 TO 3
170  FOR I = 1 TO 15
180  READ CA(I,J)
190  NEXTI
200  NEXTJ
```

Lines 210 through 230 will be the DATA statements containing the 45 parameters required, with each statement containing the 15 parameters that apply to each file.

Next, the subroutines require some alteration. First, every time LSET B$ = B1$ appears, it should be replaced with LSET B$(CA(2,FD)) = B1$, where FD is the number of the order in which the files are opened (i.e., 1 for the items, 2 for the customers, and 3 for the billing). FD should be set by the main program before any GOSUB to the key file routines. This is to be used in the place of the statements set up in Chapter 16 for selecting a file. A similar statement, using KY$(CA(2,FD)), should be used for the keys. On the GET side, every GET statement should be followed by either B$ = B$(CA(2,FD)) or KY$ = KY$(CA(2,FD)) so that the correct variable will be unpacked.

The packing and unpacking subroutines follow the same logic as presented for them in Chapter 16. Use the ON. . .GOTO with CA(2,FD) as the controlling value to branch to the proper pack or unpack subroutine. Both the subroutine that gets a record given the record number and the one that puts a record by number also require the IF statement that will effect a RETURN if CA(1), which is now CA(1,FD), is zero, as that will indicate a key-only file.

There are several other alterations that will make this subroutine set more flexible. For example, there is a way that records can be set up so that the record file may be of a selected length. This is done by combining the key-file methods with the record-linking method. Choose a standard length record (51 bytes allows five records per block and this is a fairly economical one) and set up the key file to use this length record. Use the routine to access the fields that will be in the first 49 bytes, or the record length minus 2 bytes. To add length to that record, get another record from the free list (GOSUB 6250), then pack the record number into the last two bytes of the first record. Pack the first 49 bytes of this next record. If more records are needed, repeat the procedure. This is not a bad way to tackle the problem of storing invoices, which may be of variable length. The heading information could be the first record in the file, controlled by the key-file subroutines. The line items could be added by linking to it additional records in the same file. Calculate the required file size in two parts. The total number of keys required would be the total number of invoices to be stored. The total number of records would be this number plus the total number of line items needed on all invoices. You could estimate this by multiplying the number of invoices to be stored by the average number of line items per invoice. Messages and other text may also be added to the end of the invoice with no great problem by using the first field on each record as a code to indicate the format in which the record is packed.

If the alteration described is not clear, a little experimentation with linked records will clear up most of the trouble. Create a random-access file and control it by the linked-records method. Either the one or the two pointer method can be used. The one-pointer method was used in the description because the pointer that indicated the reverse order is not really needed. When working with one invoice, simply set a selected variable equal to the number of the first record, which is the one indicated by the key.

With the ability to open and manipulate multiple files, the memory of the computer is looking smaller and smaller. There is a substantial amount of code required in memory all at the same time when the subroutine set plus all of the functions required to support the application must be in memory. Section IV, which deals with how to set up the program and data files, begins by showing a method of segmenting the code in a logical way so that only the code that is required for a given function is in memory when the function is called. Now is the time, if you haven't already done so, to buy the second disk drive.

SECTION IV

Introduction

The preceding three sections built up a very flexible set of subroutines for accessing key files. This set of subroutines may be altered for many different types of applications or may be fully parameter-controlled so that any application can use the subroutines as they are simply by defining the parameter array.

Record Number	Key	Pointer #1	Pointer #2
1	A	5	0
2	W	0	4
3	M	4	6
4	Q	2	3
5	C	7	1
6	K	3	7
7	J	6	5

Table IV.1: *An alphabetically linked record file. Pointer number two indicates reverse order as it points to the alphabetically previous record. Pointer number one indicates alphabetical order as it points to the alphabetically next record.*

There was some mention of a linked-record system that can be used in conjunction with a key file. In that type of system, one record of a fixed length is indicated by the key file. The record then points to another record in the record file that does not have a key. That second record may point to a third, etc., for as many records as needed along that chain. In effect, the key is pointing to a variable length record. After the glossary in the back of this book is the *listing of the program that produced the glossary. That program uses both the key file (WORDS) and the first record in the record file (GLOSSARY) to contain the word, which is the key (note: it is good practice to always repeat the key in the record). The record containing the key points to the first record of the definition, which points to another record, etc., until all of the definition is stored. The program has no editing capabilities—in order to change a definition, you have to delete the key and all of the linked records, then reenter them. You can edit with routines that redirect the pointers to insert a new record or to remove a record.*

Although it was not the problem with the glosssary program (for a one-time use, I decided that the extra effort would not be worth the edit feature), often the size of the computer memory will restrict the number of functions that a program can do. This is particularly limiting when the memory is additionally burdened with the long text of the key-file subroutines. The memory is even more confining when more than one key file is to be used in the application and the functions maintaining the files double in number, then add even more functions to use both or all the files at once.

Fortunately, this problem does have a simple solution. The program can be segmented so that only a small part of it is in memory at one time. This section will deal with this and then go on to more details on program and data file design and output formatting. Just presenting the tool of the key file is like putting a single diskette on a computer. It increases the power tremendously, but will very quickly become restrictive in the very power that it added. Being able to segment the programs and effectively design the data structure and output formats will add the equivalent flexibility of adding the second drive to the computer.

The references in this section to the disks will all assume a minimum of two drives. The disk use is set up so that all programs and program-related files are on the first drive and the application data is on the second drive or second and subsequent drives. Although other configurations are possible, this one has proven itself to be the most flexible and versatile for almost all applications requiring multiple drives.

CHAPTER 18

PROGRAM OVERLAYS

The key-file subroutines have added much versatility to the disk. Unfortunately, this has also added a burden to the computer memory. All of the functions and subroutines for a very large application for the microcomputer simply will not fit into memory. Fortunately, there are statements that will allow for a solution to this problem. These statements will allow for program overlays.

Most microcomputers can do part of the overlay function. The manuals refer to this action as chaining and use the BASIC verb RUN or LOAD. This allows a program to end its own execution and call another program into memory from the disk, instructing the computer to run it next. A true overlay is when only part of the code can be read into memory and the point at which execution is to begin may be specified. This would allow a program system to be written so that the subroutines all stay in memory and the text below the subroutines could be exchanged for other text from the disk. With most microcomputers this is not possible, but it can be simulated using the RUN or LOAD statement.

A typical design for a program system built of several smaller program segments involves splitting the programs by the functions. In the key-file test program, the functions were divided in memory by statement number. They could be separate programs. When one of them was completed, it would RUN (or LOAD) the control section program.

Many applications programs consist of definite sections. These sections are:

- File maintenance, which takes care of the routines to add, change, or delete information in the file
- Reports, which print the various listings required by the applications
- Posting, which usually consists of adding records to one file by extracting data from one or more other files under the direction of the operator
- Control, which allows selection of the functions

There may be other sections added for a particular application, and one or two of these sections may not be required, but the four sections listed are a good guideline and are usually all present in one form or another.

The control section is usually the first one that the operator of the system sees when the program is loaded. It will, as the section did in the key-file test program, list all of the functions available on the system. In systems where the files stay open when a program chains to another program, a small program may be used to open the files before the control section is loaded. Otherwise, each of the sections must open the files when they are loaded into memory.

On larger program systems, the control section may consist of a series of programs. The control programs are often referred to as selectors or menus because they list selections of programs much like a menu lists selections of meals. There may be one selector or menu for each of the functions and one main selector or menu that simply calls the other menus. Figure 18.1 shows a general operational flow chart of how these programs could be linked together. The main selector has a list of all of the general functions. It will chain to any one of the other selectors at the operator's option. The selector chosen will list all of the functions available under it, allowing the operator to choose one of them or to return to the main selector.

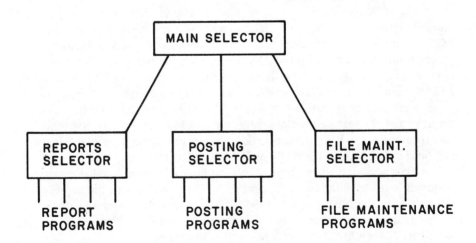

Figure 18.1: *General operational flow diagram of a program system using chaining.*

In practice, this is a very simple system to use. Unfortunately, in most microcomputers, each one of the functions except for the selectors must be saved on the disk along with the complete subroutine set. This does occupy a lot of room on the diskette, but allows the programs to be separated so that only a small amount of the whole operation is in memory at one time.

One drawback of this type of system is that if there is an error found in the subroutines, it must be corrected in every one of the function programs.

There is one clear advantage to this segmenting of the program functions: it does make it a little easier to debug the program. Each one of the program modules does one basic task. The module that adds, deletes, and alters records in file number one, for example, will not have any statements in it that refer to the printer except for, possibly, an audit trail listing. It will not refer to any of the other files in the system, either. The programs that do refer to more than one file will be the posting and reports sections. The reports will not refer to anything that will alter the files in the system. This all allows the programmer to concentrate on one small section at a time. As was often stated, computers are made of very simple parts. Computer programs are also made of very simple parts. Segmenting the programs will allow the very simple parts to become isolated from each other, which limits interference from other parts of the system.

The selectors are the easiest part of the system to program. They should be written first, as this makes it easier to program the other functions by allowing normal access to them as they are being developed. The basic format for a selector, which is a very short program, is:

```
10   CLEAR x
20   CLS
30   RESTORE
40   READ N,N$
50   PRINTAB(20);N$
60   PRINT
70   FORI = 1TON
80   READN$
90   PRINTAB(10);I;N$
100  NEXTI
110  PRINT
120  INPUT"ENTER NUMBER OF SELECTION";SN
130  IF SN< =N AND SN>OTHEN160
140  PRINT"ERROR — PLEASE ENTER A SELECTION FROM THE
          LIST"
150  GOTO120
160  FOR I = 1 TO SN
170  READ P$
180  NEXT I
190  RUN P$
```

This program can be saved on disk as a selector *skeleton* program. When there is a need for a selector, load it into memory and add DATA statements to it starting at line 190. The first DATA statement contains the number of selections and then the name of the selector. The next few entries (be careful that the number listed equals the number of selections indicated) are the selections to be displayed on the screen. Following that, in order, are the names of the programs that are to be loaded for each selection. The main selector for the program system described above would have the following DATA statements:

```
190  DATA 3,"MAIN SELECTOR"
200  DATA "ADD, DELETE AND ALTER RECORDS"
210  DATA "POSTING"
220  DATA "REPORTS"
230  DATA "MAINTSEL","POSTSEL","REPTSEL"
```

In the other selectors in the system, one of the selections must be to return to this selector. When this selector is finished, it may be saved on disk under the name selected for it. After that, form the other selectors by loading the selector skeleton (or deleting the DATA statements in this one) and adding the DATA statements for it.

If your computer will keep files open when programs are chained, write another small program that opens the files and then loads the main selector. The descriptions in this section all assume that each program that uses the files must open the files when it is loaded and close them before chaining back to a selector. This method works even on systems that keep files open during chaining.

There is one more function that may be added to the main selector. This function initializes the files. With a little reprogramming of the main selector (an IF statement as in line 125 that branches around to above the DATA statements), the selection number for it could be prevented from appearing on the list. For example, the number for the initialization program could be 27 (choose a number that will most probably not be entered by accident). Line 125 would be IF SN = 27 THEN 240. Line 240 would be a RUN statement that would chain to the initialization program given in Chapter 16. End that program by replacing the STOP statement with a RUN that refers to the main selector.

Presenting the information about program structure before the information in the chapters that follow this one does put some information out of order, but the data files must be designed first. This order of putting the information about the program segmenting first was done to make the discussions of the file design and report layouts a little easier to follow and to set up a standard approach for the listings that accompany those descriptions. To further tax the system, the next chapter will deal with additional subroutines that are used in place of certain INPUT and PRINT statements. These will make it easier to write the modules, and there is now more room for them because of the splitting up of the functions.

CHAPTER 19

GENERAL I/O SUBROUTINES

Now that there is more room in memory, you can use more
subroutines to make the task of programming the functions easier. Particularly on programs that do a lot of input, the checking of the input data
does not require many statements that have to be in the main text of the
function.

There are basically three types of input. These are alphanumeric,
numeric, and enter. In the enter type, the program waits for the operator to
hit the enter key only, and requires no input. This is the simplest routine.
The alphanumeric input in a program, particularly if it is eventually to be
packed into a record, has a length restriction. Numeric input has other
restrictions, including that it must be between two given numbers, must be
an integer or have no more than a given number of decimal places, and, in
most cases, must be entered rather than defaulted by a simple pressing of
ENTER. All of these functions may be assigned to parameter-driven
subroutines.

In addition to the above routines, a routine that displays an error
message and one that positions the cursor are also very handy to have in
the program. The error-message routine could be used by the input
subroutines so that the main program would not have to check an error
variable when an input subroutine returned. Also, a subroutine that does
the chaining can be used to display a message to the operator to explain the
delay that the chaining will cause. It is often very important to let the
operator know what is going on in the computer.

An error-message subroutine is almost a requirement in any set of
input subroutines. If you are careful about the screen layouts, you can keep
one line somewhere on the display reserved for the error messages and use a
PRINT @ statement (or the equivalent) in all subroutines to locate the
error message and return to the correct location on the screen. This
subroutine can display the message on the screen for a predetermined length
of time (governed by a FOR/NEXT loop or by checking the clock in the

computer) then erase the line and return to the calling statement. This way, old error messages do not stay on the screen. Three to five seconds is all you need, depending on the length of the statement displayed.

The input statements can use the PRINT @ to position the cursor and use an INPUT statement to get the entered data or they can use a routine based on the INKEY$ (or an equivalent) statement. You can then test the entry for the appropriate limitations. You can pass these limitations, as well as the screen position, to the subroutine in one string variable instead of a number of numeric variables. For example, in the numeric input subroutine, the values required are screen position (usually two numbers), minimum and maximum allowable values, and maximum number of decimal places allowed (zero if it is to be an integer). Instead of having to set five different numeric variables in the calling program, you can set one string equal to the alphanumeric equivalent of these values. If you request that the number to be entered be at screen position 8,10 and be between 0 and 2000 with no more than two decimal places, the calling statement could be:

xxxx PA$ = "08100000200002":GOSUB yyyy

. . .where xxxx is the statement number in the main text and yyyy is the subroutine call line number. The string breaks down into 08 and 10 as the position, 0000 and 2000 as the minimum and maximum, and 02 as the maximum number of decimal places. This is a fixed format, which means that the values are extracted by their absolute position in the string. This is as opposed to free format, which is like the INPUT statement in BASIC, where the fields are separated by a designated character, the comma (this is a *field delimeter*, defined as any character specified to separate fields). The fixed format is easier to take apart in BASIC in this application.

Note that the error routine can be called from the other subroutines. For this reason, if you use PA$ for the parameters in the other subroutines, do not use PA$ for the error message when calling the error subroutine. The easiest way to use the error subroutine is to call it when the error is detected, then GOTO the first line in the subroutine when it returns. The first line will unpack PA$. If PA$ is used to contain the error message, the contents will not be there to unpack for the second try. Try to keep the parameter string intact throughout the input subroutine.

Many of the newer microcomputers have some machine language program calls that handle some of the operations required in the input subroutines. Positioning the cursor and delaying three to five seconds may be easier when using these machine language subroutines.

Finding a place to put these new subroutines may be a problem on some computers. The record and key-file subroutines take up a significant number of program statement numbers. The numbers could be above line 10000 on computers that allow line numbers that high. Some computers are restricted to line numbers below that number, so you have to find room elsewhere. Since the main program is now split up into several smaller programs, there should be more room in the lower section of the program (lower by line number). The other subroutines are all above line 5000, so lines 4000 to 4999 could be reserved for the I/O subroutines (I/O is input-output). If you need more room, use lines 3000-3999 in addition to these. If you need still more room, rewrite the subroutines, as 2000 line numbers should provide more than enough room for accomplishing these functions.

One other note on the input routine concerns the status of the screen before and after the input is complete. The cursor positioning should always be used to position the location of the input. The reason for this will become more obvious in the chapter on screen layouts. Given this, whether an INPUT statement, a loop using the INKEY$ function, or some machine language call is used to get the input, the field should start with a question mark (?). This is a fairly standard prompt. When the input is completed, the field could be reprinted on the screen either using no mark where the question mark was or substituting another mark like a colon (:). This avoids too many question marks on the screen during sections that involve a lot of input. A screen full of phrases ending in question marks can easily confuse the operator. Looking for a question mark on a screen that has only one question mark on it is easier.

None of these general I/O subroutines must be in the program. In fact, if they are used, they do not have to appear in every program in the system. The reports, for example, may need no input or so little that the routine needs no subroutines. Obviously, keep subroutines only in the routines that use them.

CHAPTER 20

DESIGNING THE DATA FILES

The most important, as well as one of the first, tasks required in creating a system of programs is to plan out the number of data files and their contents. This tasks defines, more than any other, what the programs are to do.

There are standard approaches to designing the data files that all have the same basic steps and vary only in the resulting formats of the documentation they produce. In this chapter is one typical method of designing data files.

The first step is to find out what data are required for the entire project. This can be done by examining what the output requires. If the output is not yet known, then that should be examined first. Usually, in a programming task, the problem to be solved by the computer is expressed in what is to be printed or displayed. From the intended output, make a list of all of the different data fields that are required, and make a note of the order the reports are to be in.

Steps to Follow When Preparing Documentation

1. Identify the required data for the entire project.
2. List and order the required data files.
3. Determine the number of files required.
4. Reserve file space which will be required for computations.
5. Write out data file layout sheets.
6. Sketch "map" of the programs.
7. List all variables to be used.
8. Write descriptions of each program in the system.
9. Assemble the table of contents.
10. Fill out screen layout and printer layout sheets.
11. Describe all special tasks that are application dependent.
12. Write the program system.

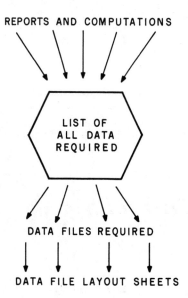

REPORTS AND COMPUTATIONS

LIST OF
ALL DATA
REQUIRED

DATA FILES REQUIRED

DATA FILE LAYOUT SHEETS

Figure 20.1: *Preparing the data-file information.*

From the various types of reports, find out how many files are required. For example, in an inventory application, there could be one file containing the items in the inventory, another file to hold information about customers, and a third file to put this information together to form invoices and packing slips. Studying how the reports are assembled will give you a good clue as to the number of files a system will need.

If the application involves some processing or other computations, inspect these to find any other values that must be entered and stored. The results of these computations will generally be on at least one of the reports, but inspect these, also, in case there are one or two values that are required in other computations and therefore must be stored. The processing or computations may also require a temporary file to store values as the operation of them progresses. These files will generally resemble a *virtual array* (an array stored on disk in a file instead of in the computer memory). The temporary file will most probably be a random-access file instead of a key file.

When the list of all of the data is complete, break it up into the different files required. The result should be lists of all of the fields required by each of the files. Next, organize these lists into something that can be used in the key-file subroutine set. There is a device that can be used to assemble this information that gives places to add other required information. This device is, appropriately, a data file layout sheet.

This data file layout sheet can be one of your own design or a copy of the one suggested (see figure 20.2). Using that format and a typewriter or short computer program, you can provide good data file layout sheets.

Listing 20.1 is the program that printed out the sheet in figure 20.2.

The basic components of a data file layout sheet include the heading information, which should include the name of the file, the type of file, the record length of the file, and supplimentary information such as, in a key file, what the key length is to be; the number of records in the file; the number of records per block; and so on. For the key files, if the parameter array is to be used, a place to put the 15 values for the DATA statement would define the file. Also include the name of the key file. If it is not a key file, a brief statement describing the method of access is appropriate.

```
                        DATA FILE LAYOUT

FILE NAME _____ FILE TYPE _____

ACCESS _____ BUFFER VARIABLE _____

RECORD LENGTH _____ NO. RECORDS PER BLOCK _____

ADDITIONAL INFORMATION _____
```

VAR. NAME	PACK START	END	VAR. TYPE	PACKING METHOD	DESCRIPTION

Figure 20.2: *Data file layout sheet generated by the program in Listing 20.1.*

```
5 REM **** PRINT DATA FILE LAYOUT SHEETS ****
10 CLEAR 1000
20 L1$=STRING$(72,"-")
30 L2$=CHR$(124)+"       "+CHR$(124)+"        "+CHR$(124)+"        "
35 L2$=L2$+CHR$(124)+"         "+CHR$(124)+"            "+CHR$(124)
40 LPRINT TAB(28);"DATA FILE LAYOUT"
50 LPRINT" "
60 LPRINT"FILE NAME ";STRING$(26,95);" FILE TYPE ";STRING$(25,95)
65 LPRINT" "
70 LPRINT"ACCESS ";STRING$(37,95);" BUFFER VARIABLE ";STRING$(11,95)
75 LPRINT" "
80 LPRINT"RECORD LENGTH ";STRING$(20,95);
85 LPRINT" NO. RECORDS PER BLOCK ";STRING$(15,95)
90 LPRINT" "
95 LPRINT"ADDITIONAL INFORMATION ";STRING$(49,95)
100 LPRINT" ":LPRINT" ":LPRINT" "
110 LPRINT L1$
120 LPRINT CHR$(124);" VAR. ";CHR$(124);"    PACK   ";CHR$(124);
125 LPRINT " VAR. ";CHR$(124);" PACKING ";CHR$(124);
126 LPRINT " DESCRIPTION";TAB(72);CHR$(124)
130 LPRINT CHR$(124);" NAME ";CHR$(124);"START";CHR$(124);
135 LPRINT " END ";CHR$(124);" TYPE ";CHR$(124);" METHOD   ";
136 LPRINT CHR$(124);TAB(72);CHR$(124)
140 LPRINT L1$
150 FOR I=1 TO 12 : FOR J=1 TO 2
160 LPRINT L2$;TAB(72);CHR$(124)
170 NEXT J
180 LPRINT L1$
190 NEXT I
200 STOP
```

Listing 20.1

The rest of the data file layout sheet is a list of the fields to be stored in the file. The various columns on the list include where in the record the field is to be packed, the type of field (and how it is to be packed, if this information is important), the name of the variable that will hold the field while it is in memory, the length of the field, and a description of the field. This information can be used directly when programming the pack and unpack subroutines for the file.

Not all of the information requested on the sheet needs to be filled in at the same time. First write the description of the field. The first field on the list of the key files should be the key. It is always good practice to put the key in the record as well as in the key file, just in case something happens to the key file. If you always do this, you'll always have a good record file and be able to write a program to recover the key file.

The data file layout sheets are also an important part of the documentation for the program system. You should also have in this documentation a map of the programs, similar to the ones presented in Chapter 18. Indicate on the map the names of the program files, and don't forget to list the subroutines used. As mentioned before, you can do this by listing the REM statements in the subroutine set. List them with spaces between so that you can write additional information about each subroutine. This will make using the subroutines a little easier. Such additional information should include the parameters that the subroutine will require (except for the parameter array, which should be assumed), what the return values are (including any returned error codes), and any special information that would be useful for using the subroutine.

Also in the documentation should be a complete list of all of the variables used. This list should show the variable name (and should be in order by the variable name), what programs use it (for this case, treat the subroutine set as if it were another program, listing it as well as the programs outside the subroutines that use the variable), and a brief description of what the variable does. Next, include a description of each of the programs in the system, except for the selectors. The selectors do not need to be described because their function is standard, and therefore pretty obvious.

The program documentation is almost complete after you finish the above parts. The rest of the documentation is the table of contents and the printer and screen layout sheets that are described in the next chapter. These will be added to the descriptions of the programs. The program descriptions should be as detailed as required so that the programming is easier. Time invested in writing good documentation will make programming easier and errors fewer. More parts can be added if required in a particular application. For example, if the program system is to assemble information for another system, details of how this information is stored and/or transmitted should occupy some space in the documentation.

Don't be afraid of overdocumenting a program. I don't think it has ever been done. Detail in the documentation makes the programming easier.

EDDIE GERMANO

CHAPTER 21

DESIGNING REPORTS AND SCREEN DISPLAYS

After you've established all of the data and program structures and are almost ready to write the program, one small matter remains to be examined: what the program will look like to the user. All the user sees is the screen and the printed reports, not any of the fancy and intricate routines used to store and manipulate the data. This chapter will help you make the program look as well organized as the documentation will allow it to be.

The screen displays of the selectors are fairly well set. The only thing to worry about is making the selection displayed on the screen clear as to what it must do. For example, a title like "FILE EDIT" may not be as clear to an operator as "ALTER ITEM RECORDS." Depending upon the application, you could invent titles even clearer than these. Time spent deciding the correct titles for the selection is not time wasted. It means less confusion for the person running the program, even if that person is you at a later date. You will recognize the functions better after being away from it if you select the titles carefully now.

Concerning the screen displays, there are two more areas that demand much attention. One is the file maintenance area, which is where the file is altered and records are added and deleted. There are screen layout forms, but they are not easy to find. Graph paper will work, but it is not exactly accurate. The number of characters per inch horizontally is greater on the screen than the number of characters per inch vertically. You could measure these two values and create your own format. I would suggest that, if you decide to do this, you make up one form, using ink or something else that can be copied, and have several of them copied. The best ones that I have used are laid out so that the long dimension is horizontal. The top has the title "SCREEN LAYOUT," or something similar, and under that are lines for filling in the name of the program and purpose of the screen display. Using the line printer to produce these forms does not work well unless the graphics on the printer can handle the resolution required to print the format.

Figure 21.1 is a typical screen layout sheet, filled out for an inventory maintenance program. In it the fields that can be entered are all named and the appropriate number of blocks is left for entry of the values. You can read the coordinates of each field directly from this sheet for the input routines described in Chapter 18. Also, you can determine the maximum length for the strings and the maximum and minimum values and maximum number of decimal places from the data file layout for that file. The program that uses that screen display is a general maintenance program that will allow altering fields within a record as well as inserting and deleting records. If the operator enters a key that is not in file, a yes-or-no question gives the operator the choice of entering it as a new record. If this is the case, the operator is requested to enter data for every field in the record. After all fields are entered or if the key is found, then the operator may enter a field number and change any of the fields listed on the screen. This is done using the "ENTER FIELD NO., DELETE OR END?" question. If the operator enters a field number, the input routine for that field is called. If the operator enters DELETE, the record is deleted from the file and the screen goes back to the beginning to request another key or END. If, after all fields are corrected, the operator enters END to the "ENTER FIELD NO, DELETE or END?" question, the program resaves the record. This is a very common structure for a maintenance program and seems to be very successful.

The other main trouble area for screen layouts is in any other interactive routine like a posting program. Posting programs are similar to the maintenance programs but are more limited in function. They also usually deal with more than one file. For example, an order posting program in an inventory system will deal with the customer file, the item file, and an order file. The screen display for this should allow for the customer name and address as well as any other pertinent information about the customer, and there should be space for the line items to be entered below this. The fancier versions of this allow the line items to roll under the customer data, updating a total as items are added. On most systems, this involves redisplaying the screen between line items and reorganizing the bottom to "roll out" excess lines.

You should also design the screen displays on other programs, such as report programs, that require interaction from the operator. If there are several reports that all require the same information, you can fill out one screen layout sheet that refers to all of the programs using the display.

The report layouts also require sheets that are not that easy to find. Again, if you can't find them, you can draw one up and have it copied. For every report in the system, there should be a layout sheet. There is no cursor position on the line printer as there is on the screen, but there are horizontal tab positions. Lining things up in the proper columns becomes routine when a layout sheet is used. Remember to place a title block and leave room for page numbering at the top of the sheet.

SCREEN LAYOUT

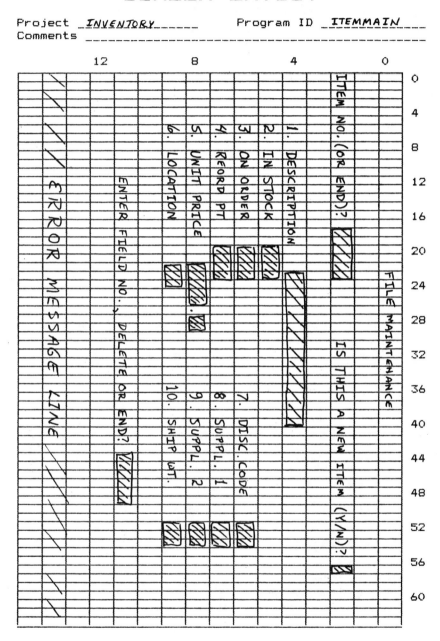

Project __INVENTORY_____   Program ID __ITEMMAIN____

Comments _____

Figure 21.1: *Sample of a screen layout sheet filled out for an inventory maintenance program.*

In the report programs, it is usually very handy to have a subroutine that handles the line counting and paging. Many computers have line counters built into the system that may be read by PEEK functions and reset by POKE, but it is just as easy to assign this function to a variable in the program. There should be two variables set up at the beginning of the report program that contain the line number and the page number. Using L9 and P9 as these two variables, set P9 to zero and L9 to the bottom line of the page. The subroutine can be called just before a line is printed. The logic of the subroutine is:

1. Increment L9. If it is less than the number of lines per page, RETURN.
2. Increment P9. Unless it is equal to one, advance the printer to top of form.
3. Print the title on the page, including the page number (the page number could be eliminated on page one, if desired).
4. Set L9 to the line number of the first line under the title block, then RETURN.

If the line numbers of the above subroutine are selected so that they do not interfere with any of the other subroutines, it can be in memory along with them. There are now three sets of subroutines. One, the longest set, controls the key and record files. Although developed as if it were two subroutine sets, it may now be thought of as one because the two parts are so interdependent. The second subroutine set is the general I/O subroutines developed in Chapter 19. The single subroutine outlined above comprises the third set. If these are saved on disk in the ASCII format, they can be added to the programs as required by use of the MERGE command.

The documentation should now be complete. It should be arranged in some understandable order, like:

1. Table of contents
2. Chart of the programs (see Chapter 18)
3. List of variable use
4. Data file layout sheets
5. Description of the subroutines used
6. Program descriptions with report and screen layouts

If there are any special calculation routines required by the program system, these can either be in with the program description of the program that will do these calculations, or, if they will appear in several parts of the program, they can be added as another section between numbers four and five on this list.

Now you can start the programming. This should also be done in order. The selectors are first and are the easiest. Next are the maintenance programs for each of the files. This order will allow all of the files to be established with some data to use for testing before the other routines are tested. Next, program the reports that do not require data from any program that is not written. The reports to write now are the ones that simply list the contents of the data files. After you do these, do the posting routines or any other routines that manipulate data from the files in some way (with the obvious exception of the maintenance programs, as they are already written). Next, write the reports that print out the information these programs produce. This should have included all of the programs in most application systems. There are some applications that will require programs that were not on the list, and these are generally done last, after the rest of the system is finished and tested. A telecommunication output, for example, will be easier to debug if you are certain that the rest of the system that supplied the data is correct.

Although it looks like an obvious point here, it is not that obvious in the middle of a programming task that there is an order to the debugging of a program system. The debugging should always follow the order that the data runs through. That path is the order described for writing the program. Each section can be corrected as it is written and should be correct before the next section is started. Working directly from good documentation will result in fewer bugs to correct.

CHAPTER 22

ASSEMBLY LANGUAGE

This book was written primarily for the BASIC language user, but the logic presented here may be used in almost any computer language. BASIC is not a fast language. There are many other languages that will outpace BASIC in a speed test. As a rule, the higher the level of the language, the slower it will run. BASIC is an interpretive language, which puts it at about the same level as the compiled languages, some of which will run faster than BASIC on the same computer. Machine language is usually the fastest on any particular computer. This could be beaten only by microcode, but that is generally not available to the programmer.

Assembly language is, for the sake of calculating the speed of operation, machine language. The only difference is that the assembly language is made of letters and symbols instead of the numbers required by the system. These must be translated into the machine language. The difference between assembly language and a compiled language is that, in assembly language, one statement will produce one machine language statement, but in a compiled language, one statement produces a fixed series of machine language statements or a series of code that will be interpreted later.

Machine language and assembly language, then, mean approximately the same thing when you're discussing the routines themselves. They are just two different ways to express the same thing.

There are two approaches to take to gain the speed of the machine language. The first and most tedious approach is to take the logic of the programs and subroutines and translate it directly into machine language (with or without an assembler). If BASIC is available, there is another approach that I consider a more efficient one.

The main programs do not require that much speed. The speed to be gained is in the key-file subroutine set. If this were in machine language, the whole system would benefit from the gained speed, but there are some problems in doing this. One problem is the passing of parameters. You could alter the use of the parameters; instead of having to pass all 15 parameters to the subroutine each time it is called, which requires making it poke the information into a designated location one byte at a time, the subroutines in machine language can be given the parameters for all files all at once. You could do this by assigning each file in the system a specific number to be used throughout the system. The file parameters could then be passed to the locations in memory in a short program that is run just before the main selector is run for the first time.

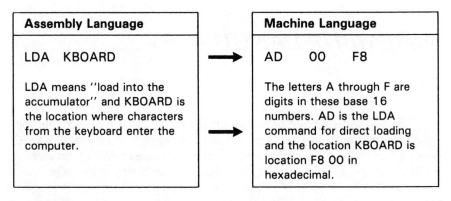

Assembly Language	Machine Language
LDA KBOARD	AD 00 F8
LDA means "load into the accumulator" and KBOARD is the location where characters from the keyboard enter the computer.	The letters A through F are digits in these base 16 numbers. AD is the LDA command for direct loading and the location KBOARD is location F8 00 in hexadecimal.

Each assembly language statement produces one machine language command.

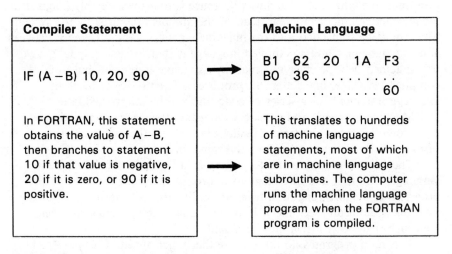

Compiler Statement	Machine Language
IF (A − B) 10, 20, 90	B1 62 20 1A F3 B0 36 60
In FORTRAN, this statement obtains the value of A − B, then branches to statement 10 if that value is negative, 20 if it is zero, or 90 if it is positive.	This translates to hundreds of machine language statements, most of which are in machine language subroutines. The computer runs the machine language program when the FORTRAN program is compiled.

Each statement in a compiled language produces many machine language commands.

Table 22.1: *Translation from a higher-level language into machine language.*

The use of the machine language subroutines will vary on different computers, but the general idea will be the same. One quick method of passing values to the subroutine is to use a section of the screen. The screen occupies a fixed area in memory, accessible to both BASIC and the machine language program. If the information were printed in a screen-acceptable format in a designated part of the screen, the machine language could read the information from the screen by memory location. If the information is printed and the machine language routine is called immediately, the subroutine could first transfer this information to some other location in memory, and then erase it from the screen. If there is not too much information being passed, the result would be only a flicker on that part of the screen.

The logic of the subroutines could be copied for the machine language routines. Some of the ways to speed up the operation that are not possible in BASIC include using shorter fields for some of the numerics (the examples are all in single precision numbers, which could also be examined for use in BASIC) and possibly using binary throughout instead of decimal, depending on the machine language. Because machine language does not have to be interpreted by machine language routines, the operation is speeded up considerably.

Most systems have a reserved area in memory that can be set up by the user. A system start-up procedure can also be defined so that the system will execute a series of commands in the disk operating system. On the program disk for the particular operation, these commands could be to load in the machine language program and then go into BASIC. Unfortunately, the operator, who may not be you, must be depended upon to enter the correct number for the reserved memory space. The machine language subroutines should be placed in this area.

Since there are many different machine languages and several different assemblers in each, there is no standard that I can use to show how this translation could take place. There are, however, some hints on logic that you can get from the material presented in this book beyond how the logic of the subroutines themselves work. These include also using subroutines within other subroutines. Various tasks that may be done very well with one command in BASIC require several machine language commands. If some of these are repeated several times, writing an additional subroutine to do that task will save time writing the subroutines and will save space in memory. For many of the subroutines, the variables to be passed include only a file number and the key. If this is to be passed by using an area on the screen, a machine language subroutine could be designed to take that information, put it somewhere else, and then erase the area on the screen and return to the calling routine. The beginning of every subroutine that requires the key and file number would be to call this subroutine before proceeding to get the rest of the information to be passed.

Passing the information back to the BASIC routine points up another problem. The error variable (E in the subroutines) is easy. Designate a fixed location for it to be used with all of the subroutines, and one statement in

BASIC, IF PEEK (xxxx) = 1 THEN ..., could check it without worrying about transferring it back. The records are a larger problem. If unpacking were left to the BASIC routines, you could set up at a specific location so that BASIC could read and write the results in a FOR/NEXT loop using PEEK and POKE, or you could give the address of the string to the machine language routine. A little experimentation in this area is in order.

The subroutines themselves can follow the same logic as that used in the BASIC versions. Understand, first, how each routine works in BASIC, then translate it statement by statement. Look for shortcuts that can be devised in the machine language version, as these will provide more speed. Also, look out for things that can more easily be done in BASIC. Instead of passing the record back and forth, for example, just program the key routines in machine language and return the locator to BASIC. Let BASIC load the record itself.

These are several suggestions on how to accomplish this task. What is really required to find out what the machine language is to do and what the BASIC is to do is to experiment on paper and on the computer with different approaches to the problem. The solution may well reflect your own abilities in each of the two languages as well as the computer's abilities in dealing with such a system.

There are several approaches and the logic of the programs in this book can be used to develop them. Extensive use of subroutines, if done correctly, makes for the easiest programming and debugging. It is this method that is used to form interpreters and some compilers. The main part of the subroutine is a series of branches to subroutines with little code between them. The concept is to set up the data, then call a subroutine, then set up the data for another subroutine. If everything is planned correctly, it becomes quite simple.

If you have a system that does not have BASIC or one in which the machine language is, for any practical purpose, impossible to access, then the question of which language to use for which function becomes irrelevant. The logic of the routines is the main message in this book, and, since the logic is independent of the language to a large extent, this book can be used as a guide to set up key-file systems in almost any language.

CHAPTER 23

WHEN THINGS GO WRONG

No matter how well planned and how well written it is, sophisticated software will probably have some bugs in it. Some will be obvious and easy to eliminate. Others will be more subtle and may not appear for some time. We will not discuss dealing with the obvious variety; they are usually just oversights or typographical errors. The more subtle problems are the ones that can really waste your time.

Debugging a system of interrelated programs that are using disk-based data files is very different from debugging the in-memory programs where all of the program statements and all of the data are in memory at the same time. For one thing, the programs are much more complicated. There are, however, several advantages to the disk-based programs and data. For example, entering an additional program statement or altering a program statement will not erase all of the data. It will only erase the variables that are being held in the computer memory. The bulk of the data is on disk and is not altered or erased. On most systems, any changes made to the program result in the computer's closing the files, but they can easily be reopened.

The major problems are with the key file and perhaps with the record file. These are all on the disk and can therefore not be printed as easily as a variable in the memory. Many commands in the so-called immediate mode can be used to control random-access files. OPEN, FIELD, LSET, RSET, GET, PUT, and CLOSE as well as the various packing and unpacking statements are usually legal immediate mode statements. These statements can be easily used to check the status of single blocks in the record and key files. The roadmap in the key file, for example, is in the variable RM$. If it is not in the memory because of some program changes, open the key file, field it, then get the first block. An immediate mode FOR/NEXT loop using the ASC and MID$ functions in a PRINT statement can then be used to show the contents of the roadmap. The following steps, in immediate mode, will display these contents of a 10-byte roadmap:

```
OPEN"R",1,"KEYFIL"
FIELD 1,255 AS KY$
GET1,1
FORI = 1TO10:PRINTASC(MID$(KY$,I,1));:NEXTI
```

For more ambitious work, you can write a small utility program to solve a particular problem. The program that is in memory is also on disk, so saving its form in memory is not that important. Clear out the memory with NEW and write a program that will open and field the file or files that are to be examined. You can then write the various routines to look at various blocks in the file or files, allow some manual corrections to the data, and resave the block that was corrected. Of course, it is wise to back up the data disk before running a utility program on it just in case there is a bug in the utility program. This limits possible loss to what you had when you started trying to correct the program. If the subroutine set is helpful in the utility program, any of the programs in the system that have the subroutine set may be loaded into memory. To get the subroutine set, just DELETE the lines below it. You may want to save the program initialization lines, also, so choose the lines for the DELETE statement carefully.

Other utility programs that do not access the data files may also be of some use. If you get into some of the habits that I have picked up, then there is one that will be invaluable. This utility decompresses a program and lists it. The habit I refer to is stacking several statements on one statement number using the colon (:). To put together this utility, first save a program in the ASCII format on the disk. The program to list it can first open this program file as an input file (sequential file). The LINE INPUT # statement will then read one statement at a time. Use a FOR/NEXT loop to examine the statement one character at a time. If it is not a colon, LPRINT the character, ending the LPRINT statement with a semicolon (;). If it is a colon, LPRINT a line feed, then print about five or six spaces and the colon, ending this LPRINT also with a semicolon. This program is in the appendix. The version there requires that the program first be saved in an ASCII file called COMPRO, for compressed program. After you save the program to be listed, load and run the decompressed listing program.

This program can be altered to give more help to you in debugging the programs. For example, you could use it to search out a certain character string and list only the statements in which this string appears. You could also alter it to store a cross-reference table for variables and/or line numbers from IF, GOTO and GOSUB statements. Another alteration could let it list a series of programs at once, if they are all saved in the ASCII format. With a little imagination and a small string array, you could also use it to list the main part of the text, replacing all GOSUB references to the subroutines with other statements that would make them easier to read. For example, have it look for all GOSUB statements and replace the line number with phrases like GET KEY, GET NEXT, etc. This way, reading the main program text will not require a list of the subroutines. It will require some kind of look-up tables so that the program can tell which phrase to print for which line number in the GOSUB statement. Don't forget to allow for printing a line number instead of a phrase for any GOSUBs that do not call one of the subroutines in the subroutine set.

All of these suggestions are only aids in the debugging process. There is no quick solution to debugging. It will not be easy to find some of the bugs no matter what utilities you have. The utilities make the process a little easier, but they will not find the bugs by themselves.

You should set up a separate diskette for storing your utility programs. You will need them for other programs systems you create. The first versions you write for these programs will also undergo many changes. If you have one diskette that contains only utility programs, then this is the only one that will need updating when you make an improvement on the utility program. It will also make them easier to find.

In addition to utility programs that help debug programs, there are some programs that help write the program. In computations that require a larger number of significant digits, you can write a program that will do the four basic functions on integers with up to 127 significant digits by using strings to contain the numbers and routines that simulate the way these functions are performed by hand. There are also programs you can write that will write parts of the text for you. The selectors are easy. First, you can save the skeleton program developed for selectors (in Chapter 18) in the ASCII format. The selector-writing program can then request the selector title and all of the selections and the programs they are to load. The selector-writing program can count the number of selections for you. Next, with all of this information stored in a string array, open the selector skeleton as an input file, then open an output file under the name of the new selector. LINE INPUT each of the lines in the selector skeleton, printing them to the output file (use a semicolon at the end of the PRINT# statement). When you've exhausted the program lines from the skeleton, form DATA statements with the entered information and use PRINT# to transfer these to the output file. CLOSE all files when this is done. The output file will then be an ASCII program containing all of the text required for that selector.

A little experimentation with generating programs like that and you will be able to generate the file maintenance programs and some of the report programs with generating programs. These are much more com- plicated than the selector, but you can generate them if the file maintenance and report programs are in standard forms. The parameter-driven I/O subroutines help in formatting the screen so that the position of everything can be entered as data in the generating program.

Remember that any program system that is complicated enough to be useful will always have bugs in it and you will always have to be looking for them. Even the subroutines and examples in this book could contain bugs that escaped my testing. You may find them and apply these utilities on them. Debugging requires patience and persistance. Utilities will only help in locating things that you think may help find errors. Realize the limits of the tools you are using, and you'll have an easier job.

WRAPPING IT UP

EDDIE GERMANO

CONCLUSION

The purpose of this book was not to make experts out of amateur programmers, but rather to give them a good background in more sophisticated disk use. The routines given in this text were of my own invention and may or may not resemble other routines written by other programmers. Programming in a computer language is much like writing prose. If you give two writers the same concept to describe, the two results will be very different. In the same way, if you give two programmers sophisticated enough programs to write, their results will vary greatly.

So the routines given here can be used as they are, or the logic of handling the key files can be improved and altered. I am sure that these routines are neither the most efficient nor the most effective. But that was not my intention. They do present some of the basics of key-file disk-access techniques, and it was my intention to explain these basics. With this information and some careful thought, most file-access problems can be solved.

To use the information presented in this book most effectively, combine the different concepts to meet different needs. Pay attention to the computer on which the programs are to be run. For example, some computers are not very good with large string arrays. They use a dynamic memory allocation system for storing these strings and will occasionally take a time out to rearrange the string area. In very large string arrays, this time out could be several minutes. During this time, even the break key is disabled. So you just have to wait. Obviously, for these machines, the alphabetical-array method is not the best one to use, particularly if the number of keys to be stored takes up a significant amount of memory. Use one of the other two methods instead. Also, be inventive. For example, take advantage of the fast access afforded by the hashing techniques where you can, but to get a sorted output from the file, write a routine for reading the key blocks into memory one at a time, and to order them use some sort of indirect sort which consists of a numeric array.

This indirect sort resembles the logic used in the roadmap of the tree-structured method. Instead of directly storing the key in the array, store in a numeric array a number or two to define its location on disk. The numeric array is to hold the alphabetical sequence of the keys. A double-subscripted array can be used with the first subscript corresponding to the element within the array and the other subscript being dimensioned to two.

For each element, the first value would then hold the block number, and the second would hold the key number within the block. To handle larger arrays with less memory, the numbers can be packed so that the integer value is the block number, and the decimal remainder, multiplied by 100, would be the number of the key on the block.

These are just a few of the many different ways that the information in this book can be combined to fit various applications. There are also methods that were not presented in full form, like the linked-record method. The program used to form the glossary is an example.

There are ways to use a random access-file with linked records instead of a key file. This, of course, depends upon the application. Insertion of a new record would involve a sequential search to find the position, as would a search for a record and deletion of a record. You could develop a pointer system that would give the positions of some of the keys to speed up the search somewhat. The linked records are best used to keep a file in order if there are no changes made to it or if the changes are minimal and the records are to always be requested in order.

The full tree-structured method was also not presented. The method is a bit high-powered for most microcomputer systems, but, once this version is understood, the full method can be implemented. You can build toward it by establishing a key file for the key file, in effect. In this extra key file, which could occupy blocks in the main key file, are blocks containing the first key and the block number of all of the blocks in the original key file. Extend this further and you can have blocks that index this level. Before everything gets too confused, I might mention that these blocks are given levels and that the level number of each block is stored in a given place on the block. Extended to the limit, these levels of blocks will end with a single block on the highest level. Instead of a roadmap, the key file needs only one pointer that indicates the block number of this *master* block. As keys are added, this block splits. When that happens, another level is added and the new master block has the first key on each of the new blocks that split.

The above explanation of a tree-structured method may seem confusing, but will become clearer after you read a little more about it. Then go back and reread it. Consider the example of a file that has 20 keys per block. Instead of leaving all of the possible blank space at the end of the block, leave one byte at the beginning. This byte will hold the block's level. Level zero is the lowest-level block and all keys on this block point to the records in the file. These blocks are the same as the ones used in the modified version presented in Section II. If there are, say, 25 of these blocks in the file, the next higher level will have two blocks. The first block on this level, after the one byte that contains the level (equal now to one), contains the first key of about half of the level-zero blocks. The pointer on these keys is not the record number. Instead, it is the block number in the key file that starts with the key. This block points to approximately the first half (approximately because the exact number depends upon how the block was split and what keys were added after the split) of the level-zero blocks in alphabetical order. The other block contains the rest of the blocks' first keys. There is also one level-two block that contains the level number two in the first byte, and the first key on each of the two level-one blocks, also in alphabetical order.

Figure C.1 shows this structure graphically. How a key is found in the method will clarify it a little more. The search starts at the highest-level block. The block number for this block is found where the roadmap was in the modified version—it is in the first physical block of the file. That block is loaded first. The key being searched will belong on one of the next lower-level blocks. In this example, the level-two block contains only two keys. The next block to load is the one that contains the highest key that is lower than the key to find. This introduces level one, where the same thing takes place again. You use the highest key on that block that is still lower than the key to find. The locator of that key will be the level-zero block. That block is then loaded and the search on that block will be the same as the search in the modified version, as that block is in the same format, except for the first byte declaring the level. The key, if it is there, contains the record number of the key.

To understand this method, reread it now. There is a simpler way to expand the number of records, and that is to invent another way to store the roadmap that will allow more blocks to be referenced. The full tree-structured method is a little faster. In it, there are only three blocks loaded in locating a key in a file that contains 25 possible locations (level-zero blocks). In the modified version, this would require loading up to five blocks. The number of blocks to load in search of a particular key equals

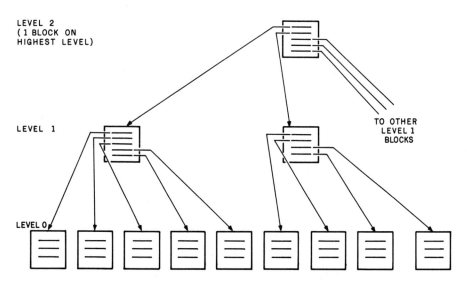

Figure C.1: *Portion of a fully tree-structured file. Each block in level zero contains keys with corresponding record numbers. On the higher levels, each block contains the first key value of every block it points to at the next lower level. At levels higher than zero, the pointers point to blocks in the key file. Only at level zero do the pointers indicate records.*

the number of levels in the full tree-structured method. The modified one depends upon the binary search method.

The manuals that accompany the disk system explain the random-access files well. Explaining the ways that the statements that random-access files access is really not enough to fully exploit the disks. The techniques given in this book will prove to be only the beginning of what you can do with the disks. Until more material is made available, you have in your favor your imagination and, if you are lucky, a lot of patience. With the material in this book and these two traits, effectively programming the disk should be far less a problem for you than it was when you started reading. I will consider this book a success if some of the under-programmed computers that are now being used become at least a little less underprogrammed.

APPENDIX A: POWERS OF TWO

1	2	11	2,048
2	4	12	4,096
3	8	13	8,192
4	16	14	16,384
5	32	15	32,768
6	64	16	65,536
7	128	17	131,072
8	256	18	262,144
9	512	19	524,288
10	1,024	20	1,048,576

APPENDIX B: PROGRAM USED TO CREATE GLOSSARY

```
10 CLEAR 5000
20 DIMCA(15)
30 OPEN"R",1,"GLOSSARY"
40 FIELD 1,255ASB$
50 OPEN"R",2,"WORDS:1"
60 FIELD 2,255ASKY$
65 GET2,1:RM$=KY$
70 RESTORE
80 FORI=1TO15
90 READCA(I)
100 NEXTI
110 DATA 50,0,5,1,188,1501,22,0,20,11,6,144,111,110,56
199 REM ** 200-999 CONTROL SECTION **
200 CLS
210 PRINT"          GLOSSARY ACCESS"
220 PRINT
230 PRINT"   1. ENTER A WORD"
```

```
240 PRINT"    2. ENTER A DEFINITION"
250 PRINT"    3. DISPLAY A WORD WITH DEFINITION"
260 PRINT"    4. DELETE A WORD AND ITS DEFINITION"
270 PRINT"    5. PRINT GLOSSARY"
280 PRINT
290 INPUT"  ENTER NUMBER OF SELECTION OR 0 TO END";N
300 IFN>=0ANDN<6THEN330
310 PRINT"ERROR - ENTER NUMBER FROM THE LIST"
320 GOTO290
330 ONN+1GOTO340,1000,1500,2000,2500,3000
340 CLOSE
350 STOP
999 REM ** 1000 - 1499 ENTER A WORD **
1000 CLS
1010 PRINT"    --- ENTER WORDS ---
1020 INPUT"ENTER WORD OR END";K$
1030 IFK$="END"THEN200
1040 IFLEN(K$)<19THEN1070
1050 PRINT"ERROR - MAXIMUM WORD LENGTH IS 18 CHARACTERS"
1060 GOTO1020
1070 R$=K$+STRING$(50,32)
1080 MID$(R$,49,2)=MKI$(0)
1090 GOSUB7000
1100 IFE=0THEN1020
1110 PRINT"ERROR -- KEY ALREADY IN FILE"
1120 GOTO1020
1499 REM ** 1500 - 1999 ENTER A DEFINITION **
1500 CLS
1510 PRINT"    --- ENTER DEFINITIONS ---"
1520 INPUT"ENTER WORD TO DEFINE, OR END";K$
1525 IFK$="END"THEN200
1530 GOSUB7500
1540 IFE=0THEN1570
1550 PRINT"ERROR -- KEY NOT FOUND"
1560 GOTO1520
1570 PRINT"ENTER DEFINITION, 48 CHARACTERS PER LINE"
1580 PRINT"AFTER THE LAST LINE, ENTER END"
1590 PRINT"POSITION 48 :";TAB(50);"!"
1595 AR=N
1590 PRINT"POSITION 48 :";TAB(50);"!"
1595 AR=N
1600 INPUTR9$
1605 IFR9$="END"THEN1520
1610 IFLEN(R9$)<=48THEN1640
1620 PRINT"--- ERROR - TOO LONG.  REENTER THAT LINE ---"
1630 GOTO1600
1640 GOSUB6250
1650 BR=FR
1660 N=AR
1670 GOSUB6150
1680 MID$(R$,49,2)=MKI$(BR)
1690 GOSUB6190
1700 R9$=R9$+STRING$(50,32)
1710 MID$(R9$,49,2)=MKI$(0)
1720 R$=R9$
1725 N=BR
1730 GOSUB6190
1740 AR=BR
1750 GOTO1600
1999 REM ** 2000 - 2499 DISPLAY A WORD AND DEFINITION **
2000 CLS
2010 PRINT"    --- DISPLAY WORD AND DEFINITION ---"
2020 INPUT"ENTER WORD OR END";K$
2030 IFK$="END"THEN200
2040 GOSUB7500
2050 IFE=0THEN2080
2060 PRINT"ERROR - WORD NOT IN FILE"
2070 GOTO2020
2080 IF"END    "=LEFT$(R$,6)THEN2020
2090 PRINTLEFT$(R$,48)
2100 N=CVI(MID$(R$,49,2))
2105 IFN=0THEN2020
```

```
2110 GOSUB6150
2120 GOTO2080
2499 REM ** 2500 - 2999 DELETE A WORD AND ITS DEFINITION **
2500 CLS
2510 PRINT"  --- DELETE A WORD AND DEFINITION ---"
2520 INPUT"WORD TO DELETE";K$
2530 GOSUB7500
2540 IFE=0THEN2570
2550 PRINT"ERROR - WORD NOT IN FILE"
2560 GOTO2520
2570 AR=CVI(MID$(R$,49,2))
2580 GOSUB8500
2590 IFAR=0THEN200
2600 N=AR
2610 GOSUB6150
2620 AR=CVI(MID$(R$,49,2))
2630 FR=AR
2640 GOSUB8610
2650 GOTO2590
2999 REM ** 3000 - 3499 PRINT GLOSSARY **
3000 CLS
3010 PRINT"       --- PRINT GLOSSARY ---"
3020 INPUT"SET UP PRINTER, THEN PRESS EXEC";N
3030 L9=55:P9=0
3040 K$=" "
3050 GOSUB8000
3060 IFE<>0THEN200
3062 L$=LEFT$(R$,48)
3064 IFP9=0THEN3080
3066 IFL9>51THENL9=L9+2:LPRINT" ":LPRINT" "
3068 GOTO3080
3070 L$="        "+LEFT$(R$,48)
3080 GOSUB3300
3090 AR=CVI(MID$(R$,49,2))
3100 IFAR=0THEN3050
3110 N=AR
3120 GOSUB6150
3130 GOTO3070
3300 L9=L9+2
3310 IFL9<55THEN3400
3320 P9=P9+1
3330 IFP9=1THEN3360
3340 FORL8=L9T065
3350 LPRINT" ":NEXTL8
3360 LPRINT"P SWANSON"
3370 LPRINT"MICROCOMPUTER DISK TECHNIQUES                    GLOSSARY -";P9
3380 LPRINT" ":LPRINT" "
3390 L9=4
3400 LPRINT" ":LPRINTL$
3410 RETURN
6000 STOP
6010 RETURN
6090 RETURN
6149 REM -- 6150-6180 GET RECORD BY NUMBER --
6150 B=INT((N-1)/CA(3)):R=N-B*CA(3)
6155 B=B+CA(4)
6160 GET 1,B
6170 R$=MID$(B$,CA(1)*(R-1)+1,CA(1))
6180 RETURN
6189 REM -- 6190-6240 PUT RECORD BY NUMBER --
6190 R1$=R$
6200 GOSUB 6150
6210 B1$=B$
6220 MID$(B1$,CA(1)*(R-1)+1,CA(1))=R1$
6230 LSET B$=B1$
6235 PUT1,B
6240 RETURN
6249 REM -- 6250-6305 GET NEXT AVAILABLE RECORD NUMBER --
6250 GET1,1:FB=0
6252 FB=FB+1:IFFB>CA(5)THEN6268
6254 IFMID$(B$,FB,1)=CHR$(255)THEN6252
6256 FA=ASC(MID$(B$,FB,1)):FR=FB*8-8:FD=0
```

```
6258 FD=FD+1:FC=INT(2[(8-FD)+.5):FA=FA-FC:IFFA>=0THEN6258
6260 FR=FR+FD:FA=ASC(MID$(B$,FB,1))+FC
6262 B1$=B$:MID$(B1$,FB,1)=CHR$(FA)
6264 LSET B$=B1$:PUT1,1
6266 RETURN
6268 FR=CA(6):E=0:RETURN
6309 REM -- 6310-6510 SEARCH FOR KEY --
6310 K1$=STRING$(CA(7),32)
6320 K$=K$+K1$:KN=0
6330 L1=0:L2=CA(15):L4=0
6340 L3=INT((L1+L2)/2+.5)
6350 IF MID$(RM$,L3,1)=CHR$(255)THEN6540
6360 KB=ASC(MID$(RM$,L3,1))
6370 GET2,KB+1
6380 IFMID$(KY$,1,CA(9))>MID$(K$,1,CA(9))THEN6540
6390 KN=0
6400 KN=KN+1:IFKN=CA(10)THEN6440
6410 IFMID$(K$,1,CA(9))=MID$(KY$,CA(7)*(KN-1)+1,CA(9))THEN6580
6415 IFMID$(KY$,CA(7)*(KN-1)+1,CA(9))=STRING$(CA(9),255)THEN6440
6420 IFMID$(K$,1,CA(9))<MID$(KY$,CA(7)*(KN-1)+1,CA(9))THEN6610
6430 GOTO 6400
6440 L1=L3
6450 L4=L4+1
6460 IFL4<CA(11)THEN6340
6470 E=1
6480 L3=L3+1
6490 KB=ASC(MID$(RM$,L3,1))
6500 K1$=STRING$(CA(7),255):IFKB=255THENRETURN
6510 GET 2,KB+1
6520 K1$=LEFT$(KY$,CA(7))
6530 RETURN
6540 L2=L3
6550 L4=L4+1
6560 IFL4<CA(11)THEN6340
6565 E=1:GOTO6490
6580 E=0
6590 K1$=MID$(KY$,CA(7)*(KN-1)+1,CA(7))
6600 RETURN
6610 E=1
6620 GOTO6590
6999 REM -- 7000-7499 PUT NEW RECORD AND KEY --
7000 GOSUB6310
7010 IFE=2THENRETURN
7020 IFE=1THEN7040
7030 E=1:RETURN
7040 GOSUB6250
7045 KZ$=KY$
7050 IFKB=255THEN7180
7060 IFLEFT$(K$,CA(7))<LEFT$(KY$,CA(7))THENKN=1
7070 FORI=CA(10)TOKN+1STEP-1:MID$(KZ$,CA(7)*(I-1)+1,CA(7))=MID$(KZ$,CA(7)
*(I-2)+1,CA(7))
7072 NEXTI
7074 MID$(KZ$,CA(7)*(KN-1)+1,CA(7))=MID$(K$,1,CA(9))+MKI$(FR)
7080 LSET KY$=KZ$
7090 PUT2,KB+1
7100 GOSUB6010
7110 N=FR:GOSUB6190
7120 E=0
7130 IFMID$(KY$,(CA(10)-1)*CA(7)+1,CA(7))=STRING$(CA(7),255)THENRETURN
7140 L4=0:FORI=1TO250:IFASC(MID$(RM$,I,1))=255THEN7144
7142 IFASC(MID$(RM$,I,1))>L4THEN L4=ASC(MID$(RM$,I,1))
7144 NEXTI
7150 FORI=CA(15)TOKB+1 STEP-1
7152 MID$(RM$,I+1,1)=MID$(RM$,I,1)
7154 NEXTI
7156 MID$(RM$,KB+1,1)=MKI$(L4+1)
7158 KZ$=KY$:KX$=MID$(KY$,CA(13),CA(12))+STRING$(CA(14),255)
7160 MID$(KZ$,CA(13),CA(12))=STRING$(CA(12),255)
7162 LSET KY$=KZ$:PUT2,KB+1
7164 LSET KY$=KX$:PUT2,L4+2
7166 LSET KY$=RM$:PUT2,1
7170 E=0:RETURN
```

```
7180 L4=0
7182 L4=L4+1:IFL4<=250THEN7184:ELSE STOP
7184 IFASC(MID$(RM$,L4+1,1))<255THEN7182
7186 KB=ASC(MID$(RM$,L4,1)):GET2,KB+1
7188 KN=0
7190 KN=KN+1:IFMID$(KY$,CA(7)*(KN-1)+1,CA(7))<STRING$(CA(7),255)THEN7190
7192 GOTO7050
7499 REM -- 7500-7999 GET RECORD --
7500 GOSUB6310
7510 IFE=0THEN7540
7520 E=1
7530 RETURN
7540 N=CVI(MID$(K1$,CA(7)-1,2))
7550 GOSUB6150
7560 GOSUB6090
7570 E=0
7580 RETURN
7999 REM -- 8000-8499 GET NEXT --
8000 K$=K$+STRING$(CA(9),32):E=ASC(MID$(K$,CA(9),1))+1
8010 MID$(K$,CA(9),1)=MKI$(E)
8020 GOSUB6310
8030 IF E=0THEN7540
8040 IF MID$(K1$,1,CA(9))<>STRING$(CA(9),255)THEN8060
8050 E=1:RETURN
8060 K$=K1$:E=0:GOTO7540
8499 REM -- 8500-8999 DELETE KEY AND RECORD --
8500 GOSUB6310
8510 IFE=0THEN8540
8520 E=1
8530 RETURN
8540 KZ$=KY$:GOSUB8600
8550 FORI=KN TO CA(10)-1
8555 MID$(KZ$,CA(7)*(I-1)+1,CA(7))=MID$(KZ$,CA(7)*I+1,CA(7))
8557 NEXTI
8560 LSET KY$=KZ$
8570 PUT2,KB+1
8580 E=0
8590 RETURN
8600 FR=CVI(MID$(K1$,CA(9)+1,2))
8610 FB=INT((FR-1)/8):FA=FR-FB*8
8620 GET1,1:B1$=B$:FB=FB+1
8630 FC=ASC(MID$(B1$,FB,1))
8640 FC=FC-INT(2[(8-FA)+.5)
8650 MID$(B1$,FB,1)=CHR$(FC)
8660 LSET B$=B1$:PUT1,1
8670 RETURN
8999 REM -- 9000-9499 RESAVE RECORD --
9000 GOSUB6310
9010 IFE=0THEN9040
9020 E=1
9030 RETURN
9040 N=CVI(MID$(K1$,CA(9)+1,2))
9050 GOSUB6010
9060 GOSUB6190
9070 E=0
9080 RETURN
```

APPENDIX C: DECOMPRESSED LISTING PROGRAM

```
10 CLEAR1000
20 NP$="COMPRO"
30 OPEN"I",1,NP$
40 AA=0
50 IFAA<>0THENSTOP
60 LINEINPUT#1,A$
70 AA=EOF(1)
80 LL=LEN(A$)
90 FORI=1TOLL
100 IFMID$(A$,I,1)=":"THENLPRINT" ":LPRINT"        ";
110 LPRINTMID$(A$,I,1);
120 NEXTI
130 LPRINT" "
140 GOTO50
```

APPENDIX D: HEXADECIMAL TO ASCII CONVERSION

		High order									
Low ord.	2		3		4		5		6		7
0	32	48	0	64	@	80	P	96	@	112	p
1	33	! 49	1	65	A	81	Q	97	a	113	q
2	34	'' 50	2	66	B	82	R	98	b	114	r
3	35	# 51	3	67	C	83	S	99	c	115	s
4	36	$ 52	4	68	D	84	T	100	d	116	t
5	37	% 53	5	69	E	85	U	101	e	117	u
6	38	& 54	6	70	F	86	V	102	f	118	v
7	39	' 55	7	71	G	87	W	103	g	119	w
8	40	(56	8	72	H	88	X	104	h	120	x
9	41	) 57	9	73	I	89	Y	105	i	121	y
A	42	* 58	:	74	J	90	Z	106	j	122	z
B	43	+ 59	;	75	K	91	[	107	k	123	{
C	44	, 60	<	76	L	92	\	108	l	124	|
D	45	– 61	=	77	M	93	]	109	m	125	}
E	46	. 62	>	78	N	94	^	110	n	126	~
F	47	/ 63	?	79	O	95	_	111	o	127	

Each box in the above table contains the decimal equivalent and the character that corresponds to the hexadecimal numbers indicated. For example, hexadecimal 41 is equivalent to the letter A and the decimal equivalent of hexadecimal 41 and the character A is 65. A lowercase A is hexadecimal 61, which is decimal 97.

APPENDIX E: APPLE SUPPLEMENT

INTRODUCTION

All of the examples in the main text of this book were written on a Radio Shack TRS-80 computer. So, what if you happen to have an Apple computer? Well, first of all, you should be aware of the several differences between the two systems, particularly in the parts of the languages that pertain to string manipulation and disk access. For example, the sections on multiple record blocks do not apply because the Apple does most of this work for you. Also, using MID$ on the left side of the equal sign will not work on the Apple. The sections in this appendix correspond to chapters in the main text, so Apple users may easily refer to the adapted listings that are presented here.

Many of the listings in this appendix will have some useful notes pertaining to the differences between the two systems. Remember that the listings in this supplement are translations of the TRS-80 listings and most of them could be made much more efficient by taking advantage of some of the features of the Apple computer. My advice is to at first use the listings the way they are now. As much as is possible, the line numbers in the Apple listings agree with the line numbers in the TRS-80 listings. This makes the text easier to follow for Apple computer users. Later, after studying the logic of the programs, modify the listings as you see fit. After the required modifications, the line numbers will not agree very closely. For this reason, I have not included more refined listings in this book.

RANDOM-ACCESS FILES

Initialization of the files on the Apple computer differs greatly from that on the Radio Shack system. The Apple computer requires the record length in the OPEN statement. In the listing for initialization of the file in this supplement, the record length is 65. Reading ahead in the main text shows that the file in the first program will have a 63-byte record length. Adding one for the RETURN character will give 64, which is the minimum length for the records. You can make the record length even longer to allow for future expansion, but remember that this practice must take into account the extra space this will require on disk. It doesn't matter on a 100-record file that has a record length this short, but it will matter on larger applications.

```
10  D$=CHR$(4):REM.CONTROL.D
20  PRINTD$;"OPEN NAMES,L65"
30  PRINTD$;"WRITE NAMES,R0"
40  PRINT0
50  PRINTD$
60  B$=CHR$(32):REM.PUT.ONE.SPACE.IN.B$
70  FORI=1TO6
80  B$=B$+B$
90  NEXTI
100   REM  B$ HAS 64 SPACES
110  FORI=1TO100
120  PRINTD$;"WRITE NAMES,R";I
130  PRINTB$
140  PRINTD$
150  NEXTI
160  PRINTD$;"CLOSE"
170  END
```

Listing E.1

The second listing on the TRS-80 uses a function that is not available on the Apple. This function, STRING$, sets a string variable to a given number of bytes equal to the same ASCII value. For example, STRING$(20,32) in line 6020 is equal to a string of 20 spaces (the ASCII value for a space is 32). To compensate, store the maximum number of spaces that you will require in a string. Using the string variable SP$, the following statements, located at the beginning of the program, will set up 255 spaces for this use:

```
SP$ = CHR$(32)
FOR I = 1 TO 254
SP$ = SP$ + CHR$(32)
NEXT I
```

Use line numbers for those statements that are appropriate for your program. There are other ways to do this that are quicker to run, and you will see some of these ways at the beginning of the sample listings in this supplement.

Line 6020 can now use SP$ to replace the STRING$ function:

```
6020 B2$ = LEFT$(SP$,20)
```

Another required function, the MID$ function, is available on the Apple, on the right side of the equal sign. The Radio Shack listing uses this function on the left side to insert some string characters into the middle of an existing string. *Concatenation*, or linking together in a series, may be used on the Apple providing that every field is given the exact length called for in the data file layout. Each field is padded with spaces, then truncated at the proper length by the LEFT$ function. This all occurs in the packing subroutine in lines 6010 through 6080. The unpacking routine requires no changes.

```
6000 END
6010 B2$=LEFT$(SP$,20)
6025 N$=N$+B2$
6030 N$=LEFT$(N$,20)
6035 A$=A$+B2$
6040 A$=LEFT$(A$,20)
6045 C$=C$+B2$
6050 C$=LEFT$(C$,16)
6055 S$=S$+"    "
6060 S$=LEFT$(S$,2)
6065 Z$=Z$+"        "
6070 Z$=LEFT$(Z$,5)
6075 B$=N$+A$+C$+S$+Z$
6080 RETURN
6090 B$=B$+LEFT$(SP$,64)
6095 N$=LEFT$(B$,20)
6100 A$=MID$(B$,21,20)
6110 C$=MID$(B$,41,16)
6120 S$=MID$(B$,57,2)
6130 Z$=MID$(B$,59,5)
6140 RETURN
```

Listing E.2

The next listing needs few changes. The CLEAR 100 statement is not required and PRINT statements must be altered to compensate for the smaller screen width. The TRS-80 has a screen that is 64 characters wide, but the Apple has only 40 characters. The PRINT statement at line 30 will fit on the Apple screen as it is in the Radio Shack listing, but will probably look better on the Apple if you split it into two lines.

```
10 SP$="  "
12 FORI=1TO63
14 SP$=SP$+"  "
16 NEXTI
18 D$=CHR$(4)
20 PRINTD$;"OPEN NAMES,L65"
22 PRINTD$;"READ NAMES,RO"
30 INPUTM
32 PRINTD$
40 HOME
50 INPUT"ENTER 1 TO WRITE OR 2 TO READ? ";N
60 IFN=1THEN100
70 IFN=2THEN300
72 IFN<>0THEN80
```

```
74 PRINTD$;"CLOSE"
76 END
80 PRINT"ERROR - PLEASE ENTER 1 OR 2"
90 GOTO50
100 HOME
110 PRINT"WRITE A NEW RECORD TO THE FILE"
120 INPUT"ENTER RECORD NO. (0 TO 100)? ";N
130 IFN>=1THEN160
140 PRINT"ERROR - RECORD NO OUT OF RANGE"
150 GOTO120
160 IFN>100THEN140
170 INPUT"NAME? ";N$
180 INPUT"ADDRESS? ";A$
190 INPUT"CITY? ";C$
200 INPUT"STATE? ";S$
210 INPUT"ZIP CODE? ";Z$
220 GOSUB6010
230 PRINTD$;"WRITE NAMES,R";N
232 PRINTB$
234 PRINTD$
240 GOTO40
300 HOME
310 PRINT"READ A RECORD FROM FILE"
320 INPUT"ENTER RECORD NUMBER";N
330 IFN>=1THEN360
340 PRINT"ERROR - RECORD NO OUT OF RANGE"
350 GOTO320
360 IFN>100THEN340
370 PRINTD$;"READ NAMES,R";N
372 INPUTB$
374 PRINTD$
380 GOSUB6090
390 PRINT"NAME : ";N$
400 PRINT"ADDRESS : ";A$
410 PRINT"CITY : ";C$
420 PRINT"STATE : ";S$
430 PRINT"ZIP CODE : ";Z$
440 GOTO50
6000 END
6010 B2$=LEFT$(SP$,20)
6025 N$=N$+B2$
6030 N$=LEFT$(N$,20)
6035 A$=A$+B2$
6040 A$=LEFT$(A$,20)
6045 C$=C$+B2$
6050 C$=LEFT$(C$,16)
6055 S$=S$+"  "
6060 S$=LEFT$(S$,2)
6065 Z$=Z$+"     "
6070 Z$=LEFT$(Z$,5)
6075 B$=N$+A$+C$+S$+Z$
6080 RETURN
6090 B$=B$+LEFT$(SP$,64)
6095 N$=LEFT$(B$,20)
6100 A$=MID$(B$,21,20)
6110 C$=MID$(B$,41,16)
6120 S$=MID$(B$,57,2)
6130 Z$=MID$(B$,59,5)
6140 RETURN
```

Listing E.3

```
10 DIMA$(5)
20 PRINT"ENTER THE FIVE LETTERS"
30 PRINT"  ONE AT A TIME"
40 FORI=1TO5
50 PRINT"ENTER LETTER NO.";I;
```

```
60  INPUTA$(I)
70  NEXTI
80  FORI=1TO4
90  FORJ=2TO6-I
100  IFA$(J)>=A$(J-1)THEN140
110  A$=A$(J)
120  A$(J)=A$(J-1)
130  A$(J-1)=A$
140  NEXTJ
150  NEXTI
160  FORI=1TO5
170  PRINTI;"  ";A$(I)
180  NEXTI
190  END
```

Listing E.4

There is a note in Chapter 4 that requires the use of the INKEY$ function. This can be replaced with an INPUT statement, as the text suggests, or with the GET statement. Use an alphanumeric variable with the INPUT statement, because a numeric will cause an error if the operator uses just the RETURN key.

All of the sections are assembled for the final listing in this chapter. There are a few other minor changes, like the PR#2 and PR#0 statements instead of the use of LPRINT. The system I used to create the examples has the printer plugged into slot number two. You will have to replace the PR#2 statements to reference the slot where your printer is connected. If you have no printer, simply replace the PR#2 statements with PR#0 statements and put the suggested PRINT and GET statements in place at lines 612 and 614.

The text also suggests adding the counter SW to the sort sequence. These statements can be added to the Apple version as they are in the text.

```
10  SP$="  "
12  FORI=1TO63
14  SP$=SP$+"  "
16  NEXTI
18  D$=CHR$(4)
20  PRINTD$;"OPEN NAMES,L65"
22  PRINTD$;"READ NAMES,R0"
30  INPUTM
32  PRINTD$
40  HOME
50  PRINT"ENTER 1 TO WRITE, 2 TO READ,"
52  INPUT"3 TO PRINT OR 4 TO SORT? ";N
54  IFN<>0THEN60
56  PRINTD$;"CLOSE"
58  END
60  IFN<1THEN80
62  IFN>4THEN80
70  ONNGOTO100,300,500,700
72  IFN<>0THEN80
74  PRINTD$;"CLOSE"
76  END
80  PRINT"ERROR - ENTER 1, 2, 3 OR 4"
90  GOTO40
100  HOME
```

```
110 PRINT"WRITE A NEW RECORD TO THE FILE"
120 INPUT"ENTER RECORD NO. (O TO 100)? ";N
130 IFN>=1THEN160
140 PRINT"ERROR - RECORD NO OUT OF RANGE"
150 GOTO120
160 IFN>100THEN140
170 INPUT"NAME? ";N$
180 INPUT"ADDRESS? ";A$
190 INPUT"CITY? ";C$
200 INPUT"STATE? ";S$
210 INPUT"ZIP CODE? ";Z$
220 GOSUB6010
230 PRINTD$;"WRITE NAMES,R";N
232 PRINTB$
234 PRINTD$
240 GOTO40
300 HOME
310 PRINT"READ A RECORD FROM FILE"
320 INPUT"ENTER RECORD NUMBER? ";N
330 IFN>=1THEN360
340 PRINT"ERROR - RECORD NO OUT OF RANGE"
350 GOTO320
360 IFN>100THEN340
370 PRINTD$;"READ NAMES,R";N
372 INPUTB$
374 PRINTD$
380 GOSUB6090
390 PRINT"NAME : ";N$
409 PRINT"ADDRESS : ";A$
410 PRINT"CITY : ";C$
420 PRINT"STATE : ";S$
430 PRINT"ZIP CODE : ";Z$
440 GOTO50
500 INPUT"START AT RECORD NO.? ";N
510 INPUT"END AT RECORD NO.? ";N1
520 IFN<1THEN640
530 IFN1<NTHEN640
540 IFN1>100THEN640
550 FORI=1TON1
560 PRINTD$;"READ NAMES,R";I
562 INPUTB$
564 PRINTD$
570 GOSUB6090
575 IFLEFT$(B$,1)=" "THEN620
580 PRINTD$;"PR#2"
582 PRINTI;"   ";N$
590 PRINTA$
600 PRINTC$;", ";S$;"   ";Z$
610 PRINT
612 PRINTD$;"PR#0"
620 NEXTI
630 GOTO40
640 PRINT"ERROR - ENTER REC. NOS. CORRECTLY"
650 GOTO500
700 PRINT"SORTING THE FILE"
710 FORI=1TO99
715 N=1
720 PRINTD$;"READ NAMES,R";N
722 INPUTB1$
724 PRINTD$
728 IFB1$=""THENB1$=LEFT$(SP$,64)
730 SW=0
740 FORJ=1TO101-I
742 PRINTD$;"READ NAMES,R";J
744 INPUTB$
746 IFB$=""THENB$=LEFT$(SP$,64)
750 PRINTD$
752 IFLEFT$(B$,1)=" "THEN800
754 IFLEFT$(B1$,1)=" "THEN770
760 IFB$>=B1$THEN800
770 PRINTD$;"WRITE NAMES,R";J-1
772 PRINTB$
```

```
774 PRINTD$
780 B$=B1$
790 PRINTD$;"WRITE NAMES,R";J
792 PRINTB$
794 PRINTD$
796 SW=SW+1
800 B1$=B$
810 NEXTJ
815 IFSW=0THENI=99
820 NEXTI
830 GOTO40
6000 END
6010 B2$=LEFT$(SP$,20)
6025 N$=N$+B2$
6030 N$=LEFT$(N$,20)
6035 A$=A$+B2$
6040 A$=LEFT$(A$,20)
6045 C$=C$+B2$
6050 C$=LEFT$(C$,16)
6055 S$=S$+"   "
6060 S$=LEFT$(S$,2)
6065 Z$=Z$+"      "
6070 Z$=LEFT$(Z$,5)
6075 B$=N$+A$+C$+S$+Z$
6080 RETURN
6090 B$=B$+LEFT$(SP$,64)
6095 N$=LEFT$(B$,20)
6100 A$=MID$(B$,21,20)
6110 C$=MID$(B$,41,16)
6120 S$=MID$(B$,57,2)
6130 Z$=MID$(B$,59,5)
6140 RETURN
```

Listing E.5

THE BINARY SEARCH

There are a few differences in the added lines in the first of the two listings from Chapter 5. Because of the smaller screen width of 40 characters instead of the 64 characters on the TRS-80, the PRINT and INPUT statements have been broken down further. These are all around line 50. The new search routine contains, in the TRS-80 listing, a STRING$ statement using the ASCII code 255. Since Apple doesn't have STRING$ and the string SP$ cannot be used (it contains only spaces), a routine has been added starting at line 1010 to fill B$ with ASCII code 255s. This routine is called at line 930. Line 920 is also different. It contains the equivalent of the TRS-80 GET statement.

```
10 SP$=" "
12 FORI=1TO63
14 SP$=SP$+" "
16 NEXTI
18 D$=CHR$(4)
20 PRINTD$;"OPEN NAMES,L65"
22 PRINTD$;"READ NAMES,R0"
30 INPUTM
32 PRINTD$
40 HOME
50 PRINT"ENTER 1 TO WRITE, 2 TO READ,"
```

```
52 PRINT"3 TO PRINT, 4 TO SORT,"
53 INPUT"OR 5 TO SEARCH? ";N
54 IFN<>OTHEN60
56 PRINTD$;"CLOSE"
58 END
60 IFN<1THEN80
62 IFN>5THEN80
70 ONNGOTO100,300,500,700,900
72 IFN<>OTHEN80
74 PRINTD$;"CLOSE"
76 END
80 PRINT"ERROR - ENTER 1, 2, 3 OR 4"
90 GOTO40
100 HOME
110 PRINT"WRITE A NEW RECORD TO THE FILE"
120 INPUT"ENTER RECORD NO. (0 TO 100)? ";N
130 IFN>=1THEN160
140 PRINT"ERROR - RECORD NO OUT OF RANGE"
150 GOTO120
160 IFN>100THEN140
170 INPUT"NAME? ";N$
180 INPUT"ADDRESS? ";A$
190 INPUT"CITY? ";C$
200 INPUT"STATE? ";S$
210 INPUT"ZIP CODE? ";Z$
220 GOSUB6010
230 PRINTD$;"WRITE NAMES,R";N
232 PRINTB$
234 PRINTD$
240 GOTO40
300 HOME
310 PRINT"READ A RECORD FROM FILE"
320 INPUT"ENTER RECORD NUMBER? ";N
330 IFN>=1THEN360
340 PRINT"ERROR - RECORD NO OUT OF RANGE"
350 GOTO320
360 IFN>100THEN340
370 PRINTD$;"READ NAMES,R";N
372 INPUTB$
374 PRINTD$
380 GOSUB6090
390 PRINT"NAME : ";N$
400 PRINT"ADDRESS : ";A$
410 PRINT"CITY : ";C$
420 PRINT"STATE : ";S$
430 PRINT"ZIP CODE : ";Z$
440 GOTO50
500 INPUT"START AT RECORD NO.? ";N
510 INPUT"END AT RECORD NO.? ";N1
520 IFN<1THEN640
530 IFN1<NTHEN640
540 IFN1>100THEN640
550 FORI=1TON1
560 PRINTD$;"READ NAMES,R";I
562 INPUTB$
564 PRINTD$
570 GOSUB6090
575 IFLEFT$(B$,1)=" "THEN620
580 PRINTD$;"PR#2"
582 PRINTI;"   ";N$
590 PRINTA$
600 PRINTC$;", ";S$;"   ";Z$
610 PRINT
612 PRINTD$;"PR#0"
620 NEXTI
630 GOTO40
640 PRINT"ERROR - ENTER REC. NOS. CORRECTLY"
650 GOTO500
700 PRINT"SORTING THE FILE"
710 FORI=1TO99
715 N=1
720 PRINTD$;"READ NAMES,R";N
```

```
722  INPUTB1$
724  PRINTD$
728  IFB1$=""THENB1$=LEFT$(SP$,64)
730  SW=0
740  FORJ=1TO101-I
742  PRINTD$;"READ NAMES,R";J
744  INPUTB$
746  IFB$=""THENB$=LEFT$(SP$,64)
750  PRINTD$
752  IFLEFT$(B$,1)=" "THEN800
754  IFLEFT$(B1$,1)=" "THEN770
760  IFB$>=B1$THEN800
770  PRINTD$;"WRITE NAMES,R";J-1
772  PRINTB$
774  PRINTD$
780  B$=B1$
790  PRINTD$;"WRITE NAMES,R";J
792  PRINTB$
794  PRINTD$
796  SW=SW+1
800  B1$=B$
810  NEXTJ
815  IFSW=0THENI=99
820  NEXTI
830  GOTO40
900  INPUT"ENTER NAME TO SEARCH? ";N1$
910  L1=0:L2=101:L4=0:L5=LEN(N1$)
920  L3=INT((L1+L2)/2+.5)
922  PRINTD$;"READ NAMES,R";L3
924  INPUTB$
926  PRINTD$
930  IFB$=""THEN1010
940  IFLEFT$(B$,L5)>N1$THENL2=L3
950  IFLEFT$(B$,L5)<N1$THENL1=L3
960  IFLEFT$(B$,L5)=N1$THEN380
970  L4=L4+1
980  IFL4<7THEN920
990  PRINT"NAME NOT FOUND - IT IS NEAR RECORD NO.";L3
1000 GOTO50
1010 B$=CHR$(255)
1015 IFL5<=1THEN940
1020 FORI=1TOL5-1
1030 B$=B$+CHR$(255)
1040 NEXTI
1050 GOTO940
6000 END
6010 B2$=LEFT$(SP$,20)
6025 N$=N$+B2$
6030 N$=LEFT$(N$,20)
6035 A$=A$+B2$
6040 A$=LEFT$(A$,20)
6045 C$=C$+B2$
6050 C$=LEFT$(C$,16)
6055 S$=S$+"  "
6060 S$=LEFT$(S$,2)
6065 Z$=Z$+"     "
6070 Z$=LEFT$(Z$,5)
6075 B$=N$+A$+C$+S$+Z$
6080 RETURN
6090 B$=B$+LEFT$(SP$,64)
6095 N$=LEFT$(B$,20)
6100 A$=MID$(B$,21,20)
6110 C$=MID$(B$,41,16)
6120 S$=MID$(B$,57,2)
6130 Z$=MID$(B$,59,5)
6140 RETURN
```

Listing E.6

The second listing adds a key field to the record. You must reinitialize the file and alter the record length in the initialization program to the new length of 74 bytes. Also, make sure you alter all of the places in the program that require the record length. Before running the initialization program, delete NAMES. After NAMES is deleted, run this new version of the initialization program:

```
10 D$=CHR$(4):REMCONTROLD
20 PRINTD$;"OPEN NAMES,L74"
30 PRINTD$;"WRITE NAMES,R0"
40 PRINT0
50 PRINTD$
60 B$=CHR$(32):REMPUTONESPACEINB$
70 FORI=1TO6
80 B$=B$+B$
90 NEXTI
100 B$=B$+LEFT$(B$,9)
110 FORI=1TO100
120 PRINTD$;"WRITE NAMES,R";I
130 PRINTB$
140 PRINTD$
150 NEXTI
160 PRINTD$;"CLOSE"
170 END
0 100,300,500,700
72 IFN<>0THEN80
74 PRINTD$;"CLOSE"
76 END
80 PRINT"ERROR - ENTER 1, 2, 3 OR 4"
90 GOTO40
100 HOME
110 PRINT"WRITE A NEW RECORD TO THE FILE"
120 INPUT"ENTER RECORD NO. (0 TO 100)? ";N
130 IFN>=1THEN160
```

Listing E.7a

Once the file is reinitialized for 74-byte records, you can make the changes to alter the first listing. The new variable, K$, will hold the value called the key, which will serve to store the name of the record. This could be the last name plus as many letters of the first name as will fit, or could be some other alphanumeric field that will uniquely identify the different records.

```
10 SP$=" "
12 FORI=1TO73
14 SP$=SP$+" "
16 NEXTI
18 D$=CHR$(4)
20 PRINTD$;"OPEN NAMES,L74"
22 PRINTD$;"READ NAMES,R0"
30 INPUTM
32 PRINTD$
40 HOME
50 PRINT"ENTER 1 TO WRITE, 2 TO READ,"
52 PRINT"3 TO PRINT, 4 TO SORT,"
```

Listing E.7b

Listing E.7b continued

```
53 INPUT"OR 5 TO SEARCH? ";N
54 IFN<>0THEN60
56 PRINTD$;"CLOSE"
58 END
60 IFN<1THEN80
62 IFN>5THEN80
70 ONNGOTO100,300,500,700,900
72 IFN<>0THEN80
74 PRINTD$;"CLOSE"
76 END
80 PRINT"ERROR - ENTER 1, 2, 3 OR 4"
90 GOTO40
100 HOME
110 PRINT"WRITE A NEW RECORD TO THE FILE"
120 INPUT"ENTER RECORD NO. (0 TO 100)? ";N
130 IFN>=1THEN160
140 PRINT"ERROR - RECORD NO OUT OF RANGE"
150 GOTO120
160 IFN>100THEN140
165 INPUT"KEY? ";K$
170 INPUT"NAME? ";N$
180 INPUT"ADDRESS? ";A$
190 INPUT"CITY? ";C$
200 INPUT"STATE? ";S$
210 INPUT"ZIP CODE? ";Z$
220 GOSUB6010
230 PRINTD$;"WRITE NAMES,R";N
232 PRINTB$
234 PRINTD$
240 GOTO40
300 HOME
310 PRINT"READ A RECORD FROM FILE"
320 INPUT"ENTER RECORD NUMBER? ";N
330 IFN>=1THEN360
340 PRINT"ERROR - RECORD NO OUT OF RANGE"
350 GOTO320
360 IFN>100THEN340
370 PRINTD$;"READ NAMES,R";N
372 INPUTB$
374 PRINTD$
380 GOSUB6090
385 PRINT"KEY : ";K$
390 PRINT"NAME : ";N$
400 PRINT"ADDRESS : ";A$
410 PRINT"CITY : ";C$
420 PRINT"STATE : ";S$
430 PRINT"ZIP CODE : ";Z$
440 GOTO50
500 INPUT"START AT RECORD NO.? ";N
510 INPUT"END AT RECORD NO.? ";N1
520 IFN<1THEN640
530 IFN1<NTHEN640
540 IFN1>100THEN640
550 FORI=1TON1
560 PRINTD$;"READ NAMES,R";I
562 INPUTB$
564 PRINTD$
570 GOSUB6090
575 IFLEFT$(B$,1)=" "THEN620
580 PRINTD$;"PR#2"
582 PRINTI;"  ";K$
584 PRINTN$
590 PRINTA$
600 PRINTC$;", ";S$;"  ";Z$
610 PRINT
612 PRINTD$;"PR#0"
620 NEXTI
630 GOTO40
640 PRINT"ERROR - ENTER REC. NOS. CORRECTLY"
650 GOTO500
700 PRINT"SORTING THE FILE"
710 FORI=1TO99
```

```
715 N=1
720 PRINTD$;"READ NAMES,R";N
722 INPUTB1$
724 PRINTD$
728 IFB1$=""THENB1$=LEFT$(SP$,73)
730 SW=0
740 FORJ=1TO101-I
742 PRINTD$;"READ NAMES,R";J
744 INPUTB$
746 IFB$=""THENB$=LEFT$(SP$,73)
750 PRINTD$
752 IFLEFT$(B$,1)=" "THEN800
754 IFLEFT$(B1$,1)=" "THEN770
760 IFB$>=B1$THEN800
770 PRINTD$;"WRITE NAMES,R";J-1
772 PRINTB$
774 PRINTD$
780 B$=B1$
790 PRINTD$;"WRITE NAMES,R";J
792 PRINTB$
794 PRINTD$
796 SW=SW+1
800 B1$=B$
810 NEXTJ
815 IFSW=0THENI=99
820 NEXTI
830 GOTO40
900 INPUT"ENTER KEY TO SEARCH? ";N1$
910 L1=0:L2=101:L4=0:L5=LEN(N1$)
920 L3=INT((L1+L2)/2+.5)
922 PRINTD$;"READ NAMES,R";L3
924 INPUTB$
926 PRINTD$
930 IFB$=""THEN1010
940 IFLEFT$(B$,L5)>N1$THENL2=L3
950 IFLEFT$(B$,L5)<N1$THENL1=L3
960 IFLEFT$(B$,L5)=N1$THEN380
970 L4=L4+1
980 IFL4<7THEN920
990 PRINT"NAME NOT FOUND - IT IS NEAR RECORD NO.";L3
1000 GOTO50
1010 B$=CHR$(255)
1015 IFL5<=1THEN940
1020 FORI=1TOL5-1
1030 B$=B$+CHR$(255)
1040 NEXTI
1050 GOTO940
6000 END
6010 B2$=LEFT$(SP$,20)
6015 K$=K$+LEFT$(SP$,10)
6020 K$=LEFT$(K$,10)
6025 N$=N$+B2$
6030 N$=LEFT$(N$,20)
6035 A$=A$+B2$
6040 A$=LEFT$(A$,20)
6045 C$=C$+B2$
6050 C$=LEFT$(C$,16)
6055 S$=S$+"  "
6060 S$=LEFT$(S$,2)
6065 Z$=Z$+"   "
6070 Z$=LEFT$(Z$,5)
6075 B$=K$+N$+A$+C$+S$+Z$
6080 RETURN
6090 B$=B$+LEFT$(SP$,73)
6092 K$=LEFT$(B$,10)
6095 N$=MID$(B$,11,20)
6100 A$=MID$(B$,31,20)
6110 C$=MID$(B$,51,16)
6120 S$=MID$(B$,67,2)
6130 Z$=MID$(B$,69,5)
6140 RETURN
```

Listing E.7b continued

SUBROUTINES

You can follow the logic presented in Chapter 6 from the Radio Shack listing in the text, but there is one problem that I should point out. The Apple computer has no MKI$ or CVI functions (or any of the others like MKS$, CVS, MKD$, and CVD). These functions pack a number into an alphanumeric string and unpack the string back into the number. The numbers are packed by using the binary values of the numbers. You can use the VAL and STR$ functions to include numbers in the records, but these will waste some space on your disk. These values convert the number to the standard ASCII representations, using one byte per digit. Or, if you are interested in saving a little space, there is a way to pack on the Apple. Two subroutines can be employed to save you some space and, with a little imagination, you can adapt your programs to use them to store most numbers.

The numbers are stored a little less efficiently than the true binary pack that is available on the TRS-80, but this method still does not waste much space. The disk controller on the Apple will allow you to use only 7 of the 8 bits available, so the numbers are packed base 100. Each byte will have a value of 1 to 100 to represent values 0 through 99 because the Apple will also not store a *null* byte (i.e., a byte equal in value to zero).

The first subroutine accepts positive integers from zero to 99999999 (eight significant digits) and packs them into 4 bytes. The second subroutine unpacks the 4 bytes back into the number. To store values that are negative, you could either add a quantity before storing (subtracting that quantity when unpacking the record), or you could assign an extra one-byte field in the record to store the sign of the number. Storing floating point numbers is also a possibility. The number of decimal places for most fields is usually fixed at two. Before packing the number, multiply it by 100 (for two decimals—1000 for three, 10000 for four, etc.) and divide it by 100 after unpacking it. This converts it to an integer for storing, then back to the floating point value when it is returned to the program.

The other two subroutines save and retrieve records. The first one, starting at line 10140, replaces the TRS-80 GET statement. The second subroutine, starting at line 10220, replaces the Radio Shack PUT statement. You have to set certain values before calling the subroutines. They all start with the letter Z, which makes it a little easier to add these to existing programs. All you do is avoid the letter in your variable names in the program. The values required are:

- Z, the numeric variable to pack or unpack.
- Z$, the packed number in the packing and unpacking routines, or the record in the GET and PUT subroutines.
- ZF$, the file name.
- ZL, the length of the record minus one. This is the length of the record, less the return character.
- ZR, the record number to GET or PUT.

Note that you must pack Z$ before calling the PUT subroutine. There will be several examples of how to use these subroutines (particularly the GET and PUT subroutines) in following chapters.

```
10 D$=CHR$(4)
12 ZF$="TEST FILE"
14 ZL=12
20 PRINTD$;"OPEN TEST FILE,L13"
30 PRINTD$;"WRITE TEST FILE,R0"
40 PRINT0
50 PRINTD$
60 HOME
70 PRINT"    NUMERIC PACKING TEST"
80 PRINT
90 FORI=1TO4
92 PRINT"ENTER VALUES FOR RECORD NO.";I
100 INPUT"FIRST NUMERIC? ";N1
110 INPUT"SECOND NUMERIC? ";N2
120 INPUT"THIRD NUMERIC? ";N3
130 Z=N1
140 GOSUB10000
150 B$=Z$
160 Z=N2
170 GOSUB10000
180 B$=B$+Z$
190 Z=N3
200 GOSUB10000
210 B$=B$+Z$
220 Z$=B$
230 ZR=I
240 GOSUB10220
250 NEXTI
260 PRINT"LOADING RECORDS"
270 FORI=1TO4
280 ZR=I
290 GOSUB10140
300 B$=Z$
310 FORJ=1TO3
320 Z$=MID$(B$,J*4-3,4)
330 GOSUB10070
340 PRINTZ,
350 NEXTJ
360 PRINT
370 NEXTI
380 PRINTD$;"CLOSE"
390 END
9998  REM *** THE SUBROUTINES ***
9999  REM ** 10000 PACK NUMERIC **
10000 Z1=INT(Z/1000000)
10005 Z=Z-Z1*1000000
10010 Z2=INT(Z/10000)
10020 Z=Z-Z2*10000
10030 Z3=INT(Z/100)
10040 Z4=Z-Z3*100
10050 Z$=CHR$(Z1+1)+CHR$(Z2+1)+CHR$(Z3+1)+CHR$(Z4+1)
10060 RETURN
10069  REM ** 10070 UNPACK NUMERIC **
10070 Z1=ASC(MID$(Z$,1,1))-1
10080 Z2=ASC(MID$(Z$,2,1))-1
10090 Z3=ASC(MID$(Z$,3,1))-1
10100 Z4=ASC(MID$(Z$,4,1))-1
10110 Z=Z1*1000000+Z2*10000+Z3*100+Z4
10130 RETURN
10139  REM ** 10140 GET ZF,ZR **
10140 PRINTD$;"READ ";ZF$;",R";ZR
10150 Z$=" "
10160 FORZ1=1TOZL
10170 GETZ1$
```

```
10180 Z$=Z$+Z1$
10190 NEXTZ1
10200 PRINTD$
10202 Z$=RIGHT$(Z$,ZL)
10210 RETURN
10219  REM ** 10220 PUT ZF,ZR **
10220 PRINTD$;"WRITE ";ZF$;",R";ZR
10230 FORZ1=1TOZL
10240 PRINTMID$(Z$,Z1,1);
10250 NEXTZ1
10260 PRINT
10270 PRINTD$
10280 RETURN
```

Listing E.8

MULTIPLE RECORD BLOCKS

Studying multiple record blocks for the record file is not a required subject on the Apple computer because this system does all of the work for you. It will be required later on the key file because you want to access that by block rather than by record. While there is no example of implementing the logic in Chapter 7 on the Apple, make sure you understand the basic logic so that you will not have any trouble when the key-file subroutines are introduced.

INDEXES

The segment of text that produces a number from one to six for any key 10 characters long works on the Apple with one minor change. The first statement contains the STRING$ function, which should be changed to read K1$ = LEFT$(SP$,10). Remember to include the FOR/NEXT loop that initializes SP$ in any program that uses this sequence.

Packing the locator is also different on the Apple. On the TRS-80, the MKI$ and CVI functions are used to pack and unpack this number, using 2 bytes at the end of the key to store it. On the Apple, you can use the same logic as that used in the subroutines in the notes for Chapter 6. The first byte is packed by taking the integer of the record number divided by 100. Add one to the result and use the STR$ function to pack it. The second byte is the remainder of this division plus one. If the record number for the locator is the variable N, and if K$ is the key, then:

K$ = LEFT$(K$,10) + STR$(INT(N/100) + 1)
K$ = K$ + STR$(N − INT(N/100) * 100 + 1)

Although the TRS-80 can handle record numbers much higher, the Apple is restricted by this method to 9999, or four-decimal digits, because only 7 bits per byte can be saved on the disk. For files with more records, you can use 3 bytes by altering the program for the packing and unpacking of the locator and compensating for the extra byte in the key.

The subroutines for packing and unpacking numbers can also be used to pack and unpack the locators. To pack, set Z equal to the record number and call the pack subroutine. Use the last two bytes of Z$. To unpack, set:

Z$ = CHR$(1) + CHR$(1) + RIGHT$(K$,2)

Then call the unpack subroutine. Z$ must be 4 bytes long for the subroutine and the two CHR$(1) bytes are the equivalent of adding left zeroes.

KEY-FILE TEST PROGRAM

The first listing in Chapter 9 is not much different for the Apple than for the TRS-80 except in the case of the subroutines which were already developed in a previous chapter. There are some minor differences, like the question mark in the INPUT statements, the HOME statement instead of CLS statement, and the different type of OPEN statement.

The second listing does show some significant differences. Almost every type of computer has its own unique way of accessing the disk. The TRS-80 can save a program on the disk in the ASCII format with a single statement. The equivalent operation on the Apple requires listing the program to a text file called PROGRAM.

The program to list the REM statements in this chapter uses the Apple GET statement. INPUT does not work because of the commas in the statements. This program looks for the carriage return (CHR$(13)). Inserting an extra PRINT statement or two just after line 160 provides some space between the lines on the listing for additional comments.

```
9   REM -- PROGRAM INITIALIZATION --
10  D$=CHR$(4)
15  GOTO100
20   REM ** THIS STATEMENT RESERVED FOR DIM'S **
30  PRINTD$;"OPEN RECORDS,L74"
40  PRINTD$
50  PRINTD$;"OPEN KEY,L255"
60  PRINTD$
99   REM -- 0100-0490 CONTROL SECTION --
100 HOME
110 PRINTTAB(10);"KEY FILE TEST
115 PRINT
120 PRINTTAB(5);"1   INITIALIZE FILES"
130 PRINTTAB(5);"2   PUT A NEW RECORD IN FILE"
140 PRINTTAB(5);"3   GET A RECORD, GIVEN THE KEY"
150 PRINTTAB(5);"4   GET NEXT RECORD, GIVEN A KEY"
160 PRINTTAB(5);"5   DELETE A RECORD"
170 PRINTTAB(5);"6   ALTER AND REPLACE A RECORD"
180 PRINT
```

```
190 INPUT"  ENTER NUMBER OF SELECTION : ";N
200 IFN<1THEN220
210 IFN<=6THEN240
220 PRINT"ERROR - ENTRY MUST BE 1 TO 6"
230 GOTO190
240 ONNGOTO500,700,900,1100,1300,1500
499  REM -- 0500-0699 INITIALIZE FILES FUNCTION --
699  REM -- 0700-0899 PUT NEW RECORD FUNCTION --
700 HOME
710 PRINTTAB(8);"PUT NEW KEY AND RECORD IN FILE"
720 PRINT
730 INPUT"NEW KEY? ";K$
740 KN$=K$
750 GOSUB7500
760 IFE=1THEN790
770 PRINT"ERROR - DUPLICATE KEY"
780 GOTO730
790 K$=KN$
795 INPUT"NAME? ";N$
800 INPUT"ADDRESS? ";A$
810 INPUT"CITY? ";C$
820 INPUT"STATE? ";S$
830 INPUT"ZIP CODE? ";Z$
840 INPUT"IS THE ABOVE CORRECT (Y/N)? ";OK$
850 IFOK$="Y"THEN890
860 IFOK$="N"THEN700
870 PRINT"ERROR - PLEASE ENTER Y OR N"
880 GOTO840
890 GOSUB7000
895 GOTO100
899  REM -- 0900-1099 GET RECORD FUNCTION --
900 HOME
910 PRINTTAB(11);"GET RECORD GIVEN THE KEY"
920 PRINT
930 INPUT"KEY? ";K$
940 GOSUB7500
950 IFE=0THEN980
960 PRINT"KEY NOT IN FILE"
970 GOTO930
980 PRINT"NAME : ";N$
990 PRINT"ADDRESS : ";A$
1000 PRINT"CITY, STATE & ZIP : ";C$;", ";S$;" ";Z$
1010 PRINT
1020 PRINT"PRESS RETURN WHEN FINISHED VIEWING"
1030 GETOK$
1040 GOTO100
1099  REM -- 1100-1299 GET NEXT FUNCTION --
1100 HOME
1110 PRINTTAB(11);"GET NEXT GREATER KEY"
1120 PRINT
1130 INPUT"KEY? ";K$
1140 GOSUB8000
1150 IFE=0THEN1180
1160 PRINT"END OF FILE":PRINT"  THERE IS NO GREATER KEY"
1170 GOTO1110
1180 PRINT"KEY : ";K$
1190 GOTO980
1299  REM -- 1300-1499 DELETE RECORD FUNCTION --
1300 HOME
1310 PRINTTAB(11);"DELETE A RECORD"
1320 PRINT
1330 INPUT"KEY TO DELETE (OR END)? ";K$
1340 IFK$="END"THEN100
1350 GOSUB8500
1360 IFE=0THEN1390
1370 PRINT"KEY NOT FOUND & NOT DELETED"
1380 GOTO1400
1390 PRINT"KEY DELETED"
1400 PRINT"PRESS RETURN WHEN FINISHED VIEWING"
1410 GETOK$
1420 GOTO100
1499  REM -- 1500-1699 ALTER RECORD FUNCTION --
```

```
1500 HOME
1502 PRINTTAB(10);"CHANGE DATA IN A RECORD"
1504 PRINT
1510 INPUT"KEY? ";K$
1520 GOSUB7500
1530 IFE=0THEN1560
1540 PRINT"ERROR - KEY NOT FOUND"
1550 GOTO1510
1560 PRINT"1. NAME : ";N$
1570 PRINT"2. ADDRESS : ";A$
1580 PRINT"3. CITY : ";C$
1590 PRINT"4. STATE : ";S$
1600 PRINT"5. ZIP CODE : ";Z$
1610 PRINT
1620 INPUT"ENTER NO. OF FIELD TO CHANGE? ";NF
1630 IFNF<1THEN1650
1640 IFNF<=5THEN1670
1650 PRINT"ERROR - ENTER NO. 1 TO 5"
1660 GOTO1620
1670 ONNFGOSUB1680,1685,1690,1695,1700
1675 GOSUB9000
1677 GOTO100
1680 INPUT"NEW NAME? ";N$
1682 RETURN
1685 INPUT"NEW ADDRESS? ";A$
1687 RETURN
1690 INPUT"NEW CITY? ";C$
1692 RETURN
1695 INPUT"NEW STATE? ";S$
1697 RETURN
1700 INPUT"NEW ZIP CODE? ";Z$
1702 RETURN
```

Listing E.9

```
10 D$=CHR$(4)
20 PRINTD$;"OPEN PROGRAM"
30 PRINTD$;"READ PROGRAM"
40 A$=" "
50 GETC$
60 IFC$=CHR$(13)THEN100
70 A$=A$+C$
80 GOTO50
100 I=0
105 IFLEN(A$)<5THEN40
110 I=I+1
120 IFMID$(A$,I,1)<CHR$(65)THEN110
130 IFMID$(A$,I,3)<>"REM"THEN40
140 PR#2
150 J=LEN(A$)
160 PRINTRIGHT$(A$,J-I-2)
170 PR#0
180 GOTO40
```

Listing E.10

```
--- PROGRAM INITIALIZATION ---
** THIS STATEMENT RESERVED FOR DIM'S **
--- 0100-0490 CONTROL SECTION ---
--- 0500-0699 INITIALIZE FILES FUNCTION ---
--- 0700-0899 PUT NEW RECORD FUNCTION ---
--- 0900-1099 GET RECORD FUNCTION ---
--- 1100-1299 GET NEXT FUNCTION ---
--- 1300-1499 DELETE RECORD FUNCTION ---
--- 1500-1699 ALTER RECORD FUNCTION ---
```

Listing E.11

THE HASHING METHOD

There are some additional system differences between the Apple and the TRS-80 that must be taken into account at this point. First, initializing to ASCII code 255 does not work on the Apple disk. The reason it doesn't work is that its most significant bit is not transmitted. Only 7 bits may be used. The highest value that can be stored on and retrieved from the disk is 127. So replace the 255 with 127 and the routines will work the same way. Second, recognize that you do not have to use record number one to store the record counter. Apple uses a record number zero for storing this counter. The scheme is the same as the one used on the TRS-80, but the numbering starts at zero instead of one. Third, the Apple uses INPUT or GET to access the disk. This GET is not the same as the Radio Shack GET statement. The subroutines section in this appendix explains this.

There is an additional change that was made in the listing to prevent a variable conflict. The variable used to store the zip code, Z$, conflicts with the variables used in the subroutines that replace the TRS-80 PUT and GET statements. The zip code is reassigned to the variable ZC$.

Note that there are two PRINT D$ statements to end the subroutine starting at line 10140. It may have been a fluke of the particular system I was using or a problem with the Applesoft language interpreter or some timing problem with the Apple computer, but the first one does not cancel the READ command. The second one will. I would suggest you experiment very carefully with statements starting with PRINT D$.

A new subroutine was appended starting at line 9500 in order to simulate the MID$ function on the left side of the equals sign. The TRS-80 allows this statement as a way of inserting characters into an existing string. To simulate this action, this subroutine uses the string array K0$(21). The subroutine inserts a key into the proper place on the key block, KY$. There is one more change related to this in line 20. Add the DIM for this array there.

On the Apple computer, you must allow time for the Applesoft interpreter to rearrange its string space. This function is a sort of garbage collection that eliminates extra space left when a string is redefined. The interpreter leaves the old string in place and adds the new value. When a statement like Z5 = FRE(0) is executed, the interpreter performs this task. It is automatic on the TRS-80, which is sometimes quite annoying in that you never can tell exactly when it will take one of these time-outs. But on the Apple, if it is important, this FRE function can be placed so that the rearranging is done at a known point. In the listings, Z5 = FRE(0) is placed at frequent intervals.

```
9   REM  -- PROGRAM INITIALIZATION --
10  D$=CHR$(4)
12  SP$=" "
14  FORI=1TO7
16  SP$=SP$+SP$
18  NEXTI
20  DIMKO$(21)
22  SP$=SP$+LEFT$(SP$,127)
24  Z5=FRE(0)
30  PRINTD$;"OPEN RECORDS,L74"
32  RF$="RECORDS":RL=73
40  PRINTD$
50  PRINTD$;"OPEN KEY,L255"
52  KF$="KEY":KL=254
60  PRINTD$
99  REM  -- 0100-0490 CONTROL SECTION --
100 HOME
110 PRINTTAB(10);"KEY FILE TEST
115 PRINT
120 PRINTTAB(5);"1  INITIALIZE FILES"
130 PRINTTAB(5);"2  PUT A NEW RECORD IN FILE"
140 PRINTTAB(5);"3  GET A RECORD, GIVEN THE KEY"
150 PRINTTAB(5);"4  GET NEXT RECORD, GIVEN A KEY"
160 PRINTTAB(5);"5  DELETE A RECORD"
170 PRINTTAB(5);"6  ALTER AND REPLACE A RECORD"
180 PRINT
190 INPUT"  ENTER NUMBER OF SELECTION : ";N
195 IFN=0THEN250
200 IFN<1THEN220
210 IFN<=6THEN240
220 PRINT"ERROR - ENTRY MUST BE 1 TO 6"
230 GOTO190
240 ONNGOTO500,700,900,1100,1300,1500
250 PRINTD$;"CLOSE"
260 END
499 REM  -- 0500-0699 INITIALIZE FILES FUNCTION --
500 K1$=CHR$(127)
502 FORZ1=1TO253
504 K1$=K1$+CHR$(127)
506 NEXTZ1
510 FORI=1TO6
520 Z$=K1$:ZF$=KF$:ZL=KL
522 ZR=I
530 GOSUB10220
540 NEXTI
550 B1$=LEFT$(SP$,RL)
560 FORI=1TO100
570 PRINTD$;"WRITE ";RF$;",R";I
572 PRINTB1$
574 PRINTD$
590 NEXTI
600 PRINTD$;"WRITE ";RF$;",R0"
610 PRINT0
620 PRINTD$
630 GOTO100
699 REM  -- 0700-0899 PUT NEW RECORD FUNCTION --
700 HOME
710 PRINTTAB(8);"PUT NEW KEY AND RECORD IN FILE"
720 PRINT
730 INPUT"NEW KEY? ";K$
740 KN$=K$
750 GOSUB7500
```

```
760 IFE=1THEN790
770 PRINT"ERROR - DUPLICATE KEY"
780 GOTO730
790 K$=KN$
792 Z5=FRE(0)
795 INPUT"NAME? ";N$
800 INPUT"ADDRESS? ";A$
810 INPUT"CITY? ";C$
820 INPUT"STATE? ";S$
830 INPUT"ZIP CODE? ";ZC$
840 INPUT"IS THE ABOVE CORRECT (Y/N)? ";OK$
850 IFOK$="Y"THEN890
860 IFOK$="N"THEN700
870 PRINT"ERROR - PLEASE ENTER Y OR N"
880 GOTO840
890 GOSUB7000
895 GOTO100
899 REM  -- 0900-1099 GET RECORD FUNCTION --
900 HOME
910 PRINTTAB(11);"GET RECORD GIVEN THE KEY"
920 PRINT
930 INPUT"KEY? ";K$
940 GOSUB7500
950 IFE=0THEN980
960 PRINT"KEY NOT IN FILE"
970 GOTO930
980 PRINT"NAME : ";N$
990 PRINT"ADDRESS : ";A$
1000 PRINT"CITY, STATE & ZIP : ";C$;", ";S$;" ";ZC$
1010 PRINT
1020 PRINT"PRESS RETURN WHEN FINISHED VIEWING"
1030 GETOK$
1040 GOTO100
1099 REM  -- 1100-1299 GET NEXT FUNCTION --
1100 HOME
1110 PRINTTAB(11);"GET NEXT GREATER KEY"
1120 PRINT
1130 INPUT"KEY? ";K$
1140 GOSUB8000
1150 IFE=0THEN1180
1160 PRINT"END OF FILE":PRINT"  THERE IS NO GREATER KEY"
1170 GOTO1110
1180 PRINT"KEY : ";K$
1190 GOTO980
1299 REM  -- 1300-1499 DELETE RECORD FUNCTION --
1300 HOME
1310 PRINTTAB(11);"DELETE A RECORD"
1320 PRINT
1330 INPUT"KEY TO DELETE (OR END)? ";K$
1340 IFK$="END"THEN100
1350 GOSUB8500
1360 IFE=0THEN1390
1370 PRINT"KEY NOT FOUND & NOT DELETED"
1380 GOTO1400
1390 PRINT"KEY DELETED"
1400 PRINT"PRESS RETURN WHEN FINISHED VIEWING"
1410 GETOK$
1420 GOTO100
1499 REM  -- 1500-1699 ALTER RECORD FUNCTION --
1500 HOME
1502 PRINTTAB(10);"CHANGE DATA IN A RECORD"
1504 PRINT
1510 INPUT"KEY? ";K$
1520 GOSUB7500
1530 IFE=0THEN1560
1540 PRINT"ERROR - KEY NOT FOUND"
1550 GOTO1510
1560 PRINT"1. NAME : ";N$
1570 PRINT"2. ADDRESS : ";A$
1580 PRINT"3. CITY : ";C$
1590 PRINT"4. STATE : ";S$
1600 PRINT"5. ZIP CODE : ";ZC$
```

```
1610 PRINT
1620 INPUT"ENTER NO. OF FIELD TO CHANGE? ";NF
1630 IFNF<1THEN1650
1640 IFNF<=5THEN1670
1650 PRINT"ERROR - ENTER NO. 1 TO 5"
1660 GOTO1620
1670 ONNFGOSUB1680,1685,1690,1695,1700
1675 GOSUB9000
1677 GOTO100
1680 INPUT"NEW NAME? ";N$
1682 RETURN
1685 INPUT"NEW ADDRESS? ";A$
1687 RETURN
1690 INPUT"NEW CITY? ";C$
1692 RETURN
1695 INPUT"NEW STATE? ";S$
1697 RETURN
1700 INPUT"NEW ZIP CODE? ";Z$
1702 RETURN
5999 REM -- 6000-6999 RECORD FILE SUBROUTINES --
6000 END
6009 REM -- 6010-6080 PACK RECORD --
6010 R2$=LEFT$(SP$,20)
6015 K$=K$+R2$
6020 K$=LEFT$(K$,10)
6025 N$=N$+R2$
6030 N$=LEFT$(N$,20)
6035 A$=A$+R2$
6040 A$=LEFT$(A$,20)
6045 C$=C$+R2$
6050 C$=LEFT$(C$,16)
6055 S$=S$+R2$
6060 S$=LEFT$(S$,2)
6065 ZC$=ZC$+"     "
6070 ZC$=LEFT$(ZC$,5)
6075 R$=K$+N$+A$+C$+S$+ZC$
6077 Z5=FRE(O)
6080 RETURN
6089 REM -- 6090-6140 UNPACK RECORD --
6090 R$=R$+LEFT$(SP$,73)
6095 K$=LEFT$(R$,10)
6100 N$=MID$(R$,11,20)
6105 A$=MID$(R$,31,20)
6110 C$=MID$(R$,51,16)
6120 S$=MID$(R$,67,2)
6130 ZC$=MID$(R$,69,5)
6135 Z5=FRE(O)
6140 RETURN
6149 REM -- 6150-6180 GET RECORD BY NUMBER --
6150 ZR=N:ZL=RL:ZF$=RF$
6160 GOSUB10140
6170 R$=Z$
6175 Z5=FRE(O)
6180 RETURN
6189 REM -- 6190-6240 PUT RECORD BY NUMBER --
6190 ZR=N
6195 ZF$=RF$
6197 ZL=RL
6200 Z$=R$
6210 GOSUB10220
6215 Z5=FRE(O)
6220 RETURN
6249 REM -- 6250-6304 GET NEXT AVAILABLE RECORD NUMBER --
6250 PRINTD$;"READ ";RF$;",RO"
6260 INPUTFR
6270 FR=FR+1
6280 PRINTD$
6290 PRINTD$;"WRITE ";RF$;",RO"
6300 PRINTFR
6302 PRINTD$
6304 Z5=FRE(O)
6306 RETURN
```

```
6309  REM -- 6310-6510 SEARCH FOR KEY --
6310 K1$=LEFT$(SP$,10)
6320 K$=K$+K1$:KN=0
6330 FORI=1TO10
6340 KN=KN+ASC(MID$(K$,I,1))
6350 NEXTI
6360 KN=KN-INT((KN-1)/6)*6
6370 ZF$=KF$:ZL=KL:ZR=KN:GOSUB10140
6372 KY$=Z$
6380 FORI=1TO21
6390 K1$=MID$(KY$,I*12-11,12)
6400 IFLEFT$(K1$,10)=LEFT$(K$,10)THEN6500
6410 NEXTI
6420 K1$=CHR$(127)
6422 FORZ1=1TO9
6424 K1$=K1$+CHR$(127)
6426 NEXTZ1
6430 FORI=1TO21
6440 IFLEFT$(K1$,10)=MID$(KY$,I*12-11,10)THEN6480
6450 NEXTI
6460 E=2
6465 Z5=FRE(0)
6470 RETURN
6480 E=1
6485 Z5=FRE(0)
6490 RETURN
6500 E=0
6505 Z5=FRE(0)
6510 RETURN
6999  REM -- 7000-7499 PUT NEW RECORD AND KEY --
7000 GOSUB6310
7010 IFE=2THENRETURN
7020 IFE=1THEN7040
7030 E=1:RETURN
7040 GOSUB6250
7050 F1=INT(FR/100)
7052 F2=FR-F1*100
7054 K$=LEFT$(K$,10)+CHR$(F1+1)+CHR$(F2+1)
7070 GOSUB9500
7080 ZF$=KF$:ZL=KL:Z$=KY$
7085 ZR=KN
7090 GOSUB10220
7100 GOSUB6010
7110 N=FR
7115 GOSUB6190
7120 E=0
7130 RETURN
7499  REM -- 7500-7999 GET RECORD --
7500 GOSUB6310
7510 IFE=0THEN7540
7520 E=1
7530 RETURN
7540 F1=ASC(MID$(K1$,11,1))-1
7542 F2=ASC(MID$(K1$,12,1))-1
7544 N=F1*100+F2
7550 GOSUB6150
7560 GOSUB6090
7570 E=0
7580 RETURN
7999  REM  -- 8000-8499 GET NEXT --
8000 STOP
8499  REM -- 8500-8999 DELETE KEY AND RECORD --
8500 GOSUB6310
8510 IFE=0THEN8540
8520 E=1
8530 RETURN
8540 K$=CHR$(127)
8542 FORZ1=2TO12
8544 K$=K$+CHR$(127)
8546 NEXTZ1
8550 GOSUB9500
8560 ZF$=KF$:ZL=KL:Z$=KY$
```

```
8565  ZR=KN
8570  GOSUB10220
8580  E=0
8585  Z5=FRE(0)
8590  RETURN
8999   REM -- 9000-9499 RESAVE RECORD --
9000  GOSUB6310
9010  IFE=0THEN9040
9020  E=1
9030  RETURN
9040  F1=ASC(MID$(K1$,11,1))-1
9042  F2=ASC(MID$(K1$,12,1))-1
9044  N=F1*100+F2
9050  GOSUB6010
9060  GOSUB6190
9070  E=0
9080  RETURN
9499   REM -- 9500 INSERT K$ AT POS I --
9500  FORZ1=1TO21
9510  KO$(Z1)=MID$(KY$,Z1*12-11,12)
9520  NEXTZ1
9530  KO$(I)=K$
9540  KY$=KO$(1)
9550  FORZ1=2TO21
9560  KY$=KY$+KO$(Z1)
9570  NEXTZ1
9580  RETURN
10139  REM  ** 10140 GET ZF,ZR **
10140  PRINTD$;"READ ";ZF$;",R";ZR
10150  Z$=" "
10160  FORZ1=1TOZL
10170  GETZ1$
10180  Z$=Z$+Z1$
10190  NEXTZ1
10200  PRINTD$
10202  Z$=RIGHT$(Z$,ZL)
10204  PRINTD$
10210  RETURN
10219  REM  ** 10220 PUT ZF,ZR **
10220  PRINTD$;"WRITE ";ZF$;",R";ZR
10230  FORZ1=1TOZL
10240  PRINTMID$(Z$,Z1,1);
10250  NEXTZ1
10260  PRINT
10270  PRINTD$
10275  PRINT
10280  RETURN
```

Listing E.12

THE ALPHABETICAL-ARRAY METHOD

Follow the Apple listing for the changes noted in the text. I've made few changes to convert to Applesoft and have described most of them. In the alphabetical-array method on the Apple, the sequential file may be written very simply and the writing and the reading are both done in fewer statements. There are also a few places where more statements are required on the Apple to replace functions such as STRING$. Although I have not run any benchmark programs to time them, it does seem that this method runs much faster on the Apple than on the TRS-80, and the hashing method runs faster on the TRS-80 than on the Apple.

```
9   REM   -- PROGRAM INITIALIZATION --
10  D$=CHR$(4)
12  SP$=" "
14  FORI=1TO7
16  SP$=SP$+SP$
18  NEXTI
20  DIMKO$(21),KY$(100)
22  SP$=SP$+LEFT$(SP$,127)
24  Z5=FRE(0)
30  PRINTD$;"OPEN RECORDS,L74"
32  RF$="RECORDS":RL=73
40  PRINTD$
50  PRINTD$;"OPEN KEY"
52  PRINTD$;"READ KEY"
60  FORI=1TO100
70  INPUTKY$(I)
80  NEXTI
90  PRINTD$;"CLOSE KEY"
99  REM   -- 0100-0490 CONTROL SECTION --
100 HOME
110 PRINTTAB(10);"KEY FILE TEST
115 PRINT
120 PRINTTAB(5);"1  INITIALIZE FILES"
130 PRINTTAB(5);"2  PUT A NEW RECORD IN FILE"
140 PRINTTAB(5);"3  GET A RECORD, GIVEN THE KEY"
150 PRINTTAB(5);"4  GET NEXT RECORD, GIVEN A KEY"
160 PRINTTAB(5);"5  DELETE A RECORD"
170 PRINTTAB(5);"6  ALTER AND REPLACE A RECORD"
180 PRINT
190 INPUT"  ENTER NUMBER OF SELECTION : ";N
195 IFN=0THEN250
200 IFN<1THEN220
210 IFN<=6THEN240
220 PRINT"ERROR - ENTRY MUST BE 1 TO 6"
230 GOTO190
240 ONNGOTO500,700,900,1100,1300,1500
250 PRINTD$;"CLOSE"
260 END
499 REM   -- 0500-0699 INITIALIZE FILES FUNCTION --
500 BK$=CHR$(127)
502 FORI=2TO12
504 BK$=BK$+CHR$(127)
506 NEXTI
508 FORI=1TO100
510 KY$(I)=BK$
520 NEXTI
530 GOSUB6450
550 B1$=LEFT$(SP$,73)
560 FORI=1TO100
570 Z$=B1$:ZL=RL
572 ZR=I:ZF$=RF$
574 GOSUB10220
580 NEXTI
600 PRINTD$;"WRITE RECORDS"
610 PRINT0
620 PRINTD$
650 GOTO100
699 REM   -- 0700-0899 PUT NEW RECORD FUNCTION --
700 HOME
710 PRINTTAB(8);"PUT NEW KEY AND RECORD IN FILE"
720 PRINT
730 INPUT"NEW KEY? ";K$
740 KN$=K$
750 GOSUB7500
760 IFE=1THEN790
770 PRINT"ERROR - DUPLICATE KEY"
780 GOTO730
790 K$=KN$
792 Z5=FRE(0)
795 INPUT"NAME? ";N$
800 INPUT"ADDRESS? ";A$
810 INPUT"CITY? ";C$
```

```
820 INPUT"STATE? ";S$
830 INPUT"ZIP CODE? ";ZC$
840 INPUT"IS THE ABOVE CORRECT (Y/N)? ";OK$
850 IFOK$="Y"THEN890
860 IFOK$="N"THEN700
870 PRINT"ERROR - PLEASE ENTER Y OR N"
880 GOTO840
890 GOSUB7000
895 GOTO100
899  REM  -- 0900-1099 GET RECORD FUNCTION --
900 HOME
910 PRINTTAB(11);"GET RECORD GIVEN THE KEY"
920 PRINT
930 INPUT"KEY? ";K$
940 GOSUB7500
950 IFE=0THEN980
960 PRINT"KEY NOT IN FILE"
970 GOTO930
980 PRINT"NAME : ";N$
990 PRINT"ADDRESS : ";A$
1000 PRINT"CITY, STATE & ZIP : ";C$;", ";S$;" ";ZC$
1010 PRINT
1020 PRINT"PRESS RETURN WHEN FINISHED VIEWING"
1030 GETOK$
1040 GOTO100
1099  REM  -- 1100-1299 GET NEXT FUNCTION --
1100 HOME
1110 PRINTTAB(11);"GET NEXT GREATER KEY"
1120 PRINT
1130 INPUT"KEY? ";K$
1140 GOSUB8000
1150 IFE=0THEN1180
1160 PRINT"END OF FILE":PRINT"  THERE IS NO GREATER KEY"
1170 GOTO1120
1180 PRINT"KEY : ";K$
1190 GOTO980
1299  REM  -- 1300-1499 DELETE RECORD FUNCTION --
1300 HOME
1310 PRINTTAB(11);"DELETE A RECORD"
1320 PRINT
1330 INPUT"KEY TO DELETE (OR END)? ";K$
1340 IFK$="END"THEN100
1350 GOSUB8500
1360 IFE=0THEN1390
1370 PRINT"KEY NOT FOUND & NOT DELETED"
1380 GOTO1400
1390 PRINT"KEY DELETED"
1400 PRINT"PRESS RETURN WHEN FINISHED VIEWING"
1410 GETOK$
1420 GOTO100
1499  REM  -- 1500-1699 ALTER RECORD FUNCTION --
1500 HOME
1502 PRINTTAB(10);"CHANGE DATA IN A RECORD"
1504 PRINT
1510 INPUT"KEY? ";K$
1520 GOSUB7500
1530 IFE=0THEN1560
1540 PRINT"ERROR - KEY NOT FOUND"
1550 GOTO1510
1560 PRINT"1. NAME : ";N$
1570 PRINT"2. ADDRESS : ";A$
1580 PRINT"3. CITY : ";C$
1590 PRINT"4. STATE : ";S$
1600 PRINT"5. ZIP CODE : ";ZC$
1610 PRINT
1620 INPUT"ENTER NO. OF FIELD TO CHANGE? ";NF
1630 IFNF<1THEN1650
1640 IFNF<=5THEN1670
1650 PRINT"ERROR - ENTER NO. 1 TO 5"
1660 GOTO1620
1670 ONNFGOSUB1680,1685,1690,1695,1700
1675 GOSUB9000
```

```
1677 GOTO100
1680 INPUT"NEW NAME? ";N$
1682 RETURN
1685 INPUT"NEW ADDRESS? ";A$
1687 RETURN
1690 INPUT"NEW CITY? ";C$
1692 RETURN
1695 INPUT"NEW STATE? ";S$
1697 RETURN
1700 INPUT"NEW ZIP CODE? ";Z$
1702 RETURN
5999  REM -- 6000-6999 RECORD FILE SUBROUTINES --
6000 END
6009  REM -- 6010-6080 PACK RECORD --
6010 R2$=LEFT$(SP$,20)
6015 K$=K$+R2$
6020 K$=LEFT$(K$,10)
6025 N$=N$+R2$
6030 N$=LEFT$(N$,20)
6035 A$=A$+R2$
6040 A$=LEFT$(A$,20)
6045 C$=C$+R2$
6050 C$=LEFT$(C$,16)
6055 S$=S$+R2$
6060 S$=LEFT$(S$,2)
6065 ZC$=ZC$+"       "
6070 ZC$=LEFT$(ZC$,5)
6075 R$=K$+N$+A$+C$+S$+ZC$
6077 Z5=FRE(0)
6080 RETURN
6089  REM -- 6090-6140 UNPACK RECORD --
6090 R$=R$+LEFT$(SP$,73)
6095 K$=LEFT$(R$,10)
6100 N$=MID$(R$,11,20)
6105 A$=MID$(R$,31,20)
6110 C$=MID$(R$,51,16)
6120 S$=MID$(R$,67,2)
6130 ZC$=MID$(R$,69,5)
6135 Z5=FRE(0)
6140 RETURN
6149  REM -- 6150-6180 GET RECORD BY NUMBER --
6150 ZR=N:ZL=RL:ZF$=RF$
6160 GOSUB10140
6170 R$=Z$
6175 Z5=FRE(0)
6180 RETURN
6189  REM -- 6190-6240 PUT RECORD BY NUMBER --
6190 ZR=N
6195 ZF$=RF$
6197 ZL=RL
6200 Z$=R$
6210 GOSUB10220
6215 Z5=FRE(0)
6220 RETURN
6249  REM -- 6250-6304 GET NEXT AVAILABLE RECORD NUMBER --
6250 PRINTD$;"READ ";RF$;",R0"
6260 INPUTFR
6270 FR=FR+1
6280 PRINTD$
6290 PRINTD$;"WRITE ";RF$;",R0"
6300 PRINTFR
6302 PRINTD$
6304 Z5=FRE(0)
6306 RETURN
6309  REM -- 6310-6510 SEARCH FOR KEY --
6310 K1$=LEFT$(SP$,10)
6320 K$=K$+K1$:KN=0
6330 L1=0:L2=101:L4=0
6340 L3=INT((L1+L2)/2)
6350 IFLEFT$(K$,10)<LEFT$(KY$(L3),10)THENL2=L3
6360 IFLEFT$(K$,10)>LEFT$(KY$(L3),10)THENL1=L3
6370 IFLEFT$(K$,10)=LEFT$(KY$(L3),10)THEN6430
```

```
6380 L4=L4+1
6390 IFL4<7THEN6340
6400 E=2:IFLEFT$(KY$(100),1)=CHR$(127)THENE=1
6410 IFLEFT$(K$,10)>LEFT$(KY$(L3),10)THENL3=L3+1
6415 IFL3=0THENL3=1
6420 RETURN
6430 E=0:K1$=KY$(L3)
6440 RETURN
6449 REM --  6450-6540 RESAVE KEYS ON DISK --
6450 PRINTD$;"OPEN KEY"
6452 PRINTD$;"WRITE KEY"
6460 FORI=1TO100
6470 PRINTKY$(I)
6480 NEXTI
6490 PRINTD$;"CLOSE KEY"
6540 RETURN
6999  REM -- 7000-7499 PUT NEW RECORD AND KEY --
7000 GOSUB6310
7010 IFE=2THENRETURN
7020 IFE=1THEN7040
7030 E=1:RETURN
7040 GOSUB6250
7050 F1=INT(FR/100)
7052 F2=FR-F1*100
7054 K$=LEFT$(K$,10)+CHR$(F1+1)+CHR$(F2+1)
7070 FORI=99TOL3STEP-1
7075 KY$(I+1)=KY$(I)
7080 NEXTI
7085 KY$(L3)=K$
7090 GOSUB6450
7100 GOSUB6010
7110 N=FR
7115 GOSUB6190
7120 E=0
7130 RETURN
7499  REM --- 7500-7999 GET RECORD --
7500 GOSUB6310
7510 IFE=0THEN7540
7520 E=1
7530 RETURN
7540 F1=ASC(MID$(K1$,11,1))-1
7542 F2=ASC(MID$(K1$,12,1))-1
7544 N=F1*100+F2
7550 GOSUB6150
7560 GOSUB6090
7570 E=0
7580 RETURN
7999  REM  -- 8000-8499 GET NEXT --
8000 GOSUB6310
8002 K1$=CHR$(127)
8004 FORI=2TO12
8006 K1$=K1$+CHR$(127)
8008 NEXTI
8010 IFE=1THEN8030
8020 L3=L3+1
8030 IFL3>100THEN8050
8040 IFKY$(L3)<K1$THEN8060
8050 E=1
8055 RETURN
8060 F1=ASC(MID$(KY$(L3),11,1))-1
8062 F2=ASC(MID$(KY$(L3),12,1))-1
8064 N=F1*100+F2
8070 GOSUB6150
8080 GOSUB6090
8090 E=0
8100 RETURN
8499  REM -- 8500-8999 DELETE KEY AND RECORD --
8500 GOSUB6310
8510 IFE=0THEN8540
8520 E=1
8530 RETURN
8540 FORI=L3TO99
```

```
8550 KY$(I)=KY$(I+1)
8560 NEXTI
8562 KY$(100)=CHR$(127)
8564 FORI=2TO12
8566 KY$(100)=KY$(100)+CHR$(127)
8568 NEXTI
8570 GOSUB6450
8580 E=0
8585 Z5=FRE(0)
8590 RETURN
8999  REM -- 9000-9499 RESAVE RECORD --
9000 GOSUB6310
9010 IFE=0THEN9040
9020 E=1
9030 RETURN
9040 F1=ASC(MID$(K1$,11,1))-1
9042 F2=ASC(MID$(K1$,12,1))-1
9044 N=F1*100+F2
9050 GOSUB6010
9060 GOSUB6190
9070 E=0
9080 RETURN
9499  REM -- 9500 INSERT K$ AT POS I --
9500 FORZ1=1TO21
9510 KO$(Z1)=MID$(KY$,Z1*12-11,12)
9520 NEXTZ1
9530 KO$(I)=K$
9540 KY$=KO$(1)
9550 FORZ1=2TO21
9560 KY$=KY$+KO$(Z1)
9570 NEXTZ1
9580 RETURN
10139  REM  ** 10140 GET ZF,ZR **
10140 PRINTD$;"READ ";ZF$;",R";ZR
10150 Z$=" "
10160 FORZ1=1TOZL
10170 GETZ1$
10180 Z$=Z$+Z1$
10190 NEXTZ1
10200 PRINTD$
10202 Z$=RIGHT$(Z$,ZL)
10204 PRINTD$
10210 RETURN
10219  REM  ** 10220 PUT ZF,ZR **
10220 PRINTD$;"WRITE ";ZF$;",R";ZR
10230 FORZ1=1TOZL
10240 PRINTMID$(Z$,Z1,1);
10250 NEXTZ1
10260 PRINT
10270 PRINTD$
10280 RETURN
```

Listing E.13

THE TREE-STRUCTURED METHOD

Some additional differences between the TRS-80 and the Apple computers show up in this method. The roadmap on the Apple can have ASCII codes only as high as 127 instead of the 255 allowed on the TRS-80. This restricts the Apple to 126 key-file blocks instead of the 254 available on the TRS-80.

There are several places in the new parts of the subroutines that require alterations from the TRS-80 listing, but I've covered most of these, such as the use of the K0$ array to replace the MID$ function.

Note that the string variable KW$ is introduced in the subroutine starting at line 7000 to replace one of the STRING$ functions. KW$ is filled with ASCII 127s to fill in the parts of the two blocks created from the split where the keys were removed. The TRS-80, you might remember, uses the code 255 in the STRING$ functions that are being replaced.

On the Apple, do not use RESET where the text suggests you hit the BREAK key after initialization. There is a provision for ending the program by entering the selection number zero. This closes the files, which is required on the Apple because of the way the system writes to the disks.

```
9  REM  -- PROGRAM INITIALIZATION --
10 D$=CHR$(4)
12 SP$=" "
14 FORI=1TO7
16 SP$=SP$+SP$
18 NEXTI
20 DIMKO$(21)
22 SP$=SP$+LEFT$(SP$,127)
24 Z5=FRE(O)
30 PRINTD$;"OPEN RECORDS,L74"
32 RF$="RECORDS":RL=73
40 PRINTD$
50 PRINTD$;"OPEN KEY,L255"
52 KF$="KEY":KL=254
60 PRINTD$
70 PRINTD$;"READ KEY,R1"
72 GETRM$
74 FORI=1TO254
76 GETZ$
78 RM$=RM$+Z$
80 NEXTI
82 PRINT
90 PRINTD$
99  REM  -- 0100-0490 CONTROL SECTION --
100 HOME
110 PRINTTAB(10);"KEY FILE TEST
115 PRINT
120 PRINTTAB(5);"1  INITIALIZE FILES"
130 PRINTTAB(5);"2  PUT A NEW RECORD IN FILE"
140 PRINTTAB(5);"3  GET A RECORD, GIVEN THE KEY"
150 PRINTTAB(5);"4  GET NEXT RECORD, GIVEN A KEY"
160 PRINTTAB(5);"5  DELETE A RECORD"
170 PRINTTAB(5);"6  ALTER AND REPLACE A RECORD"
180 PRINT
190 INPUT" ENTER NUMBER OF SELECTION : ";N
195 IFN=0THEN250
200 IFN<1THEN220
210 IFN<=6THEN240
220 PRINT"ERROR - ENTRY MUST BE 1 TO 6"
230 GOTO190
240 ONNGOTO500,700,900,1100,1300,1500
250 PRINTD$;"CLOSE"
260 END
499  REM  -- 0500-0699 INITIALIZE FILES FUNCTION --
500 RM$=CHR$(1)
502 FORI=2TO254
504 RM$=RM$+CHR$(127)
506 NEXTI
508 ZF$=KF$:ZL=KL:Z$=RM$:ZR=1
510 GOSUB10220
512 Z$=LEFT$(SP$,12)+RIGHT$(RM$,242)
514 ZR=2
516 GOSUB10220
```

```
550 Z$=LEFT$(SP$,RL)
552 ZF$=RF$:ZL=RL
560 FORZR=1TO100
570 GOSUB10220
580 NEXTZR
590 PRINTD$;"WRITE ";RF$;",RO"
600 PRINTO
610 PRINTD$
620 GOTO100
699  REM  -- 0700-0899 PUT NEW RECORD FUNCTION --
700 HOME
710 PRINTTAB(8);"PUT NEW KEY AND RECORD IN FILE"
720 PRINT
730 INPUT"NEW KEY? ";K$
740 KN$=K$
750 GOSUB7500
760 IFE=1THEN790
770 PRINT"ERROR - DUPLICATE KEY"
780 GOTO730
790 K$=KN$
792 Z5=FRE(0)
795 INPUT"NAME? ";N$
800 INPUT"ADDRESS? ";A$
810 INPUT"CITY? ";C$
820 INPUT"STATE? ";S$
830 INPUT"ZIP CODE? ";ZC$
840 INPUT"IS THE ABOVE CORRECT (Y/N)? ";OK$
850 IFOK$="Y"THEN890
860 IFOK$="N"THEN700
870 PRINT"ERROR - PLEASE ENTER Y OR N"
880 GOTO840
890 GOSUB7000
895 GOTO100
899  REM  -- 0900-1099 GET RECORD FUNCTION --
900 HOME
910 PRINTTAB(11);"GET RECORD GIVEN THE KEY"
920 PRINT
930 INPUT"KEY? ";K$
940 GOSUB7500
950 IFE=0THEN980
960 PRINT"KEY NOT IN FILE"
970 GOTO930
980 PRINT"NAME : ";N$
990 PRINT"ADDRESS : ";A$
1000 PRINT"CITY, STATE & ZIP : ";C$;", ";S$;" ";ZC$
1010 PRINT
1020 PRINT"PRESS RETURN WHEN FINISHED VIEWING"
1030 GETOK$
1040 GOTO100
1099  REM  -- 1100-1299 GET NEXT FUNCTION --
1100 HOME
1110 PRINTTAB(11);"GET NEXT GREATER KEY"
1120 PRINT
1130 INPUT"KEY? ";K$
1140 GOSUB8000
1150 IFE=0THEN1180
1160 PRINT"END OF FILE":PRINT"  THERE IS NO GREATER KEY"
1170 GOTO1120
1180 PRINT"KEY : ";K$
1190 GOTO980
1299  REM  -- 1300-1499 DELETE RECORD FUNCTION --
1300 HOME
1310 PRINTTAB(11);"DELETE A RECORD"
1320 PRINT
1330 INPUT"KEY TO DELETE (OR END)? ";K$
1340 IFK$="END"THEN100
1350 GOSUB8500
1360 IFE=0THEN1390
1370 PRINT"KEY NOT FOUND & NOT DELETED"
1380 GOTO1400
1390 PRINT"KEY DELETED"
1400 PRINT"PRESS RETURN WHEN FINISHED VIEWING"
```

```
1410 GETOK$
1420 GOTO100
1499  REM  -- 1500-1699 ALTER RECORD FUNCTION --
1500 HOME
1502 PRINTTAB(10);"CHANGE DATA IN A RECORD"
1504 PRINT
1510 INPUT"KEY? ";K$
1520 GOSUB7500
1530 IFE=OTHEN1560
1540 PRINT"ERROR - KEY NOT FOUND"
1550 GOTO1510
1560 PRINT"1. NAME : ";N$
1570 PRINT"2. ADDRESS : ";A$
1580 PRINT"3. CITY : ";C$
1590 PRINT"4. STATE : ";S$
1600 PRINT"5. ZIP CODE : ";ZC$
1610 PRINT
1620 INPUT"ENTER NO. OF FIELD TO CHANGE? ";NF
1630 IFNF<1THEN1650
1640 IFNF<=5THEN1670
1650 PRINT"ERROR - ENTER NO. 1 TO 5"
1660 GOTO1620
1670 ONNFGOSUB1680,1685,1690,1695,1700
1675 GOSUB9000
1677 GOTO100
1680 INPUT"NEW NAME? ";N$
1682 RETURN
1685 INPUT"NEW ADDRESS? ";A$
1687 RETURN
1690 INPUT"NEW CITY? ";C$
1692 RETURN
1695 INPUT"NEW STATE? ";S$
1697 RETURN
1700 INPUT"NEW ZIP CODE? ";Z$
1702 RETURN
5999  REM -- 6000-6999 RECORD FILE SUBROUTINES --
6000 END
6009  REM -- 6010-6080 PACK RECORD --
6010 R2$=LEFT$(SP$,20)
6015 K$=K$+R2$
6020 K$=LEFT$(K$,10)
6025 N$=N$+R2$
6030 N$=LEFT$(N$,20)
6035 A$=A$+R2$
6040 A$=LEFT$(A$,20)
6045 C$=C$+R2$
6050 C$=LEFT$(C$,16)
6055 S$=S$+R2$
6060 S$=LEFT$(S$,2)
6065 ZC$=ZC$+"        "
6070 ZC$=LEFT$(ZC$,5)
6075 R$=K$+N$+A$+C$+S$+ZC$
6077 Z5=FRE(O)
6080 RETURN
6089  REM -- 6090-6140 UNPACK RECORD --
6090 R$=R$+LEFT$(SP$,73)
6095 K$=LEFT$(R$,10)
6100 N$=MID$(R$,11,20)
6105 A$=MID$(R$,31,20)
6110 C$=MID$(R$,51,16)
6120 S$=MID$(R$,67,2)
6130 ZC$=MID$(R$,69,5)
6135 Z5=FRE(O)
6140 RETURN
6149  REM -- 6150-6180 GET RECORD BY NUMBER --
6150 ZR=N:ZL=RL:ZF$=RF$
6160 GOSUB10140
6170 R$=Z$
6175 Z5=FRE(O)
6180 RETURN
6189  REM -- 6190-6240 PUT RECORD BY NUMBER --
6190 ZR=N
```

```
6195 ZF$=RF$
6197 ZL=RL
6200 Z$=R$
6210 GOSUB10220
6215 Z5=FRE(0)
6220 RETURN
6249  REM -- 6250-6304 GET NEXT AVAILABLE RECORD NUMBER --
6250 PRINTD$;"READ ";RF$;",R0"
6260 INPUTFR
6270 FR=FR+1
6280 PRINTD$
6290 PRINTD$;"WRITE ";RF$;",R0"
6300 PRINTFR
6302 PRINTD$
6304 Z5=FRE(0)
6306 RETURN
6309  REM -- 6310-6510 SEARCH FOR KEY --
6310 K1$=LEFT$(SP$,10)
6320 K$=K$+K1$:KN=0
6330 L1=0:L2=10:L4=0
6340 L3=INT((L1+L2)/2)
6350 IFMID$(RM$,L3,1)=CHR$(127)THEN6540
6360 KB=ASC(MID$(RM$,L3,1))
6370 ZF$=KF$:ZR=KB+1:ZL=KL
6372 GOSUB10140
6374 KY$=Z$
6380 IFLEFT$(KY$,10)>LEFT$(K$,10)THEN6540
6390 KN=0
6400 KN=KN+1:IFKN=21THEN6440
6410 IFLEFT$(K$,10)=MID$(KY$,KN*12-11,10)THEN6580
6420 IFLEFT$(K$,10)<MID$(KY$,KN*12-11,10)THEN6610
6430 GOTO6400
6440 L1=L3
6450 L4=L4+1
6460 IFL4<4THEN6340
6470 E=1
6480 L3=L3+1
6490 KB=ASC(MID$(RM$,L3,1))
6500 K1$=CHR$(127)
6502 FORZ1=2TO12
6504 K1$=K1$+CHR$(127)
6506 NEXTZ1
6508 IFKB=127THENRETURN
6510 ZF$=KF$:ZL=KL:ZR=KB+1
6512 GOSUB10140
6514 KY$=Z$
6520 K1$=LEFT$(KY$,12)
6530 RETURN
6540 L2=L3
6550 L4=L4+1
6560 IFL4<4THEN6340
6565 E=1:IFL1>0THEN6500
6570 PRINT"KEY FILE INITIALIZATION ERROR!"
6572 STOP
6580 E=0
6590 K1$=MID$(KY$,KN*12-11,12)
6600 RETURN
6610 E=1
6620 GOTO6590
6999  REM -- 7000-7499 PUT NEW RECORD AND KEY --
7000 GOSUB6310
7010 IFE=2THENRETURN
7020 IFE=1THEN7040
7030 E=1:RETURN
7040 GOSUB6250
7045 KZ$=KY$
7050 IFKB=127THEN7180
7060 IFLEFT$(K$,10)<LEFT$(KZ$,10)THENKN=1
7062 FORI=1TO21
7064 K0$(I)=MID$(KZ$,I*12-11,12)
7066 NEXTI
7068 FORI=21TOKN+1STEP-1
```

```
7070 KO$(I)=KO$(I-1)
7072 NEXTI
7074 F1=INT(FR/100)
7076 F2=FR-F1*100
7078 KO$(KN)=LEFT$(K$,10)+CHR$(F1+1)+CHR$(F2+1)
7080 KY$=KO$(1)
7082 FORI=2TO21
7084 KY$=KY$+KO$(I)
7086 NEXTI
7088 ZF$=KF$:ZL=KL:ZR=KB+1
7090 Z$=KY$
7092 GOSUB10220
7100 GOSUB6010
7110 N=FR:GOSUB6190
7120 E=0
7130 IFMID$(KY$,241,1)=CHR$(127)THENRETURN
7132 KW$=CHR$(127)
7134 FORI=1TO7
7136 KW$=KW$+KW$
7138 NEXTI
7140 KW$=KW$+LEFT$(KW$,127)
7142 L4=0:FORI=1TO10:IFASC(MID$(RM$,I,1))=127THEN7144
7143 IFASC(MID$(RM$,I,1))>L4THENL4=ASC(MID$(RM$,I,1))
7144 NEXTI
7146 I=0
7148 I=I+1:IFASC(MID$(RM$,I,1))<>KBTHEN7148
7150 RW$=RM$
7152 RM$=LEFT$(RW$,I)+CHR$(L4+1)+RIGHT$(RW$,10-I-1)
7154 KX$=MID$(KY$,121,134)+LEFT$(KW$,120)
7156 KZ$=MID$(KY$,1,120)+LEFT$(KW$,134)
7158 ZF$=KF$:ZL=KL:ZR=KB+1:Z$=KY$
7160 GOSUB10220
7162 Z$=KX$:ZR=L4+2:GOSUB10220
7164 Z$=RM$+LEFT$(KW$,244):ZR=1:GOSUB10220
7170 E=0:RETURN
7180 L4=0
7182 L4=L4+1:IFL4<=10THEN7184:ELSESTOP
7184 IFASC(MID$(RM$,L4+1,1))<127THEN7182
7186 KB=ASC(MID$(RM$,L4,1)):ZF$=KF$:ZL=KL:ZR=KB:GOSUB10140
7187 KY$=Z$
7188 KN=0
7190 KN=KN+1:IFMID$(KY$,KN*12-11,1)<CHR$(127)THEN7190
7192 GOTO7050
7499  REM  -- 7500-7999 GET RECORD --
7500 GOSUB6310
7510 IFE=0THEN7540
7520 E=1
7530 RETURN
7540 F1=ASC(MID$(K1$,11,1))-1
7542 F2=ASC(MID$(K1$,12,1))-1
7544 N=F1*100+F2
7550 GOSUB6150
7560 GOSUB6090
7570 E=0
7580 RETURN
7999  REM  -- 8000-8499 GET NEXT --
8000 K$=K$+LEFT$(SP$,10):E=ASC(MID$(K$,10,1))+1
8010 K$=LEFT$(K$,9)+CHR$(E)
8020 GOSUB6310
8030 IFE=0THEN7540
8040 IFLEFT$(K1$,1)<CHR$(127)THEN8060
8050 E=1:RETURN
8060 E=0:GOTO7540
8070 GOSUB6150
8080 GOSUB6090
8090 E=0
8100 RETURN
8499  REM -- 8500-8999 DELETE KEY AND RECORD --
8500 GOSUB6310
8510 IFE=0THEN8540
8520 E=1
8530 RETURN
```

```
8540 FORI=1TO21
8542 K0$(I)=MID$(KY$,I*12-11,12)
8544 NEXTI
8550 FORI=KNTO20
8555 K0$(I)=K0$(I+1)
8557 NEXTI
8560 K0$(21)=CHR$(127)
8562 FORI=2TO12
8564 K0$(21)=K0$(21)+CHR$(127)
8566 NEXTI
8570 KY$=K0$(1)
8572 FORI=2TO21
8574 KY$=KY$+K0$(I)
8576 NEXTI
8578 Z$=KY$:ZF$=KF$:ZL=KL:ZR=KB+1
8580 GOSUB10220
8590 E=0
8600 Z5=FRE(0)
8610 RETURN
8999  REM -- 9000-9499 RESAVE RECORD --
9000 GOSUB6310
9010 IFE=0THEN9040
9020 E=1
9030 RETURN
9040 F1=ASC(MID$(K1$,11,1))-1
9042 F2=ASC(MID$(K1$,12,1))-1
9044 N=F1*100+F2
9050 GOSUB6010
9060 GOSUB6190
9070 E=0
9080 RETURN
9499  REM -- 9500 INSERT K$ AT POS I --
9500 FORZ1=1TO21
9510 K0$(Z1)=MID$(KY$,Z1*12-11,12)
9520 NEXTZ1
9530 K0$(I)=K$
9540 KY$=K0$(1)
9550 FORZ1=2TO21
9560 KY$=KY$+K0$(Z1)
9570 NEXTZ1
9580 RETURN
10139  REM  ** 10140 GET ZF,ZR **
10140 PRINTD$;"READ ";ZF$;",R";ZR
10150 Z$=" "
10160 FORZ1=1TOZL
10170 GETZ1$
10180 Z$=Z$+Z1$
10190 NEXTZ1
10200 PRINTD$
10202 Z$=RIGHT$(Z$,ZL)
10204 PRINTD$
10210 RETURN
10219  REM  ** 10220 PUT ZF,ZR **
10220 PRINTD$;"WRITE ";ZF$;",R";ZR
10230 FORZ1=1TOZL
10240 PRINTMID$(Z$,Z1,1);
10250 NEXTZ1
10260 PRINT
10270 PRINTD$
10280 RETURN
```

Listing E.14

TRACKING FREE RECORDS

The restriction of being able to use only 7 bytes on the Apple makes using the bit map, suggested for the TRS-80, less practical. Instead, I have included the subroutines required for using a LIFO (last in, first out) buffer kept in a separate file. You could develop the routines to use the first part of the record file as the LIFO buffer, but keeping it in a separate file simplifies the programming.

The buffer must be initialized first. You can add this to the file initialization routine in the main program. The number in record zero can be the pointer and is initialized to one. The rest of the records contain all of the numbers from 1 to 99. One hundred records can be written if you change the 100 in line 15240 to 101. This IF statement should contain the number of records plus one.

Popping consists of taking one number off the list and updating the counter accordingly. That routine starts at line 15200. Record number zero is read (it contains the stack pointer) and, in memory, incremented. It is then checked against the maximum number of records in the file. If it is greater (greater or equal to one more than the number of records), the subroutine simply sets E equal to one to indicate that there are no records left, and returns. If there are records left in the stack, the incremented pointer is saved and the next available free record number is read from record number NR − 1. Setting E equal to zero indicates that the subroutine was successful.

Pushing onto the stack works in a similar manner. This time the pointer is decremented and the new record number is written to this file as record number NR, which is the stack pointer.

Implementing these subroutines is not very complicated. You can replace the subroutine starting at line 6250 by a GOTO 15200, using the RETURN in that subroutine, or alter the other subroutines to call 15200 instead of 6250. Use the SEARCHER program to find the string 6250 and it will return all of the statements containing it.

The only call to 15000 (push onto the stack) occurs in the delete subroutine starting at line 8500. First, in order to salvage the record number that is to be placed on the free list, insert line 8546 K$ = K0$(KN). Eliminate the RETURN at line 8610 and write a routine starting there to extract the record number from K$, assigning it to FR. Then call the subroutine at line 15000 to return the record to the free list.

```
14999  REM -- 15000 PUSH FR --
15000  PRINTD$;"READ FREE LIST,R0"
15010  INPUTNR
15015  PRINTD$
15020  IFNR>1THEN15050
15030  E=1
15040  RETURN
15050  E=0
15060  NR=NR-1
15070  PRINTD$
```

```
15080 PRINTD$;"WRITE FREE LIST,R0"
15090 PRINTNR
15100 PRINTD$
15110 PRINTD$;"WRITE FREE LIST,R";NR
15120 PRINTFR
15130 PRINTD$
15140 E=0
15150 RETURN
15199   REM -- 15200 POP FR --
15200 PRINTD$;"READ FREE LIST,R0"
15210 INPUTNR
15220 PRINTD$
15230 NR=NR+1
15240 IFNR<=100THEN15270
15250 E=1
15260 RETURN
15270 PRINTD$;"WRITE FREE LIST,R0"
15280 PRINTNR
15290 PRINTD$
15300 PRINTD$;"READ FREE LIST,R";NR-1
15310 INPUTFR
15320 PRINTD$
15330 E=0
15340 RETURN
```

Listing E.15

PARAMETERS

Chapter 14 developed an array used to control the subroutine set. By varying the values of the array, you can access different key-file systems. The TRS-80 set uses more parameters than this Apple version. The subroutine set for the Apple does not require the number of records per block, because it does not block the records, and the first block in the record file will always be record number one.

The Apple also requires the file name in the subroutines. This is passed to the subroutines that replaced the TRS-80 GET and PUT statements as ZF$. The subroutines that call these subroutines use KF$ and RF$. These are also parameters and must be set in the initialization section. The key-file subroutines also use RL and KL for the lengths of the records in the record and key files. You can replace these variables in the subroutines with the array elements CA(1) and CA(7). In the OPEN statements, remember to add one to these values as you must leave room for the carriage return character.

```
6149   REM -- 6150-6180 GET RECORD BY NUMBER --
6150  ZR=N:ZL=RL:ZF$=RF$
6160  GOSUB10140
6170  R$=Z$
6175  Z5=FRE(0)
6180  RETURN
6189   REM -- 6190-6240 PUT RECORD BY NUMBER --
6190  ZR=N
6195  ZF$=RF$
6197  ZL=RL
6200  Z$=R$
```

```
6210 GOSUB10220
6215 Z5=FRE(O)
6220 RETURN
6249  REM -- 6250-6304 GET NEXT AVAILABLE RECORD NUMBER --
6250 PRINTD$;"READ ";RF$;",RO"
6260 INPUTFR
6270 FR=FR+1
6280 PRINTD$
6290 PRINTD$;"WRITE ";RF$;",RO"
6300 PRINTFR
6302 PRINTD$
6304 Z5=FRE(O)
6306 RETURN
6309  REM -- 6310-6510 SEARCH FOR KEY --
6310 K1$=LEFT$(SP$,CA(9))
6320 K$=K$+K1$:KN=0
6330 L1=0:L2=CA(9):L4=0
6340 L3=INT((L1+L2)/2)
6350 IFMID$(RM$,L3,1)=CHR$(127)THEN6540
6360 KB=ASC(MID$(RM$,L3,1))
6370 ZF$=KF$:ZR=KB+1:ZL=KL
6372 GOSUB10140
6374 KY$=Z$
6380 IFLEFT$(KY$,CA(9))>LEFT$(K$,CA(9))THEN6540
6390 KN=0
6400 KN=KN+1:IFKN=CA(10)THEN6440
6410 IFLEFT$(K$,CA(9))=MID$(KY$,(KN-1)*CA(7)+1,CA(9))THEN6580
6420 IFLEFT$(K$,CA(9))<MID$(KY$,(KN-1)*CA(7)+1,CA(9))THEN6580
6430 GOTO6400
6440 L1=L3
6450 L4=L4+1
6460 IFL4<CA(11)THEN6340
6470 E=1
6480 L3=L3+1
6490 KB=ASC(MID$(RM$,L3,1))
6500 K1$=CHR$(127)
6502 FORZ1=2TOCA(7)
6504 K1$=K1$+CHR$(127)
6506 NEXTZ1
6508 IFKB=127THENRETURN
6510 ZF$=KF$:ZL=KL:ZR=KB+1
6512 GOSUB10140
6514 KY$=Z$
6520 K1$=LEFT$(KY$,CA(7))
6530 RETURN
6540 L2=L3
6550 L4=L4+1
6560 IFL4<CA(11)THEN6340
6565 E=1:IFL1>0THEN6500
6570 PRINT"KEY FILE INITIALIZATION ERROR!"
6572 STOP
6580 E=0
6590 K1$=MID$(KY$,(KN-1)*CA(7)+1,CA(7))
6600 RETURN
6610 E=1
6620 GOTO6590
6999  REM -- 7000-7499 PUT NEW RECORD AND KEY --
7000 GOSUB6310
7010 IFE=2THENRETURN
7020 IFE=1THEN7040
7030 E=1:RETURN
7040 GOSUB6250
7045 KZ$=KY$
7050 IFKB=127THEN7180
7060 IFLEFT$(K$,CA(9))<LEFT$(KZ$,CA(9))THENKN=1
7062 FORI=1TOCA(10)
7064 KO$(I)=MID$(KZ$,(I-1)*CA(7)+1,CA(7))
7066 NEXTI
7068 FORI=CA(10)TOKN+1STEP-1
7070 KO$(I)=KO$(I-1)
7072 NEXTI
7074 F1=INT(FR/100)
```

```
7076 F2=FR-F1*100
7078 KO$(KN)=LEFT$(K$,CA(9))+CHR$(F1+1)+CHR$(F2+1)
7080 KY$=KO$(1)
7082 FORI=2TOCA(10)
7084 KY$=KY$+KO$(I)
7086 NEXTI
7088 ZF$=KF$:ZL=KL:ZR=KB+1
7090 Z$=KY$
7092 GOSUB10220
7100 GOSUB6010
7110 N=FR:GOSUB6190
7120 E=0
7130 IFMID$(KY$,(CA(10)-1)*CA(7)+1,1)=CHR$(127)THENRETURN
7132 KW$=CHR$(127)
7134 FORI=1TO7(
7136 KW$=KW$+KW$
7138 NEXTI
7140 KW$=KW$+LEFT$(KW$,127)
7142 L4=0:FORI=1TOCA(15):IFASC(MID$(RM$,I,1))=127THEN7144
7143 IFASC(MID$(RM$,I,1))>L4THENL4=ASC(MID$(RM$,I,1))
7144 NEXTI
7146 I=0
7148 I=I+1:IFASC(MID$(RM$,I,1))<>KBTHEN7148
7150 RW$=RM$
7152 RM$=LEFT$(RW$,I)+CHR$(L4-1)+RIGHT$(RW$,CA(15)-I-1)
7154 KX$=MID$(KY$,CA(13),CA(12))+LEFT$(KW$,CA(14))
7156 KZ$=MID$(KY$,1,CA(14))+LEFT$(KW$,CA(12))
7158 ZF$=KF$:ZL=KL:ZR=KB+1:Z$=KY$
7160 GOSUB10220
7162 Z$=KX$:ZR=L4+2:GOSUB10220
7164 Z$=RM$+LEFT$(KW$,254-CA(15)):ZR=1:GOSUB10220
7170 E=0:RETURN
7180 L4=0
7182 L4=L4+1:IFL4<=10THEN7184
7183 STOP
7184 IFASC(MID$(RM$,L4+1,1))<127THEN7182
7186 KB=ASC(MID$(RM$,L4,1)):ZF$=KF$:ZL=KL:ZR=KB:GOSUB10140
7187 KY$=Z$
7188 KN=0
7190 KN=KN+1:IFMID$(KY$,(KN-1)*CA(7)+1,1)<CHR$(127)THEN7190
7192 GOTO7050
7499  REM  -- 7500-7999 GET RECORD --
7500 GOSUB6310
7510 IFE=0THEN7540
7520 E=1
7530 RETURN
7540 F1=ASC(MID$(K1$,CA(9)+1,1))
7542 F2=ASC(MID$(K1$,CA(7),1))
7544 N=F1*100+F2
7550 GOSUB6150
7560 GOSUB6090
7570 E=0
7580 RETURN
7999  REM  -- 8000-8499 GET NEXT --
8000 K$=K$+LEFT$(SP$,CA(9)):E=ASC(MID$(K$,CA(9),1))
8010 K$=LEFT$(K$,CA(9)-1)+CHR$(E)
8020 GOSUB6310
8030 IFE=0THEN7540
8040 IFLEFT$(K1$,1)<CHR$(127)THEN8060
8050 E=1:RETURN
8060 E=0:GOTO7540
8070 GOSUB6150
8080 GOSUB6090
8090 E=0
8100 RETURN
8499  REM -- 8500-8999 DELETE KEY AND RECORD --
8500 GOSUB6310
8510 IFE=0THEN8540
8520 E=1
8530 RETURN
8540 FORI=1TOCA(10)
8542 KO$(I)=MID$(KY$,(I-1)*CA(7)+1,CA(7))
```

```
8544 NEXTI
8550 FORI=KNTOCA(10)-1
8555 KO$(I)=KO$(I+1)
8557 NEXTI
8560 KO$(21)=CHR$(127)
8562 FORI=2TOCA(7)
8564 KO$(CA(10))=KO$(CA(10))+CHR$(127)
8566 NEXTI
8570 KY$=KO$(1)
8572 FORI=2TOCA(10)
8574 KY$=KY$+KO$(I)
8576 NEXTI
8578 Z$=KY$:ZF$=KF$:ZL=KL:ZR=KB+1
8580 GOSUB10220
8590 E=0
8600 Z5=FRE(O)
8610 RETURN
8999 REM -- 9000-9499 RESAVE RECORD --
9000 GOSUB6310
9010 IFE=0THEN9040
9020 E=1
9030 RETURN
9040 F1=ASC(MID$(K1$,CA(9)+1,1))
9042 F2=ASC(MID$(K1$,CA(7),1))
9044 N=F1*100+F2
9050 GOSUB6010
9060 GOSUB6190
9070 E=0
9080 RETURN
9499 REM -- 9500 INSERT K$ AT POS I --
9500 FORZ1=1TOCA(10)
9510 KO$(Z1)=MID$(KY$,(Z1-1)*CA(7)+1,CA(7))
9520 NEXTZ1
9530 KO$(I)=K$
9540 KY$=KO$(1)
9550 FORZ1=2TOCA(10)
9560 KY$=KY$+KO$(Z1)
9570 NEXTZ1
9580 RETURN
10139 REM ** 10140 GET ZF,ZR **
10140 PRINTD$;"READ ";ZF$;",R";ZR
10150 Z$=" "
10160 FORZ1=1TOZL
10170 GETZ1$
10180 Z$=Z$+Z1$
10190 NEXTZ1
10200 PRINTD$
10202 Z$=RIGHT$(Z$,ZL)
10204 PRINTD$
10210 RETURN
10219 REM ** 10220 PUT ZF,ZR **
10220 PRINTD$;"WRITE ";ZF$;",R";ZR
10230 FORZ1=1TOZL
10240 PRINTMID$(Z$,Z1,1);
10250 NEXTZ1
10260 PRINT
10270 PRINTD$
10280 RETURN
```

Listing E.16

KEY-ONLY AND MULTIPLE-KEY FILES

A key-only file is simply a key-file system that is missing the record file. Putting together the subroutine set for a key-only file requires the same subroutine set developed in Chapter 14, replacing the record file subroutines (the ones between lines 6000 and 6309) with return statements and altering the control array.

The key-only file requires, as the name implies, only one file, and that is the one that contains the keys. TRS-80 listing 15.1 can be used to create the key-only file program for the Apple. The initialization section in the lines prior to line 100 is the same as for the Apple listing in Chapter 14, except that the OPEN statement is not required for the record file and the DATA statement contains values for the key-only file. The file initialization section, in lines 100 through 160, can be modified in the same way as the subroutines were. The STRING$ function must be replaced with a FOR/NEXT loop or other equivalent coding and the PUT and GET statements can be replaced with calls to the appropriate subroutines.

Using more than one key file requires the same types of alterations as are required on the TRS-80. You can double-subscript the CA array or write other subroutines that transfer the contents. For the extra parameters needed by the Apple, the same two options are possible. With the double-subscripted version, two alpha arrays, KF$ and RF$, can hold the file names. Using the subroutines, just set the values of KF$ and RF$ when you redefine the CA array. Using a double-subscripted CA array and two alpha arrays is a more effective solution. If you find a need to have more files accessed by one program than the Apple allows, use the subroutine to redefine the parameters and have it close the files and again open the ones in the file that are to be accessed next. This is a slow method, but you will probably never run into the situation, as the 16 files allowed on the Apple allow for eight key-file sets (five if you use the LIFO file) open at the same time.

PROGRAMMING

The information given in this section contains few listings, most of which can be easily translated to Applesoft. There are some advantages in the Apple system that you should incorporate into your programs. The general input and output subroutine set is easier to program on the Apple, using HTAB, VTAB, and GET, than the INKEY$ routine suggested for the TRS-80 (see listing 19.1). Creating screen layout sheets and data file layout sheets are also simple tasks. The assembly language on the Apple is probably the place where you can improve the performance of your programs more than on the TRS-80.

The Apple has an assembler built into the integer BASIC system. Using the assembly language to access the disk requires some very fancy routines and is probably not worth the effort. You may be able to use a data diskette, located in a second drive, in much the same way as the TRS-80 uses the disk, to pack and save numerics more efficiently or to compress out the field delimeters by doing your own blocking. This can be done by making use of the RWTS subroutine described in Chapter 9 of your Apple's DOS manual. This subroutine allows you to access the disk by sector and track numbers. Remember that BASIC will use the DOS controller, which involves an index (the directory) and a dynamic allocation system that is a little more complicated than using the disk as if it were a large array.

The assembler can be used to program the input/output subroutines, or at least part of them. The product of the assembler is machine language, which is much faster than BASIC. If you have some screen control subroutines that operate too slowly in BASIC, try the assembler. To save and load the machine language program, either use the BSAVE and BLOAD commands, or, if it is short enough, use POKE statements in a BASIC program. If you use BSAVE to store your program, remember that it will not load or save with your BASIC program. You must use BSAVE or BLOAD it separately.

Using the assembler for string handling is not very simple. Finding the string in memory may prove to be an impossible task. Using POKE to place the string in a known area in memory will probably prove slower than manipulating it in BASIC.

As far as what to do when things go wrong is concerned, there are many utilities you can use on the Apple, such as the ones that follow. BASIC can manipulate programs for listings, searches, and other debugging functions if the program is first stored on the disk in a text file. The next section has a routine for doing this, plus two routines for handling the stored program.

UTILITY PROGRAMS

Some utility programs are helpful in creating and debugging programs on the Apple computer. In the preparation of this book, I have used a few. Listed in this section are three programs. The first is used to form the text file from a program, which is used to set up a file for the other two programs. The text file is called PROGRAM and should be deleted from the disk prior to running the first program.

This first program, called SAVER, is a text file and so is easier to append to an existing program. You first load into memory the program that you want to run through one of the utilities. Next, enter EXEC SAVER (assuming you saved the first program on disk as SAVER). When it has been read into memory, you will see that it resides below the program you want to save by line number. Then enter the command RUN and your program will be listed to the text file PROGRAM. Now you can load into memory the utility you want to run.

```
1 D$=CHR$(4)
2 PRINTD$;"OPEN PROGRAM"
3 PRINTD$;"WRITE PROGRAM"
4 LIST10,
5 PRINTD$;"CLOSE"
6 END
```

Listing E.17

LISTER will give you a listing of the program. You can alter it to modify the spacing, split the line at colons (to form a decompressed listing as in Appendix C for the TRS-80), or any of a number of other things that may prove helpful in debugging or writing the programs.

```
10 D$=CHR$(4)
12 INPUT"TITLE? ";T$
14 PR#2
16 PRINTT$
20 PRINT:PRINT
21 PR#0
22 INPUT"PRESS RETURN TO LIST? ";Q$
23 D$=CHR$(4)
24 PRINTD$;"OPEN PROGRAM"
30 PRINTD$;"READ PROGRAM"
40 A$=" "
45 SC=1
50 GETC$
60 IFC$=CHR$(13)THEN100
70 A$=A$+C$
80 GOTO50
100 PR#2
110 PRINTA$
120 PR#0
130 GOTO40
```

Listing E.18

SEARCHER is very useful in debugging. It is a modification of LISTER. It will list only those statement lines that contain a string equal to the one you enter. It will not ignore spaces, which is its one drawback. You could add some code that would cause it to ignore the spaces, but then it would be more difficult to enter a string that requires spaces.

```
10 D$=CHR$(4)
12 INPUT"STRING TO SEARCH? ";SS$
14 LS=LEN(SS$)
24 PRINTD$;"OPEN PROGRAM"
30 PRINTD$;"READ PROGRAM"
```

```
40 A$=" "
50 GETC$
60 IFC$=CHR$(13)THEN100
70 A$=A$+C$
80 GOTO50
100 Z1=LEN(A$)
105 L=0
110 FORI=1TOZ1-LS+1
120 IFMID$(A$,I,LS)=SS$THENL=1
130 NEXTI
140 IFL=0THEN40
145 PR#2
150 PRINTA$
155 PR#0
160 GOTO40
```

Listing E.19

There are some very fancy alterations that can be done to these programs. You can first write a renumbering routine, reading the program and keeping a simple cross-reference list of the old and new statement numbers, then rereading the program, writing it to a new text file, and changing the old line numbers to the ones on the cross-reference list. Remember to change the statement numbers in the GOTO and GOSUB statements.

GLOSSARY

ALPHANUMERICS

The set of all numbers, letters, and other symbols used by the computer. One character of this set (i.e., one alphanumeric) is stored by the computer in 1 byte.

ASCII

American Standard Code for Information Interchange. It defines how a set of characters is encoded into the bit patterns for storage in the computer memory, mass storage devices, and on transmission lines. It seems to be standard for just about everyone except IBM, which uses its own code, EBCDIC.

BASIC

Beginner's All-Purpose Symbolic Instruction Code. Originally written to teach the basics of computer programming, BASIC is now a widely used language of the smaller mini- and microcomputers.

BINARY DIGIT

Same as binary integer. See BINARY INTEGER.

BINARY INTEGER

One or zero. The decimal integers are the numbers 0 through 9. Counting in binary, using binary integers, to five is: 0, 10, 11, 100, 101. Also called BIT.

BINARY SEARCH

A method of searching through a list that has been set into alphabetical or numerical order. See Part Two, Chapter 2.

BIT

Abbreviation of Binary Integer. See BINARY INTEGER and BINARY DIGIT.

BUBBLE

A method of sorting a list by swapping the positions of elements that are out of order. The process is repeated until all elements are in the proper order. Also called the Push Down sort.

BYTE

A collection of bits (usually 8 bits) used by the computer as one unit. One byte will store one character.

CHIP

An integrated circuit. This is a small device that contains many logic circuits used in the computer.

CPU
Abbreviation for Central Processing Unit. This is the brain of the computer.

CURSOR
The indicator on the computer's display that tells where the next character will print.

CURSOR POSITIONING
Placing the cursor at some chosen place on the screen to control where the next character(s) will be printed.

DATA FILE
A file in which is stored information in the form of data. See FILE.

DEBUG
To correct programming errors.

DISK
A platter coated with a magentic material that is used to store data from the computer. Disk can also be used to mean the device used to read and write the data, or to mean both the device and the platter as one unit.

DYNAMIC
Always changing. A dynamic file allocation system is one in which the deleted record's space is immediately made available for any new records that may require it.

FILE
Any collection of information. On disk, a file is generally a specified area, which can be referenced by name, containing data (a data file), a program (a program file), system commands (a system file), or other collection of information that can be stored like data.

FLOW CHART
A chart using symbols and lines to represent the logic of a program.

FORMAT
(1) As applied to a disk, the act of putting certain system information on the platter so that the operating system can locate the data. (2) A design or arrangement.

HARD DISK
Any one of a number of disk platters that are rigid, as opposed to flexible. This term is also used sometimes to refer to the disk drive that uses that type of disk.

HASHING METHOD
One type of key-file system where the position of the key is determined by a formula applied to the key itself.

JUNK VARIABLE
Any variable that is used as a temporary place to store data during some processing, but is not required before or after the processing.

K
Abbreviation for kilobytes. See KILOBYTE.

KEY FILE	The index for a record file. This could also be used to refer to both the key and the record file.
KILOBYTE	1024 bytes. This is a unit used to measure the size of memory, disks, tapes, and other storage devices. 8 K means 8 × 1024, or 8192.
M	Abbreviation for megabyte. See MEGABYTE.
MACRO-STATEMENT	Any statement that calls up a series of other statements, particularly in an assembly language program, that are inserted into the text in its place.
MEGABYTE	1,048,576 bytes. This is another storage unit like the kilobyte, but about 1,000 times larger. See also KILOBYTE.
MEMORY	A data storage area. Usually, this refers to the random-access memory (RAM) that is used in the processor of the computer, but could also refer to the mass storage devices (i.e., disk memory).
MICROCOMPUTER	Any computer using a microprocessor as its main CPU. See also MICROPROCESSOR; CPU.
MICROPROCESSOR	A single integrated circuit ("chip") with all of the logic functions for a computer. It is the base for a microcomputer.
MINIFLOPPY	A trademark of Shugart Associates, now in common use, meaning a 5¼-inch diskette or minidiskette.
NESTING	A programming technique. The most common nesting is in loops, where one loop will be inside the other, and in subroutines, where one subroutine is called by another.
NYBBLE	A collection of 4 bits used by a computer as one unit. Nybble started as a pun on the word byte, as a nybble is 4 bits instead of the 8 bits in a byte, and it stuck. See BIT; BYTE.
PARAMETER	In subroutines, a variable whose value controls, to a greater or lesser extent, what the subroutine is to do.
PROGRAM FILE	A file in which is stored program statements. See FILE.
PUSH DOWN	This is another term for a bubble sort. See BUBBLE.
RAM	Random-access memory. This is the memory in the computer that stores the program statements and user data. This does not refer to disk memory nor does it refer to ROM memory. See also DISK; MEMORY; MASS STORAGE.

READ/WRITE HEAD   On a disk or tape drive, the device that actually magnetizes the surface when writing and converts the magnetic pulses to electrical pulses when reading.

ROADMAP   In the tree-structured method, an indicator that shows the order in which the blocks are to be read to maintain the sorted order.

ROM   Read-only memory. This is special memory set up in the computer with set values that can never be altered. This is usually used to store the information needed by the computer to operate before any commands are given, like the BASIC interpreter program, and the instructions on how to load in the disk operating system.

SECTOR   A division of the disk, usually equal to 256 bytes. One sector is read from or written to the disk in one operation by the computer.

SEQUENTIAL   By number, with no number left out in the order.

SUBROUTINE   A series of statements that can be called from a single statement. When the subroutine is completed, it will return and resume execution of the program at the statement immediately following the statement calling the subroutine.

TRACK   A division of a disk that contains several sectors (the number varies depending on the disk). Physically, the track is in the shape of a circle on the disk platter.

TREE-STRUCTURED   A type of key-file method where the search for a key involves making several decisions on the block within the key file to load next in pursuit of the key.

WORK VARIABLE   A junk variable. See JUNK VARIABLE.

INDEX